MIRANDA

MIRANDA

The Story of America's Right to
Remain Silent

Gary L. Stuart

With a Foreword by
Janet Napolitano, Governor of Arizona

The University of Arizona Press

Tucson

The University of Arizona Press
© 2004 Gary L. Stuart

First paperback printing 2008

ISBN 978-0-8165-2763-2 (pbk. : alk. paper)
Library of Congress Cataloging-in-Publication Data
Stuart, Gary L., 1939–
Miranda : the story of America's right to remain silent /
Gary L. Stuart.—1st ed.
p. cm.
Includes bibliographical references and index.
ISBN 0-8165-2313-4 (cloth : alk. paper)
1. Miranda, Ernesto—Trials, litigation, etc. 2. Trials
(Rape)—Arizona. 3. Right to counsel—United States.
4. Self-incrimination—United States. 5. Confession (Law)—
United States. 6. Police questioning—United States. I. Title.
KF224.M54S78   2004
345.73'056—DC22 2004008436

Publication of this book is made possible in part by
generous financial support from Lewis and Roca, LLP.

Manufactured in the United States of America
on acid-free, archival-quality paper.

13   12   11   7   6   5   4   3

A judicious reticence is hard to learn,

but it is one of the great lessons of life.

—Chesterfield

CONTENTS

To the memory of John P. Frank

FOREWORD

The Age of Frank came to the legal world when John P. Frank insisted that the full potential of the U.S. Constitution be realized and extended to every American.

It did not extend to Ernesto Miranda in 1963, nor to millions of Americans like him. John found this abhorrent and went to work applying the virtues of the Age of Frank to American constitutional law. Three years later he triumphed, as the U.S. Supreme Court agreed with him by establishing Miranda Rights.

There was potential in the U.S. Constitution that the American justice system had left untapped, and John was there to fix that deficiency. In doing so, he welcomed millions of Americans into the Age of Frank.

John P. Frank tapped every ounce of potential in his life. He created a one-man movement to ensure that none of life's potential joy or justice was denied to those who orbited his larger-than-life existence.

In the Age of Frank, strawberries were not just for eating—they were to be dipped in champagne, rolled in powdered sugar, and devoured. Secretary's Day meant more than flowers on a desk. It meant taking everyone out for a long, leisurely lobster lunch. And opera began and ended with Wagner.

That was how the Age of Frank came to the people who knew John personally. John Frank is gone, but his era lives in the legacy of *Miranda v. Arizona*. Long live the Age of Frank.

—Janet Napolitano
Governor of Arizona

PREFACE

Whether innate or acquired early in life, the desire to confess—to take responsibility for a perceived misdeed—is no doubt a deep-seated impulse in us all; perhaps we want, as Sartre suggests, to return the world to a "harmony of minds," an agreement on the principles that bind us to the society in which we live. Why we wish to do this seems visceral, as immutable as physical law, and as basic to our sense of justice as the concept of right and wrong. The act of confession, it would seem, restores the world (and our psyches) to a state of balance: For every action there must be an equal reaction—an eye for an eye, and a tooth for a tooth.

There is, however, a curious aspect to our impulse to confess. We feel that in the act of contrition resides an implicit covenant: If I confess, I will be forgiven by the authority with which I have formed this covenant, for in the confession itself I make restitution.

Confess, and all will be forgiven—this is what the police interrogator conveys to the suspect. Not in so many words, but the message is there—in the tone of voice, in the proffered kindness of a cigarette or cup of coffee—and in truth the suspect will be forgiven by the cop, whose only real requirement for achieving harmony is the confession. For the higher authority, however, the admission of wrongdoing is not the end. The ancient god of retribution must be served; the wrongdoer must pay for what he did, with his wealth, his liberty, or his life.

But does he understand this? As he sits in the interrogation room and the hours pass, and the cop repeats the same unspoken message over and over—does he understand that this whole problem can end if he simply admits to the crime? Does the suspect always know, always remember, and always understand that what he says can be used against him in a court of law? Does the suspect know that he has the legal right to remain silent and to refuse to answer the interrogator's questions? Do we as a society have the obligation to make sure he knows, understands, and does not forget?

The answers to these questions may seem self-evident today, but before the United States Supreme Court handed down *Miranda v. Arizona,* our system of justice operated under a different set of assumptions. Prior to *Miranda,* a well-informed citizen might be aware of the constitutional protection against self-incrimination, but few understood that this protection extended beyond the courtroom. In a very real sense, most Americans—certainly most white, middle-class Americans—assumed that a suspect, once in custody, was most likely guilty, and that police interrogation could and should continue, in private, isolated from counsel, until the suspect confessed. In general, police held this conviction as well and saw no wrong in concealing the fact that the suspect's confession *would* be used to incriminate him, nor did they see any wrong in pandering to the suspect's desire to confess. Scarcely anyone outside the realm of psychology believed a man would confess to something he had not done. And even those who knew better could find comfort in the belief that such false confessions would easily be discovered and never used unscrupulously to convict an innocent man.

In the middle of the last century, however, American society began to change and, with that change, to question some deep-rooted assumptions about race, about gender, and about law. The war, to some extent, had desegregated the army, and returning black GIs, having fought for their country, could not help but resent their lack of freedom at home. Then, too, the war effort had brought women into sectors of the workforce long reserved for men. Suddenly they were being asked to surrender their independence and pretend they could not handle a man's job. Finally, in movies like *The Last Angry Man,* audiences were shown what can happen when juries make the lazy assumption that the accused must be guilty as charged.

As the forces of change manifested in the struggle for civil rights and greater social and economic equity, there began a growing demand for higher education. Across the country, the university system expanded to include the children of lower- and middle-class parents, and to provide them the opportunity to enter professions that had been traditionally the province of the upper class—especially the professions of law and academe. As a new crop of lawyers and professors came of age, they pushed for egalitarian reforms, and for the first time, the state took on the responsibility of providing legal counsel for citizens who could not afford it. Soon thereafter, that right was extended to include pretrial procedures. But even so, the suspect had to invoke this right to have a lawyer present, and if he did not know he had the right, well, that was his fault.

Then one afternoon in March of 1963, a Phoenix police detective arrested a young, poor, and uneducated Hispanic man in connection with a series of sexual assaults. Within a few hours the man had willingly confessed to the crimes. His subsequent trials and convictions on two of the charges were swift and certain, and it seemed that, like so many others before it, the case would end there.

But there is, of course, more to this story. What happened that afternoon in the Phoenix police station began a chain of events that came to bear on a central precept of our system of justice, and upon a core belief of the American way of life. Ernesto Miranda was a poor, illiterate American convicted of a crime not on the strength of eyewitness testimony or physical evidence, but almost entirely because he had incriminated himself without knowing it, and without knowing that he didn't have to.

I undertook the writing of this book not simply because *Miranda v. Arizona* stands as one of the most important events in the annals of American legal history; I was also drawn to the story because I've spent my career practicing, teaching, and writing about the law in the state where the story began, unfolded, and ultimately concluded. In 1966, when *Miranda* came down, I was a third-year law student at the University of Arizona. Although the case at first received virtually no attention from the media or the legal community, Miranda's lawyers, John P. Frank and John J. Flynn, were among the most prominent in the Arizona bar, and their work soon focused the entire country on the issue of Miranda's rights. A great many Arizona lawyers followed the story closely, ingesting the daily reading and discussing—arguing vehemently sometimes—the points of the case. Arizona was at that time a politically conservative, law-and-order state—the state of Barry Goldwater and John Rhodes. Sentiments against the lawyers representing Miranda ran high.

Just as high, however, ran the groundswell pushing for a true and universal recognition of civil liberties and a reinterpretation of that essential tenet of American justice, the right of all citizens to be treated equally under that law. Ernest Miranda figures centrally in this story partly because he was an uneducated, ethnically disenfranchised citizen with virtually no voice to defend himself. But also, and even more important, he is central precisely because he was so obviously the perpetrator of the crimes for which he was arrested. For it is in cases when evidence and common sense so strongly dictate guilt—when all involved seem willing to waive rights set forth in our constitution—that the law must step forward to protect the presumed innocence of the accused and provide him the legal protection to which all innocent American citizens can lay claim.

This basic tenet had been invoked many times before *Miranda,* but never before had anyone drawn such a clear rationale from the various precedents, and never before had the argument been carried so eloquently before the Supreme Court. It is fair to say that the social and political climate of the day offered proponents of the Miranda Doctrine an environment receptive to their reasoning. Nevertheless, without the dedication of those responsible, and if not for the unique combination of skills they possessed, the chance might have passed, and the course of American justice might have remained unaltered for an unknowable time.

Miranda represented a 1966 sea change in that the "totality of the circumstances" test for the admissibility of a confession was eschewed and a new bright-line was established by the now-famous Miranda warnings. The necessity for such a change came about because police interrogation techniques were developed forty years ago that were specifically designed to induce suspects into unknowingly giving up their Fifth and Sixth Amendment rights.

The *Dickerson* decision in 2000 cemented that change by declaring that the *Miranda* warnings were not simply judicially created rules that protected constitutional rights but were themselves mandated by the Constitution.

The sad truth is that forced or coerced confessions were commonplace in rural America before the *Miranda* decision and were usually the product of unprofessional police conduct, which by definition was often difficult to prove. Even when it could be proved, it took a lawyer to prove it. As the late John P. Frank said, "[T]he right to counsel and the freedom not to be a witness against oneself are a shield by which our Constitution protects persons in our society from suffering the broken bodies, not merely of distant centuries but of today, broken bodies of persons whom some government seeks to compel to testify against themselves. The minimal safeguard against such abuses, a safeguard that has been demonstrably necessary in our own country, is to declare that no confession may be used unless it is clear that it was made by a person who knew his constitutional rights and chose to waive them."

History was made again in 2004 when the Supreme Court handed down several decisions expanding the *Miranda* doctrine in domestic criminal cases and expanding the right to access to counsel to suspects apprehended in the ongoing war against terrorism. The domestic cases dealt with new police interrogation techniques that were designed to produce confessions by avoiding the strictures set down in *Miranda*. The terrorist cases dealt with the right of access to American courts for both citizens and non-citizens alike.

Yarborough v. Alvarado supported *Miranda*'s basic promise of protection of Fifth Amendment rights but carefully distinguished pre-custody situations in juvenile cases. While affirming a criminal conviction obtained through an unwarned confession, the court enunciated for the first time that the Constitution does not require that special consideration be given to age when deciding whether to grant or withhold *Miranda* warnings.

Fellers v. United States produced a rare unanimous Supreme Court decision that suppressed a suspect's in-custody confession after he had been read and had waived his *Miranda* rights. His "warned" confession in the police station was suppressed because it came from an earlier confession taken by the same officers at the defendant's home. The police had gone to the suspect's home for the express purpose of arresting him pursuant to an indictment in a drug case. While at his home, without reading him his rights and knowing that he was already represented by counsel on the drug charge, the officers engaged him in a conversation in which he incriminated himself. The Court held that the second confession must be suppressed because it was the "fruit" of the first confession and thus a violation of both Fifth and Sixth Amendment rights.

United States v. Patane tested the admissibility of physical evidence obtained by the police as a result of an unwarned confession. In this instance, the police had "accidentally" violated Patane's *Miranda* rights. The suspect had been arrested and interrogated at home and had admitted possessing a gun in violation of his parole status. The Court ruled that prosecutors may use physical evidence against a suspect even if it was obtained by officers who had not given the suspect a *Miranda* warning. A narrow plurality of the Court stated that the *Miranda* rule could not be violated unless the statements were introduced in court. In this case, only the gun was admitted, not the suspect's actual statements.

Missouri v. Seibert involved an "intentional" withholding of *Miranda* rights by police. The officers who arrested Patrice Seibert consciously elected not to inform her of her constitutional rights as part of a strategy to get the suspect to incriminate herself. Only after securing her first unwarned confession did they read the *Miranda* rights card to her. Having already confessed, she waived her rights and confessed a second time. The Court soundly denounced the intentional violation of *Miranda* and ordered both confessions stricken. The 5–4 vote against the strategy, in an opinion by Justice

David H. Souter, was a "plurality" decision since the five justices in the majority did not fully agree on a single rationale for holding both confessions inadmissible. Justice Souter said, "Strategists dedicated to draining the substance out of *Miranda* cannot accomplish by training instructions what *Dickerson* held Congress cannot do by statute."

Thus in these domestic criminal cases the Court firmly continued to support the uniquely American right to remain silent, the more general right to be informed, and the somewhat global right to be represented by counsel. The entry of foreign and domestic suspects in the war against terrorism brings an unpredictable consequence of *Miranda*'s legacy. In the past few years, the notion that an individual should have a right to remain silent has spread from police stations in America to custodial interrogations of foreign nationals in foreign countries. The fact that no other country in the world requires its police to issue *Miranda* warnings therefore creates a conundrum for the FBI and other American law enforcement agencies, for if a foreign suspect is Mirandized on foreign soil in a nation that does not recognize the right to remain silent or to receive counsel in pretrial settings, then *Miranda* warnings are inherently misleading.

The larger question of the extent to which domestic *Miranda* rights should be respected on foreign soil or on American sovereign territory is the subject of three recent decisions handed down along with the domestic *Miranda* decisions in the last two days of the Court's October 2003 term. In *Rasul v. Bush*, the Court held that non-citizen detainees held at the U.S. naval base at Guantanamo Bay, Cuba, have a right to file *habeas corpus* petitions in federal courts to challenge the legality of their detention. In *Hamdi v. Rumsfeld*, the Court clarified American citizen Yaser Hamdi's rights. Hamdi had been detained as an "enemy combatant" for two years without access either to the courts or his lawyer. The court held that his detention was proper and could be continued but that he had a right to challenge the justification for his detention (i.e., his status as an enemy combatant) before a neutral decision maker. In *Rumsfeld v. Padilla*, the Court held that Padilla—another American citizen being held as an enemy combatant—had filed his *habeas* petition in the wrong court. Presumably, when Padilla re-files his petition in the right court, he will be given the same rights as Mr. Hamdi.

The three cases involving the war on terrorism thus invite the comparison between the well-known *Miranda* rights and what may become known as Hamdi rights.

The devastation inflicted upon New York City and, psychologically, on the rest of the nation on September 11, 2001, understandably created a need for changes in the ways we prosecute foreign criminals such as the al Qaeda terrorists. What we see as constitutional rights for ourselves may have to be withheld from those who would take all rights away by terror and violence rather than by the due process of the democratic system. We would do well to remember, however, that if, in the effort to solve the problems *Miranda* has posed to law enforcement, we return to the days when law enforcement was silent on the rights of suspects—be they home-grown thieves or foreign-trained terrorists—then those people seeking to destroy democracy itself and replace it with a radically fundamental theocracy will have obtained one of their objectives.

Justice O'Connor is as close to these large questions as anyone could possibly be. She is at the center of the Court and the center of American thought when she says, as she did in the Hamdi case, "Striking the proper constitutional balance . . . is of great importance to the nation during this period of ongoing combat. But it is equally vital that our calculus not give short shrift to the values that this country holds so dear or to the privilege that is American citizenship."

The last day of the Supreme Court's October 2003 term was, as Anthony Lewis said in the *New York Times*, "As profound a day in the court as any in a long time." *Miranda* rights were, once again, constitutionally confirmed, and Hamdi rights were, for the first time, constitutionally created.

I wanted to write this book because I know many of the principal figures personally. I took advanced constitutional law from John P. Frank in 1966, practiced law with Rex E. Lee, and tried cases before all of the judges involved in Miranda's many trials. Over the years, I tried cases with other lawyers involved in the case and came to know some of the police officers and other *Miranda* "insiders." I knew starting out that I would be accorded a level of access and trust that few others could enjoy.

The book is arranged to accommodate two different but not mutually exclusive audiences: the general reader, for whom the story of Ernest Miranda might well be the most interesting, and the student of the law, who will find interest in the way our justice system worked before, during, and after the *Miranda* decision. Consequently, the first part recounts the events of Ernest Miranda's capture, conviction, and first appeal, as well as the entry of Bob Corcoran, John P. Frank, and John Flynn into the story and their parts in creating the argument brought before the Supreme Court.

Part Two is a more categorical discussion of the aftermath. It includes not only chapters about subsequent test cases and the ongoing debate but also an account of what finally happened to Ernest Miranda. In a final chapter I offer my summation, contemplating the legacy as well as the fate of *Miranda* in the twenty-first century, now that we face new challenges to our criminal code beyond our national borders.

PART ONE
Miranda

Chapter 1

CRIMES, CONFESSIONS, AND CONVICTIONS

Ernest Miranda Confesses to Carroll Cooley

On the night of November 27, 1962, a young bank teller whom I will call "Barbara Doe," to protect her privacy, was abducted from a parking lot in downtown Phoenix, Arizona. She had stayed late to attend a training class at the downtown branch of the bank where she had worked for just over two months. The class ended around 8:30, and soon afterward, Barbara left the building and crossed the street to her car parked on the corner of Second Street and Monroe. As she would describe the events later to police, she had just unlocked the driver's side door and gotten in behind the wheel when the assailant surprised her, first gripping her arm, then putting a hand over her mouth and pressing a small knife into her side. He would not hurt her, he promised, so long as she didn't cry out.

The man, whom Barbara described as a short, slender Hispanic in his twenties, then shoved her across the bench seat, got in behind the wheel, and started the car. He drove a short distance before turning into an alley, where he shut off the ignition and lights. He had put away the knife by this time, and now he moved across the seat toward her, telling her she was very pretty. He began to fumble at her blouse and tried to slide a hand up her thigh. Barbara began to struggle, first tentatively and then more forcefully, sensing the man's uncertainty. For several more minutes the struggle continued, Barbara repeatedly begging her attacker not to hurt her, and the man telling her he wouldn't. Finally, when Barbara told him he could have the money in her purse, the man gave up his assault. After collecting eight dollars, all that Barbara had, the man got out of the car and disappeared.

Nearly three months later, on February 22, an eighteen-year-old telephone dispatcher, whom I'll call "Sylvia Doe," left the telephone company in downtown Phoenix at the end of her late-evening shift. Sylvia was abducted by a man who approached her as she was getting into her car on North Fourth Avenue. Jerking the driver's door open before she could lock it, he placed a small knife against her throat and demanded the car and her money. Then he seemed to decide he wanted more. Climbing into the car, he began to tear at her clothes, at which time she began to scream. The young woman told the police that the short, slender Hispanic man seemed nervous to begin with and her screams apparently frightened him enough that he backed off and then ran.

A little over a week later, on March 2, the would-be rapist tried again. This time the victim was a shy eighteen-year-old who worked at the downtown Paramount Theater. At 11:45 "Patricia Doe" caught a bus traveling up Central toward midtown, where she lived with her parents. The bus dropped her three blocks from their house at just after midnight. She was less than a block from her front door when a car passed, pulled over in front of her, and stopped. Then the driver got out and approached on the sidewalk. Once he was within striking distance, he grabbed hold of her hand, spun her around, and placed something sharp to her throat. He told her he wouldn't hurt her unless she screamed. Then he pushed her into his car, forcing her to lie face down on the back seat. He drove to a desert area near 20th Street and Bethany Home Road on the east side of Phoenix. This time he would not be dissuaded or scared off. At the end of a dirt road just south of Squaw Peak, he assaulted and raped Patricia Doe, then drove her back to her neighborhood and let her go.

The next day, Monday, March 4, Sergeant Seymour Nealis, head of the Crimes Against Persons Detail for the Phoenix Police Department, assigned Detective Carroll Cooley to the case. Cooley, a sandy-haired, fit young man in his fifth year on the police force, had already proven himself an able investigator. Patient, methodical, and at times wary, Cooley was nevertheless a gregarious man, at ease with suspects and helpful to victims. He was known around the precinct as a good team player but also an independent thinker. By the time he and Sgt. Nealis sat down to go over the case, they had already connected Patricia Doe's assault to the two earlier incidents. The physical descriptions of the assailant matched, and in each case, his weapon had apparently been a small knife. Also the victims' descriptions of his mannerisms and several of his remarks coincided. Unfortunately, Cooley had virtually no physical evidence, and Patricia Doe's description of the assailant's car could scarcely help them. The Phoenix area was full of older-model four-door sedans. As Cooley remarked in his own account of the case,[1] the chances of finding the vehicle were "slim."

Cooley then got the break that many cases depend on. Ever since the attack on Patricia Doe, a cousin who also lived at Patricia's parents' house had begun to meet her at the bus stop each night and escort her home. One week after the rape, as he sat on the bus-stop bench waiting, he saw an older model car drive slowly past on the cross street. Was it the same car? Patricia's bus pulled up minutes later. From her cousin's description of the car, Patricia thought it might be the same one. And as they neared home, walking along the curb, the car reappeared, coming slowly down the street. When the cousin ran toward it, trying to get a look at the driver, it sped away, but not before he got a partial license plate number, and he told Detective Cooley he could definitely identify the car as an old-model Packard sedan.

The next morning, Detective Cooley and Patricia's cousin visited the local Packard dealership and found a 1953 Packard sedan that the cousin swore was nearly identical. Carroll Cooley knew there wouldn't be many such cars in the area. Sure enough, in the vehicle registration records he soon found a similar 1953 Packard, with a similar though not identical license number. It belonged to a woman named Twila Hoffman, living in nearby Mesa, Arizona. Yes, she told Cooley, when he telephoned, the man living with her, whose name was Ernesto Miranda, sometimes borrowed her car.

Cooley knew better than to jump to conclusions, but his suspicions increased considerably when he ran a routine record check. Ernesto Arthur Miranda had had frequent run-ins with the Phoenix Police Department, a fact that, as Cooley said, made him "look good" for the crime. Since he was the only suspect they had, two days later Cooley and his partner, Detective Wilfred Young, drove out to the house in Mesa. Their knock on the front door was responded to by a woman carrying a small baby. She said her name was Twila Hoffman. Miranda was still asleep, but she offered to wake him up. A few minutes later, a young Hispanic man, wearing only a pair of khaki trousers, came to the door. Dark, unruly hair framed his not-quite pretty face. His dark eyes and heavy brows were furrowed with suspicion but quickly gave way to a quiet smile. Yes, he was Ernesto Arthur Miranda, he told them. He did not seem overly concerned that they were police officers. When Young informed him that he did not have to talk to the officers if he did not want to, Miranda told them he did not mind talking. Would he accompany them down to the police station? Sure, he responded.

During the thirty-minute drive from Miranda's home in Mesa to Phoenix police headquarters, Miranda continued to appear perfectly at ease, and Cooley's doubts increased. As he said later, "All they had on this guy was his access to a car that might have been the one seen under suspicious circumstances a full week later. The license number, although similar, was not the one the witness originally gave police and the car was not the same color Patricia reported at the time of the crime."[2] But Miranda had a record and he fit the general description of the man involved in all three assaults.

When they arrived at the station, Cooley escorted his suspect into Interrogation Room Number Two. Aptly named the "sweat room," Number Two was a twelve-foot-square cubicle with pale green walls, fluorescent tubes set into acoustic tile overhead, and a two-way mirror in the door for viewing lineups. Miranda's interview began at approximately 10:30 A.M. Without hesitating, Cooley and Young confronted Miranda with selective facts of Patricia Doe's rape. Miranda denied any involvement and said he was at work the night Patricia was abducted. When they asked him about Barbara Doe's robbery, he denied any knowledge or participation. Cooley then asked Miranda to stand in a lineup for the victims of both crimes, telling him they would take him home as soon as the victims cleared him. Cooley later freely admitted to misleading Miranda about his knowledge of the crimes under investigation but noted that the cordial, sympathetic approach he used in talking to Miranda helped establish a rapport with the suspect. Besides, it was common for officers to engage in a certain amount of deception. Good detectives, for instance, usually implied that they knew more about a case than they actually did.

Unfortunately, although Patricia and Barbara both thought number one (Miranda) looked like the man, they couldn't be positive. "I was somewhat dejected and frustrated," Cooley recalled in his later account, and, unsure what approach to use next, he returned to the interview room where Miranda waited alone. Noting the gravity of the officer's demeanor, Miranda shifted uneasily in his chair and asked, "How did I do?"

"Not too good, Ernie," replied Cooley, noticing Miranda's concern.

"They identified me then?" Miranda asked.

"Yes, Ernie, they did," Cooley replied gravely.

"Well," said Miranda resignedly, "I guess I'd better tell you about it then."

Somewhat surprised, Cooley gave Miranda a copy of the standard statement form, having already filled in the top four lines: SUBJECT: Rape DR 63-08380, STATEMENT OF: Ernest Arthur Miranda; TAKEN BY: C. Cooley #413-W. Young #182; DATE: 3-13-63; TIME: 1:30 P.M.; PLACE TAKEN: Interr Rm #2. At the top of this standard form was a paragraph that read:

I, _____, do hereby swear that I make this statement voluntarily and of my own free will, with no threats, coercion, or promises of immunity, and with full knowledge of my legal rights, understanding any statement can be used against me. I, _____, am _____ years of age and have completed the _____ grade in school.[3]

Miranda wrote his name, recorded his age as twenty-three, and the grade completed as eighth. Then, in the provided space below, he wrote:

Seen a girl walking up street stopped a little ahead of her got out of car walked towards her grabbed her by the arm and asked to get in car. Got in car without force tied hands and ankles. Drove away for a few mile. Stopped asked to take clothes off. Did not, asked me to take her back home. I started to take clothes off her without any force and with cooperation. Asked her to lay down and she did. Could not get penis into vagina got about 1/2 (half) inch in. Told her to get clothes back on. Drove her home. I couldn't say I was sorry for what I had done but asked her to pray for me.[4]

When he'd finished, Miranda signed the form again at the bottom, beneath the statement: "I have read and understand the foregoing statement and hereby swear to its truthfulness." Detectives Cooley and Young signed the document as witnesses.

Miranda also confessed, although not in writing, to robbing Barbara Doe in November 1962 and admitted attempting to rob Sylvia Doe in February 1963. Cooley, not wanting to risk jeopardizing Miranda's successful prosecution in the rape case by opening his written confession to attack because of the mention of other, unrelated crimes,"[5] did not ask Miranda for a written confession in these other two cases. After Miranda signed his handwritten confession, Cooley brought Patricia Doe into Interrogation Room Number Two, and Cooley asked Miranda to state his name. Miranda did so and, in Patricia's presence, told Cooley and Young that he recognized her. "She's the one I was talking about," he said. Patricia later remembered that he said, "She's the one." Barbara Doe was then led into the interrogation room, and in her presence Miranda told Cooley and Young that he recognized her as well. Both young women later testified that based on this interaction they were "sure" he was the man who had accosted them.[6]

It is also important to note that only at this point of the interrogation did Cooley and Young place Miranda under arrest and book him into the fourth-floor jail. Previously, he had merely been "in custody." From their perspective, as Cooley said later, it would have been difficult to hold Miranda "if he had demanded that they either charge or release him."

Despite Miranda's having confessed to crimes involving Barbara, Patricia, and Sylvia, the prosecutor filed charges involving only Barbara and Patricia. By merely arresting Miranda, the police and prosecutors "cleared" the docket and file involving Sylvia. Accordingly, Miranda went to jail to await trial on the two cases involving Barbara and Patricia, and Sylvia was spared the necessity of a public trial and confronting Miranda in open court. The trial on Barbara's robbery case was scheduled first because it had occurred earlier.

Miranda's Robbery Trial

Judge Yale McFate presided over the case of the State of Arizona versus Ernesto A. Miranda on one count of robbery in the second degree. A former county attorney, McFate had sat on the Maricopa County Superior Court bench for the last twelve years. A kindly, courteous man, Judge McFate was known to all trial lawyers as a fair and able arbiter of justice. County Attorney Robert Corbin assigned Larry Turoff as lead counsel for the state. Turoff, a young but skilled lawyer, had tried scores of these "one-day" confession cases and had a long string of convictions under his belt. For the defense, Judge McFate assigned Alvin Moore, a seventy-three-year-old lawyer in a one-man firm, who had volunteered to accept the judicial assignment of indigent-criminal cases despite the fact that he possessed little experience in criminal law, having spent most of his career in civil court. The reality was that judge, prosecutor, and defense lawyer all knew that these one-day confession cases involved little challenge and usually resulted in easy convictions. Certainly, Moore was not motivated by money, as the state paid volunteer advocates a fee not to exceed fifty dollars (Moore, in this instance, was paid a total of fifty dollars for his entire representation of Miranda).

The robbery trial lasted but a single day, and a cursory examination of the proceedings would lead to the facile conclusion that this was an open-and-shut case, the entire event serving at best as an example of the sort of halfhearted and inept defense that indigents often received from their court-assigned lawyers. However, in several ways, the testimony and several inadvertent gaffs committed by the defense set the stage for what was to come in the second trial, involving the rape of Patricia Doe.

Moore had filed a single motion in the case, one indicating that Miranda would plead insanity at the time of the robbery and at the time of trial.[7] In response to the motion, the court selected two prominent Phoenix psychiatrists, Dr. James Kilgore and Dr. Leo Rubinow, to examine Miranda in jail and report back to the court.[8] Judge McFate's intent was to ensure that two "disinterested medical witnesses" examined the defendant.

Accordingly, Dr. James Kilgore had examined Miranda and issued a report on May 28, 1963. His diagnostic impression was that "Mr. Miranda has an emotional illness . . . a schizophrenic reaction [of the] chronic, undifferentiated type." Notwithstanding his emotional illness, Dr. Kilgore told the court, "he was aware of the nature and quality of his acts and he was aware that what he did was wrong."[9]

Dr. Leo Rubinow had examined Miranda in jail on May 22 and again on May 23. He described Miranda as heavily tattooed and "very immature, psychologically, and somewhat inadequate." Dr. Rubinow was struck by Miranda's instability and inability to control his acts. "[H]is id takes over and dominates him completely, especially in the sexual area, even though he denies any sexual conflicts, problems, or deviations," the doctor wrote. Rubinow also noted that, notwithstanding Miranda's impaired judgment and reasoning, he found no evidence of psychotic manifestations. Miranda was neither insane nor mentally defective, in his opinion, and knew the difference between right and wrong. Dr. Rubinow's official diagnosis for Miranda was "sociopathic [sic] personality disturbance."[10]

Following opening statements, the state called two witnesses, Detective Carroll Cooley, and the victim, Barbara Doe. Cooley was up first.[11] Under questioning from Larry Turoff, Cooley confirmed that he had first met Ernesto Miranda at his home on March 13, 1963, and he also identified Miranda as the man he had interviewed in Interrogation Room Number Two at the Phoenix police station on March 13, 1963. He said nothing, however, about Miranda's rape case and did not mention that he had actually closed three cases based on Miranda's incriminating statements.

At this point, when Turoff asked Cooley whether the defendant was one of the men in the March 13 police lineup, Alvin Moore objected, asking that the answer be stricken because it reflected negatively on the defendant. If Miranda was in a lineup at that time, Moore argued, then he must have been charged with some crime.

Judge McFate overruled this objection but Moore persisted, somewhat vaguely, arguing, "If the Court please, I think it has the same affect [sic] as a mug shot reference."

"I hardly think so," Judge McFate replied to Moore. Then, in an effort to be helpful, he said to Turoff, "You should perhaps lay a better foundation."

Whereupon Turoff turned back to Cooley and said, "I am trying to think in my mind what foundation we need. Where was this held? Officer, would you describe to us what you mean by a lineup?"

In answering, Cooley reported that the lineup had taken place at the Detective Bureau in Interrogation Room Number Two, and he described a lineup as "consisting of three other persons approximately the same age and description as the defendant . . . and the lineup room has a two-way mirror in the door so that you can look into the room and you cannot see out," he added.

"Did you cause a photo to be taken of the room with these gentlemen in it?" Turoff asked next.

Cooley answered yes and went on to explain that he had taken a photo of all four men in the lineup and that Barbara was present when the photo was taken.

"Did she make any identification of any of the gentlemen in that lineup?"

"Yes, sir," Cooley said, "She said the suspect looked like the Number One in the lineup."

When Turoff offered the photo of the four men in evidence, Moore objected again but was once again overruled and the court accepted the photo as State's Exhibit 1.[12]

Cooley then testified that Barbara had actually met with Miranda in Interrogation Room Number Two after the lineup. At that time, he said, Barbara told him, "That is the man there." As he said this, Cooley pointed toward Miranda, seated next to his lawyer in the courtroom.

"Did the defendant make any reply either to you or to her at that time?" Turoff asked.

"He made a reply to us," Cooley answered.

Again Moore objected. In his opinion, the answer, having occurred in the interrogation room, in the presence of the officer, "was not shown it was made voluntarily."

Judge McFate sustained this objection, but Cooley, under further questioning, testified that he did not make any threats, use any force, or offer Miranda immunity of any kind. And he confirmed that, after the lineup and meeting in the interrogation room, he arrested Miranda.

Moore then asked that he be allowed to examine Cooley on *voir dire*, which means, literally, "to speak the truth." Defense lawyers are permitted to interrupt the examination of a witness on the stand if there is a legitimate dispute regarding the qualifications or competence of the witness. However, a lawyer must ask questions limited to the witness's qualification or capacity to answer a direct examiner's questions. When Judge McFate allowed this interruption to Turoff's direct examination, Moore approached the witness and asked, "Did you say to the defendant at any time before he made the statement you are about to answer to, that anything he said would be held against him?"

"No, sir," Cooley answered.

"You didn't warn him of that?"

Again Cooley answered in the negative.

"Did you warn him of his rights to an attorney?"

"No, sir."

Abruptly, Moore turned to the bench. "We object, not voluntarily given."

"I don't believe that is necessary," Turoff responded just as quickly, and Judge McFate agreed, overruling Moore's objection.

When Turoff resumed his direct examination, he apparently felt no need to bolster his witness's qualifications, probably sensing that Moore's inept voir dire interruption had strengthened rather than weakened the jury's perception of Detective Cooley. "Would you tell us, Officer," he asked immediately, "what you said to the defendant after the victim made her statement and what the defendant said to you regarding this charge?"

In response, Cooley said, "I asked him, I said, 'Is this the woman that you took the money from?' and he said, 'Yeah, this is her.'"

"Did you ask him anything else? Was there any further conversation regarding the taking of this money?"

When Cooley said no, Turoff announced he was finished with the witness. Turoff likely knew that Moore caused his client further damage when he took the witness on cross-examination. After asking several innocuous questions about the robbery, the only issue before the jury, Moore carelessly asked, "You discussed rape during this particular case?"

Up to this point in the robbery trial, no one had said anything about the attempted rape of Barbara or even that the police had discussed the subject with Miranda. Moore's error thus opened the door for the prosecutor to ask additional questions of Detective Cooley, and Turoff was quick to accept the gift. Immediately he stood and asked Cooley, "Now, relating solely to this victim, will you tell us *now*, Officer, what the conversation was concerning rape?"

Cooley was able to reply that Miranda had already talked about rape before he talked about robbery. Then Moore seemed to catch on to the significance of his mistake and reminded the court that the defendant was not charged with rape. Apparently, Judge McFate decided to give the defense lawyer a little help, for he directed the jury to disregard all references to rape, but then he allowed Cooley to answer the question.

"We asked him if he had attempted to rape this victim," Cooley duly explained, "and he said that was his first thought and he was going to do what he originally intended to do." Cooley then went on to tell the court that he and Young had asked Miranda why he had not raped her, and Miranda had said that she had "kind of talked him out of it, and he told us about what—he said she had told him she worked for a lawyer—and had given him quite a lengthy story and he changed his mind and he said he decided just to take her money."

Thus the jury, having begun with the understanding that this was a simple robbery trial involving a mere eight dollars, discovered that much more had happened that night. It is safe to say that Miranda's fate was sealed, for Turoff could not present the jury with a much more sympathetic case. Even though the attempted rape of Barbara Doe was not material to the robbery charge, Turoff could now elicit testimony about it from the victim of the "robbery." Accordingly, When Turoff called Barbara Doe as his next witness, he quickly established the background details and then began questioning her in detail about the actual encounter, establishing that Barbara had been attacked as she was getting into her car, and that the man had put his hand over her mouth and held a knife against her side. Then he had pushed her to the passenger side, she told the jury, and started the car, and driven into a nearby alley where he shut off the ignition and the lights. And then what had happened? They had "struggled" for some time, Barbara said, during which time she had pleaded with the man not to hurt her. Finally, he had given up attacking her, taken what money she had in her purse, and left.[13]

Up to this point the testimony had all gone against Miranda, but now came a small mistake on the part of the prosecution, one that Moore could have capitalized on had he been more experienced. After asking his witness how much money she had given to the defendant, Turoff asked, "Did you give it to him voluntarily?"

"Yes," Barbara answered.

One can surmise that Barbara considered her action voluntary only in the sense that she was choosing the lesser evil, paying a price to get a dangerous man out of her car. But it was not the answer Turoff expected or wanted, for the sole issue in the case, robbery, depended on the *involuntary* taking of money from the victim.

Incredibly, however, Moore posed an objection, arguing that the line of questioning was leading and suggestive. Then, as if to compound the gaff, Judge McFate asked Turoff to repeat his question.

Turoff was happy to oblige, and this time Barbara did much better. "I just gave it to him because I was afraid," she responded.

After Turoff rested his case, Moore called Ernesto Miranda as his first witness. After establishing that Miranda had been in the courtroom all morning and had heard Barbara's testimony, Moore then asked Miranda when he had first seen the woman. Miranda explained that he had seen her for the first time on the 27th day of November 1962, on Second Street one block north of Van Buren.[14] He further explained that he had seen that "the lady" could not get her car started and that he offered to help. In turn, Miranda claimed, she had asked him if he wanted to go home with her, so he had driven her car two blocks and then pulled into a driveway. "She asked me what I was going to do," Miranda said, "and I said, well, if I was going to rape you, I would have tried it at the other lot, but since I want to go to work, that is what I have to do."

Miranda also claimed that Barbara was worried that police might be in the area and "if we are caught, we could go to jail." Then he volunteered, "[I] put my hand on her thigh; that is when she bit me,"[15] at which time he "got disgusted, got out of the car and went around the back of the car and asked her if she had any money. She grabbed her purse . . . took the money out and gave it to me."

On that low note, Moore turned to the prosecutor and said, "Your witness, that is all."

On cross-examination, Turoff quickly established Miranda's felony record and that he had spent two hours drinking coffee at the bus depot before he walked to the area where he found Barbara getting into her car. Turoff then led Miranda into confirming that he had used the word "rape" in talking to Barbara. When, however, Turoff accused Miranda of "fighting" with the victim, "pressing a knife against her ribs," Miranda denied grabbing her and only admitted to putting his hand on her thigh. Turoff then asked, "While you were fighting in the car, you put your hand on her thigh, and she bit you on the cheek?"

"Yes," Miranda said.

"Was this before or after she asked you to go to her apartment?"

"It was before and after. She asked me twice."

"What did she say when she bit you on the lip?"

"She said, 'I'm sorry.'"

"Did you tell the police about this?"

"Not all of it."

"[Did you tell them] about your conversation with her about if you wanted to rape her?"

"Yes, I did."

"Did you tell the officers also that you took approximately $8 from her and that you were broke at the time and had numerous bills to pay?"

"I told them she gave me $8," Miranda replied.

Turoff had no further questions and neither did Moore. In his closing argument, Turoff outlined the facts from the state's perspective and then moved on to Miranda's confession, reminding the jury that the defendant had admitted that he took the money from the young woman. The prosecutor also reminded the jury that in his cross-examination of Miranda, Miranda had denied confessing to the police.

Moore began his closing argument saying, "I don't know whether this defendant is guilty or not. . . . That is your problem, not mine." He then attempted to discredit the police officers regarding Miranda's confession, reminding the jury that, "One officer came in and testified he never warned the defendant in the interrogation room that the evidence would be held against him. He never told him he was entitled to an attorney before he interrogated him." Then, as if to foreshadow what was to become the most crucial question in the years to come, Moore said, "Did or did they not warn him? One said they did and one said they did not. Which one is telling the truth? . . . They take him down in this room . . . and without warning . . . they didn't tell him he has a right to call an attorney and an attorney be present when he made any statement."[16]

In conclusion Moore told the jury members to remember that they lived in a "free America." Then he said, "When two officers will take a Mexican boy in a room and interrogate him and not tell him whether he has any rights at all, you think that is fair?"

In answer to this question, Turoff in his rebuttal admonished Moore for implying that Cooley and Young had abused Miranda. "Counsel knows that it is not necessary for them [the police] to tell him [about] rights," he said. "We have a good police force and these men aren't jumping on poor innocent boys and forcing them to make confessions. You wouldn't have heard a confession if that was a requirement; they wouldn't have been able to testify if that was a requirement."[17] Turoff also made reference to one of the key issues when, in referring again to the police officers, he said, "They are not taking away any rights, and I don't think you think they are, regardless of what the defendant says."

Apparently, the jury members felt as Turoff did. Well before the dinner hour they returned a unanimous finding of guilty. Since Miranda was scheduled to be tried on the rape charge the next day, and since both cases involved the same confession, lawyers, and courtroom, Judge McFate deferred sentence on the robbery case, pending completion of the rape case.

Miranda's Rape Trial

Miranda's second consecutive day in court began with Judge McFate assuming the bench quietly, his bailiff making only the terse announcement: "Case Number 41948."[18] The judge nodded down to Larry Turoff at the prosecutor's table, which was the one closest to the jury box, and said, "The State versus Ernest Arthur Miranda. Is the State ready?"

"State is ready," Turoff responded. Once again assigned to prosecute Miranda, he, too, was quite certain, at this point, that Miranda's trial for rape would proceed quickly and last but one day.

Then Alvin Moore stood to address the court. "Defense is ready, except for the record; we would like to renew our motion made before the trial for violation of substantial rights in delaying of the trial more than sixty days, as set forth in our motion."

Judge McFate denied the motion and directed his clerk to call the roll of the jury panel. After the jury was summarily selected, empanelled, and sworn, the clerk read the charges and recorded the defendant's plea of not guilty. Knowing that this was to be another "one-day" trial, Judge McFate turned to the prosecutor and indicated that he could begin his opening statement to the jury. However, Turoff waived the state's right to open and immediately Moore stood and said, "We reserve our opening."

The jury may have been confused by the waiver of an opening statement by the prosecutor, but Judge McFate, a veteran of hundreds of such felony trials involving appointed counsel for indigent defendants, was unfazed. Without pause he told Turoff to call his first witness, Patricia Doe. Before this moment, the jury members would not have known whether the case was notorious or insignificant. They would have gleaned little from the dry reading of the "information," the legal document handed to them. An "information" is just one of several ways a defendant can be charged in a criminal case. It is similar to the "indictment" handed up by grand jury, but it is easier for the prosecutor since he can simply file the charge with the clerk of the court without the formality of empanelling a grand jury. In retrospect, had anyone guessed that *Miranda* would become a landmark in American law, this case would likely have been handled via a grand jury.

At any rate, although the jury members likely did not know she was the victim of the crime in question, they could easily guess it. Turoff certainly intended to encourage such a supposition. And most assuredly he succeeded, as he carefully led his witness through the preliminaries—the jury learned that the witness was eighteen years old, single, and employed at the Paramount Theatre concession stand in downtown Phoenix, and that her shift on a particular night had ended around 10:30, at which time she had caught a bus to midtown and then walked alone down a darkened street for three blocks. By the time Patricia had reached this point in recounting the crime, it is likely that most of the members of the jury, without any inkling of their growing prejudice, would have begun to assume that Patricia was indeed a victim of rape.

And by the time Patricia described the car that passed her and then pulled over, and the man who got out suddenly to come walking swiftly toward her, the jury would surely have guessed that the young Hispanic male slouched at the defense table, dressed in a brand-new suit, next to a much older man in a white shirt and tie, was the accused. More important, their presumption of innocence until proven guilty would have begun to erode.

At this point Turoff moved to confirm what the jury had already decided. "Then what happened?" he asked quietly.

"He told me not to scream," Patricia answered softly. "That he wouldn't hurt me. He had my hand behind my back and one hand over my mouth and he started pulling me towards the car."

Whereupon Turoff, without turning from her asked, "Is this man you have just referred to in the courtroom today?"

"Yes, sitting over there," Patricia answered, gesturing toward the defense table.

Turoff turned now toward the table where Miranda and Alvin Moore sat, along with a court police officer. "The one next to the bookcase, the gentleman in the white shirt, or the officer?"

"On the left," Patricia answered.

"On the left, that is the man in the white shirt?"

"In the suit."

"In the suit next to the bookcase?"

"Yes."

Having thus successfully created a facsimile of a police lineup, Turoff faced the bench again and stated, "Let the record show the witness has identified the defendant, Mr. Miranda." Then he resumed his businesslike examination, establishing that the witness was not married to Miranda, was not related to him in any way, and had not met him before. Afterward, if there were any lingering doubt about the full nature of the crime, Patricia dispelled it, describing how her assailant had pressed something sharp to her neck, forced her onto the back seat of his car, and then driven east for about twenty minutes as she lay face down. Somewhere in the mountains east of Phoenix, she said, he had stopped and told her to take off her clothes. She had not done anything willingly—she made this clear. She had screamed, cried, pleaded to be let go, and told her attacker "No!" and "Don't do that!"

Turoff next led his witness through a recounting of the assault itself, not so much to provide the jury with the details as to show the jury that Patricia was a decent and very proper young girl from a respectable family. As the trial transcripts indicate, Patricia fit the desired image perfectly. She showed great reluctance in answering the next series of questions—the standard "penetration" queries put to the victim in every rape case.

"Well, when he was over me," she said finally, "and I was undressed and he was undressed, and then he tried to make penetration."

"Did he make penetration?" Turoff asked.

"At first he didn't succeed, and then he sat, he waited for about five minutes and he started again."

"Did he succeed at that time?"

"Yes."

After the victim reluctantly gave more detail, Turoff finally asked, "Did you permit him to do this voluntarily?"

"Well, he was a lot stronger than I was," Patricia answered.

Turoff was satisfied. With his final questions he moved her past the rape, allowing her to describe how Miranda had moved back to the front seat and driven her back to Phoenix, dropping her off around 2:00 A.M. near where he had picked her up. This one indication of her attacker's kindness, such as it was, probably served better to imply that the perpetrator felt no guilt and feared no recrimination.

After recess, when the trial resumed, Moore began his cross-examination by asking the witness to retell her story, probably hoping to catch her in a clear contradiction. Perhaps he also hoped that in this second telling Patricia would speak more easily and thus undermine the jury's first impressions of her. Accordingly, after assuring the witness he would try not to embarrass her, and asking her not to break down, he said, "Just give me a few truthful answers and we will get along just fine." Then he plowed the same ground, dealing with time, distance, direction traveled, how she was dressed, her age, and details of the rape. Like Turoff, Moore spent some time on the "penetration" details, establishing that the witness was unsure of exactly when or how penetration had occurred.

Unfortunately for Moore, none of what he hoped for occurred. Instead, he came across as the inept lawyer he was, and as if to emphasize this, at one point, he called the rape "an unfortunate occurrence."[19] Whether intentional or not, such a woeful understatement, coming at this point in the trial, could only have worked against him and his client. He fared no better in closing and, in fact, compounded the mistake. "You are a young girl," he said. "Do you know the difference between rape and seduction?"

"Yes," Patricia answered.

"If you know the difference," Moore continued, "did the defendant rape you or did he seduce you?"

"He raped me," Patricia answered immediately and firmly.

Perhaps Moore had wanted to put the question into the minds of the jury in the hope that some of them might begin to think this a case of revenge—a tale of a girl of loose morals going willingly into the desert and then, when her seducer failed to continue the relationship, turning wrathful. Such was not an uncommon strategy. Perhaps he had also expected his preamble to create enough hesitation in his timid witness that even though she would likely call the act rape, the jury might think she wasn't so sure or so honest. Whatever the truth, Patricia's prompt and firm answer obviously wasn't what Moore wanted, for he abruptly ended his cross-examination. Turoff also wisely declined further questions, and Judge McFate excused the witness.

The next witness called to the stand, the victim's sister, confirmed much of what Patricia had just told the jury. Turoff ended his examination by asking what had happened after Patricia arrived home on the night of the attack. "I called the police," her sister said. The prosecutor did not ask what she told the police and the defense lawyer declined any cross-examination.

Turoff called Officer Carroll Cooley as his next witness.[20] Cooley testified that he had been a police officer for five years and was assigned to the

"Crimes Against Persons Detail." He identified Ernesto Miranda in open court, explaining that he had gone to Miranda's home to investigate a rape and, along with Detective Wilfred Young, had taken Miranda to Interrogation Room Number Two in the Phoenix Police Department. He described putting Miranda in a lineup and hearing the victim identify him as the rapist. He stated that this had been done before beginning their interrogation at 11:30 A.M. on March 13, 1963.

Cooley then told the jury that Miranda was in his custody during the lineup and the interrogation. He did not use any threats or force on the defendant, he said, and did not make any promises of immunity, nor did he hear anyone else do so that day.

Turoff then asked Cooley for the "substance" of his conversation in the interrogation room.

"After a short time, he said he was the person that had raped this girl we were questioning him about," Cooley answered. "However, he did not know her name. He said that—he related that—he had been up in the northeast area of Phoenix driving around when he saw a girl walking on a street."

At this point, Moore interrupted, requesting "questions and answers instead of a story,"[21] but Judge McFate overruled the objection and Turoff told Detective Cooley to continue. Afterward, Cooley related what Miranda had told him in some detail and told the judge and jury that their entire conversation had been reduced to writing.

"Who wrote it down, Officer?" Turoff asked.

"He wrote his own statement down."

"He wrote it down?" Turoff feigned surprise. "Were you present, Officer, when he wrote this?"

"Yes, sir, I was."

"Officer, I will show you what has been marked as State's Exhibit Number 1 for identification and ask you to look at that and tell us whether or not you can identify that."

Turoff held out a copy of the written confession. With a glance Cooley identified it and then told the jury that he had signed the statement after Miranda completed it, noting the date and time as "1:30 P.M. on 3-13-63." The interrogation of Miranda had taken about two hours.

Alvin Moore, in his cross-examination of Cooley, had but one objective: to keep Miranda's confession out of the record. Consequently, he began by asking Cooley if Miranda had had an attorney present. Cooley admitted that Miranda hadn't spoken with a lawyer but that he, Cooley, had "warned

Miranda of his rights." Nevertheless, Moore immediately objected to the admission of the confession into evidence because "the Supreme Court of the United States says a man is entitled to an attorney at the time of his arrest."[22] However, Judge McFate summarily overruled; there would be no further argument on the matter. The confession was admitted as Exhibit 1. Disappointed, Moore paused, as though trying to gather his concentration, and then posed a final question to Cooley: "It is not your practice, is it, to advise people you arrest that they are entitled to the services of an attorney before they make a statement?"[23]

"No, sir," Cooley admitted.

That ended the morning's testimony. There seemed nothing further Moore could do to help his client, and the afternoon's testimony was uneventful. Detective Wilfred Young confirmed that Miranda had given a statement of his own free will; no one had forced him and no one had promised him immunity, Young said. Like Cooley, he admitted on cross-examination that an attorney was neither present nor offered, and that the defendant was not told he had a right to have an attorney present.[24]

Turoff began his jury summation at 2:30 P.M. and ended a few minutes later. He recounted the testimony of the victim and her sister. Then he reminded the jury that, while Detective Cooley was securing the defendant's statement, he had asked Miranda "whether or not he had in fact raped this girl."[25]

At this point, interrupting to object, Moore managed one more mistake. "Mr. Young and Mr. Cooley testified he raped the girl," he argued, "but there is nothing in the *confession* to that effect."[26]

No one, up to that point, had actually described State's Exhibit 1 as a "confession." Turoff, Cooley, and Young had all referred to it as a "statement." Miranda's own lawyer was thus the first person to name it as such. The court record is silent as to whether this error on Moore's part went unnoticed by the jury. However, it likely did not escape the notice of Judge McFate, who quickly overruled the objection. Accordingly, Turoff resumed his closing argument. "He admits it," Turoff told the jury, waving Miranda's handwritten "confession" at them. "You have this to take into the deliberation room. This is his written statement. You have read it all."

It is worth noting that Moore began his summation with an effective strategy. He conceded the obvious, saying, "As an attorney, and as a father, this is one of the cases I don't like to be involved with." He also excused his own ineptness as a trial lawyer, saying that he was not going to spellbind them with his oratory or try to show how intelligent he was in an attempt to influence them. Thus, he put aside any intention of playing on the jury's sympathies and cleared a path to the crucial question of legal procedure. "Regardless of the type of case," he told the jury, "the defendant is entitled to the best defense that he can have."

Then, unaccountably, Moore abandoned this ground as quickly as he had prepared it. Over the next several minutes he read aloud from the formal written complaint in the case, not only admitting to the proof that his client had "accosted the victim" in Maricopa County on the day in question, but also no doubt dulling the senses of the jury members, who had already heard the facts of the case several times. From this point onward, Moore's closing continued to disintegrate into a haphazard and eventually blatant and chauvinistic attempt to smear the reputation of the victim. He talked briefly about "resistance" and about the vagueness in the victim's testimony on "penetration." Calling the case both "pitiful" and "sorrowful," he argued that the state "didn't have the facts to send a man to prison for rape of someone who should have resisted and resisted and resisted, until her resistance was at last overcome by the force and violence of the defendant."[27] He then closed his argument with an insensitive and nearly incoherent characterization of the victim:

> I could be wrong and that is either this young lady—and she is a nice looking young lady—but she is human like you and I—and that is whether or not she resisted until she could resist no longer. That is the meat of the coconut, and I want to say this to you: You men don't know too much about that because you are not nervous and you don't thread needles, but a nervous person can't thread a needle if the needle is moving. Thank you.[28]

Judge McFate ended the proceedings by reading the law regarding confessions, as it existed in 1963. Then he gave the jury his final instructions, which state in part:

> if you find that a voluntary confession was made, you are the exclusive judges as to whether or not the confession was true. . . . Nevertheless, the fact that a defendant was under arrest at the time he made a confession or that he was not at the time represented by Counsel, or that he was not told that any statement he might make could or would be used against him in and of themselves will not render such confession involuntary.[29]

Thus, the jury got the case on the testimony of the victim, the police, and

Miranda's written confession. Neither Miranda nor his attorney had disputed the confession or offered any opposing evidence other than to cross-examine the victim regarding penetration and resistance issues. The jury resolved the case within minutes and returned a unanimous guilty verdict.

Judge McFate delayed sentencing for seven days and then sentenced Ernesto Miranda to twenty to thirty years on each count (kidnapping and rape) with the terms to be served concurrently. McFate also sentenced Miranda to spend twenty to twenty-five years in the Arizona State Penitentiary on the eight-dollar robbery charge. The sentence on the robbery case was to run concurrently with the sentence on the rape case.

The Case File of Coerced Confessions

If common sense alone had dictated, the story would have ended on June 20, 1963. It did not matter that Ernesto Miranda's appointed counsel had mounted an ineffective and at times damaging defense. No one, including Alvin Moore, disbelieved the simple truth that Miranda was a serial rapist who had confessed to his crimes. It did not matter that he had made his confession in the absence of counsel and without knowing that he had a right to remain silent, and that, therefore, most of the evidence used to convict him had come out of his own mouth. He had not been tortured, unduly tricked, or cleverly manipulated into admitting his guilt. The police had acted consistently and in accordance with standards that had been deemed acceptable for many years.

However, by 1963 America's criminal justice system, and the nation in general, had entered an era of civil unrest. Under pressure from liberal and activist groups all over the country, appellate courts had begun an active reexamination of the laws of the land—of their basis in the Constitution and their application in the course of meting out justice. The central issue had actually already come to rest squarely on two questions: When could a "suspect" assert his constitutional rights under the Fifth and Sixth Amendments, and must he be appraised of those rights by the police before anything he said could be used against him?

Thus, it is not surprising that Miranda's handwritten confession, while it had not helped him at all in Judge McFate's courtroom, or on appeal in the Arizona Supreme Court, nevertheless caught the attention of the U.S. Supreme Court, as well as most law-review writers in the country. Four similar cases involving the coerced-confession issue were subjected to the judicial scrutiny of the United States Supreme Court.

Sylvester Cassidy and Stanley Johnson

One involved two New Jersey men, Sylvester Cassidy and Stanley Johnson. Sylvester Cassidy had been arrested at his home in Camden at about 4:00 A.M. on January 29, 1958, for a murder that ostensibly had occurred during the course of a robbery five days earlier.[30] He was taken to the police station in Newark and interrogated until about 10:30 A.M., when he made a partial confession. The police continued to interrogate him, took three formal statements, and, at 11:40 P.M., took him to the chief detective for a final round of questions.

Stanley Johnson was taken into custody in Newark at 5:00 P.M. on January 29, 1958, for the same crime as Cassidy. At about 2:00 A.M., the police drove him to Camden, some eighty miles from Newark. There his questioning continued before the same chief detective who had questioned Cassidy. He made a full confession to felony murder about 6:00 A.M.

The seven police officers who converged on Sylvester Cassidy's home had no warrant. Cassidy had no police record, no prior arrests, and no experience of any kind with the police; he had an eighth-grade education. During the four days preceding his arrest, as he later acknowledged, Cassidy had been using drugs "pretty heavy" and was under the influence of severe marijuana intoxication.

Chief of County Detectives Dube took several statements from Cassidy, all in the presence of a court stenographer. At some point during the questioning, Chief Dube warned Cassidy, "I am going to ask you some questions as to what you know about the holdup, but before I ask you these questions, it is my duty to warn you that everything you tell me must be of your own free will, must be the truth, without any promises or threats having been made to you, and knowing anything you tell me can be used against you, or any other person, at some future time."[31] The record shows no effort was made at any time to inform Cassidy that he had any right to talk to an attorney before he made any statement.

Meanwhile, Stanley Johnson was also photographed, fingerprinted, and interrogated without a warrant and taken before a municipal judge so that he could be transferred to the Camden jail, where Cassidy was being held. His interrogation continued during the ride to Camden. When he arrived, he was turned over to Chief Dube.

Throughout this period of his incarceration Johnson repeatedly requested that he be allowed to speak to family and counsel, but his requests were denied by the New Jersey police. Chief Dube gave Johnson the same "warning" that had been given to Cassidy. So far as the record shows, he never mentioned any right to counsel. Both men had confessed, both were tried, found guilty of murder, and sentenced to death. The New Jersey Supreme Court upheld their convictions. The issue of coerced confessions was not raised at trial or in the appellate courts. It was raised for the first time in a motion for new trial and then denied by each successive court up the appellate ladder.

Michael Vignera

The second case involved a Brooklyn man named Michael Vignera who, armed with a knife, robbed a dress shop in Brooklyn on October 11, 1960. Three days later, a man tried to buy some jewelry using the dress shop owner's credit card. When caught, the man said he had received the card from Vignera. The police picked up Vignera and took him to the dress shop, where the owner identified him as the man who had robbed his store and stolen his credit card.

After Vignera was placed under formal arrest and detained at the 66th Squad Room in Manhattan, where Detective John Gillen questioned him, he admitted that he had committed the holdup. Shortly thereafter, Vignera confessed to an assistant district attorney in the presence of a stenographer. Both the oral confession and the written confession were accepted in evidence at the trial.

Vignera's lawyer cross-examined Detective Gillen at trial, asking whether he had advised Vignera of his right to counsel before taking his confession. The judge sustained an objection, ruling that such evidence would be irrelevant.[32] The judge immediately told the jury, "The law doesn't say that the confession is void or invalidated because the police officer didn't advise the defendant as to his rights. Did you hear what I said? I am telling you what the law of the State of New York is."

Vignera was adjudged a "third-felony" offender after being found guilty of the single count of robbery and was sentenced to thirty to sixty years' imprisonment.[33] When he challenged the validity of the "prior" felony conviction, he was successful but was resentenced as a "second-felony" offender to the same term of imprisonment he had been given as a "third-felony" offender. When he appealed his conviction to the New York Court of Appeals, that court affirmed the conviction, holding that he had no constitutional right to be advised of his right to counsel or his privilege against self-incrimination.

Roy Allen Stewart

In the third case involving the question of coerced confessions, Roy Allen Stewart was charged with robbing five women—and murdering one of them—between December 21, 1962, and January 30, 1963. He first came to the attention of the Los Angeles police as the man who had cashed dividend checks stolen in one of the robberies. On January 31, 1963, Stewart and four other men were arrested at Stewart's home in Los Angeles. A search of the home turned up property stolen in each of the five robberies.

Between January 31 and February 5, 1963, Stewart was placed in a cell and interrogated nine different times. He initially denied all involvement in the crimes, but on February 5 he confessed to robbing the murder victim. Two of Stewart's confessions were tape-recorded. His confessions were admitted in evidence at his trial, and he was found guilty of robbery and murder and sentenced to death.

During interrogation, Stewart had never requested counsel, nor had he been warned about his statements; however, the door to custodial interrogation law had been partially opened by two previous cases. In *Escobedo v. Illinois*,[34] the U.S. Supreme Court had established a suspect's right to counsel during custodial interrogation, as long as the suspect asked for a lawyer. That decision had led to a California Supreme Court decision in the case of *People v. Dorado*,[35] which expanded the warnings first discussed in *Escobedo* into a general Sixth Amendment right to counsel. *Dorado*'s expansion, at least in California, confirmed the suspect's right to counsel both at and after his arrest.

Consequently, the California Supreme Court reversed Stewart's convictions on the ground that his confessions were constitutionally inadmissible.[36] Citing *Escobedo* and *Dorado*, the California Supreme Court held that Stewart should have been advised of his right to remain silent and his right to counsel and stated that it would not presume, in the face of a silent record, that the police had advised Stewart of his rights.

Carl Calvin Westover

While Miranda, Vignera, Johnson, Cassidy, and Stewart were "in the system," Westover was arrested in Kansas City, Missouri, on March 20, 1963, and charged with two robberies. The police soon learned that he was wanted in California on a felony warrant. He was placed in a lineup and booked on "investigation" of the local robberies and "possible outside warrants, California."

Around the time Westover was being booked, the FBI called and asked that Westover "be held for them also." Two photographs of him were taken and transmitted to Sacramento, California. The Kansas City police interrogated Westover until shortly before noon on March 21. In the afternoon, three FBI agents arrived and continued to interrogate him. Eventually, the FBI secured a longhand confession in which Westover admitted to several different robberies. Eleven days later Westover was officially released from state custody in Kansas City and turned over to federal officials under an indictment returned on April 1 in Sacramento.

Westover's lawyers did *not* object to the admission of his confession during his trial or to his lack of counsel at the time he confessed. He was convicted and sentenced to fifteen years on each of two counts of bank robbery. The United States Court of Appeals for the Ninth Circuit affirmed his conviction.[37]

The Ninth Circuit found that "The agents made no threats or promises to the appellant. The appellant made detailed statements as to how he had committed the two Sacramento robberies for which he was later indicted and tried." The circuit court concluded,[38] "The FBI agents advised the appellant that he did not have to make a statement; that any statement he made could be used against him in a court of law; and that he had the right to consult an attorney."

Chapter 2

THE LAW

Law and Order in '64

At the time Miranda and his companion defendants went to prison, public opinion rested firmly on the side of law and order.[1] It was, in fact, Arizona's Richard G. Kleindienst, who later served as President Richard Nixon's attorney general, and was one of the principal architects of Barry Goldwater's unsuccessful presidential campaign, who coined the phrase "law and order" as a way of taking Goldwater's "violence in our streets" theme to the voters. However, former president Dwight D. Eisenhower had already set the political tone in his August 1964 address to the Republican National Convention, when he said,

> Let us not be guilty of maudlin sympathy for the criminal who, roaming the street with switchblade knife and illegal firearms seeking a helpless prey, suddenly becomes upon apprehension a poor, underprivileged person who counts upon the compassion of our society and the laxness or weakness of too many courts to forgive his offense.[2]

The next day, in his now-famous speech accepting his party's presidential nomination, Barry Goldwater, a man noted for speaking plainly, responded to Eisenhower's challenge: "[I will] do all I can," he promised, "to see that women can go out in the streets of this country without being scared stiff." He went on to warn, "Security from domestic violence, no less than foreign aggression is the most elementary and fundamental purpose of any government and a government that cannot fulfill this purpose is one that cannot long command the loyalty of its citizens."[3]

Furthermore, when Goldwater opened his national campaign in Prescott, Arizona, on September 3, 1964, with a rousing speech in the town square, he made clear not only the problem as he saw it but also who was to blame. "[T]hose that break the law are accorded more consideration than those who try to enforce the law," he fumed. "Law enforcement agencies . . . are attacked for doing their jobs."

Alluding to the *Escobedo* decision in another speech, Goldwater said, "If there is any flaw in one confession, all confessions . . . must be thrown out. . . . Something must be done to swing this obsessive concern for the rights of the criminal defendant."

After Goldwater lost to Johnson in the 1964 election, others took up Goldwater's thunderous call for "law and order." The Senate Judiciary Committee met in the summer of 1966 to explore the implications of *Miranda*. Truman Capote, the author of *In Cold Blood,* testified that had the *Miranda* rulings been in effect when the murderers of the Clutter family were captured, the two killers would have gone "scot-free."[4]

Then, in 1966, Georgetown University's prestigious Institute of Criminal Law and Procedure published *From Escobedo to Miranda.*[5] This comprehensive treatment of the pertinent "law" and the political "order" stood in sharp opposition to the prevailing opinion, as Samuel Dash wrote in the foreword:

> The cases for this presentation deal with one of the most fundamental and at the same time most controversial issues of American criminal justice—the application of the Fifth Amendment privilege to in-custody police interrogation of persons suspected of crime. The resolution of this issue by a five-member majority of the Supreme Court dramatically closed a period of national debate, sometimes frenzied in nature, over the competing interests of the police and the individual in police custody.

The debate did not end there, however. Goldwater's "law and order" campaign resonated with then–private citizen Richard Nixon, who, in 1964, was neither radical conservative nor social adventurer. He was said to be "the likeliest man to weld the dissident elements of right and left, the choice of a lukewarm South, a traditionally Republican West and Midwest, and a reluctant Northeast."[6] Two years after the Warren Court made *Miranda* a household word by reversing the Arizona Supreme Court decision that confirmed Miranda's conviction, Nixon ran for the presidency on Goldwater's "law and order" ticket and won.

It is possible to trace the need for "law and order" all the way back to the framing of the Constitution of the United States.[7] As originally crafted, the Constitution contained relatively few protections of individual rights, apart from those resulting from the diffusion of power in the federal system. Article one dealt with *habeas corpus* and *ex post facto* laws. An order of habeas corpus, or, "You should have the body," requires the government to produce prisoners and answer challenges to the legality of their detention. Ex post facto, or, "after the fact," refers to laws passed after the occurrence of an act, laws that retrospectively change the legal consequences of the act. Article three assured a jury trial in criminal cases.

Apart from these two articles, the American Constitution is silent on individual rights in criminal cases, but the essential First Amendment freedoms, those of speech, religion, and assembly, were assured during the ratification process, and James Madison introduced the proposed amendments to the Constitution at the first session of Congress, which ratified the Bill of Rights in 1791.

The first ten amendments to the Constitution have been crucial to the development of the political and legal systems of the United States. Collectively, they portray an important ideal: that the people have rights, which no government may withhold. It was for the express purpose of preventing tyrants from restricting the rights of citizens that the framers of the Constitution embedded this ideal and also pragmatically provided the basis for actually securing the rights they envisioned. In a letter to Madison in 1787, Jefferson wrote that a bill of rights "puts into the hands of the judiciary" a "legal check" against tyranny by the legislature or the executive.

However, one of the first United States Supreme Court decisions to discuss the constitutional framework of the 1791 amendments (the Bill of Rights) observed that they applied only to the national government and did not limit the states.[8] Chief Justice John Marshall delivered the opinion of the Court: "The Constitution was ordained and established by the people of the United States for themselves, for their own government, and not for the government of the individual states." This view, which enjoyed near universal approval at the time and continued to guide lawmakers for nearly two centuries, ultimately proved a crucial point of contention: the issue of federalism.

The American Right to Counsel

Procedural rights define how people accused of crimes are treated in our criminal justice system. The major emphasis rests on the specific safeguards set out in the Bill of Rights, but many U.S. Supreme Court cases address the related issue of federalism.[9]

The word *federal,* from the Latin term *fidere,* meaning "to trust," refers simply to the federal government's expectation that states will surrender some of their political power to the federal government, relying on it to act for the common good of the union. Such a trust becomes imperative when both levels of government control the same territory and citizens. Our constitutional history is rife with conflicts over the exact boundary between state and national power. The conflicts proliferated after the Civil War, when the Supreme Court began to allow Congress more and more control over the states, often basing its decisions on the Commerce Clause in article one, section eight of the Constitution. Thus occurred a gradual increase in the authority of the federal government, accompanied by a growth in power at all levels of government, with the result that crime, once strictly a problem dealt with locally, became a national issue by the early part of the twentieth century.

Today, when conflicts, criminal and civil, arise, the courts must decide how to balance states' rights with the needs of the nation.

Consistent with federalism, the United States has a dual system of federal and state courts that is independent of one another. Because each state has its own legal structure, there are essentially fifty-two court systems in the United States (the federal system, fifty state systems, and the District of Columbia). The most controversial arguments arise when the legal issue at hand concerns whether the federal court system controls an issue or whether it must defer to a state court. This is, for lack of a better term, federalism within the court system. Those who defend the growth in the power of the federal government insist that public interest demands federal control in cases involving more than one state. Opponents fear that the continued expansion of federal authority will create an inefficient and possibly dangerous concentration of power in federal hands.

The combination of federalism within the court system, the right to counsel, and the culture of the Deep South made the 1932 case of *Powell v. Alabama*[10] pivotal in the story of America's right to remain silent. This case involved two African-American men charged—in a state court—with raping two white women. The ethnicity of both the accused and the victims is relevant because men and women of color were treated differently in the criminal justice system in some states during the thirties.

The men were accused of attacking the two women on a train passing through Alabama. When the train arrived in Scottsboro, Alabama, the women identified the two men. The men were arrested, charged, tried by the State of Alabama, and found guilty within a matter of days. The proceedings "from beginning to end, took place in an atmosphere of tense, hostile, and excited public sentiment." Also the defendants were acknowledged both "ignorant and illiterate." Both men appealed and, eventually, the case reached the United States Supreme Court, where the issue of federalism was central to the Court's decision.

The 1932 reversal of the convictions in *Powell* comes as close to a short-tempered opinion as has ever been handed down:

> To be kind, the record also suggested that the right to counsel for a black man accused of raping a white woman was a matter of humor, not law, in Scottsboro, Alabama, in the thirties.[11] . . . It is hardly necessary to say that, the right to counsel being conceded, a defendant should be afforded a fair opportunity to secure counsel of his choice. Not only was that not done here, but such designation of counsel as was attempted was either so indefinite or so close upon the trial as to amount to a denial of effective and substantial aid in that regard.[12]

In reaching its historic decision, the Court said, "Under the circumstances disclosed, we hold that the defendants were not accorded the right of counsel in any substantial sense. . . . The prompt disposition of criminal cases is to be commended and encouraged. But in reaching that result a defendant, charged with a serious crime, must not be stripped of his right to have sufficient time to advise with counsel and prepare his defense."

In another significant case regarding the right to counsel, *Betts v. Brady*,[13] the core issue concerned whether the appointment of counsel in state criminal cases was a "fundamental right, essential to a fair trial." The U.S. Supreme court found that in the great majority of the states the appointment of counsel was not a fundamental right, and therefore not required as a matter of due process. The Court recognized, however, that "want of counsel" in a particular case might result in a conviction lacking "fundamental fairness." Furthermore, in his sharply worded dissent, Justice Hugo Black stated that the Fourteenth Amendment made the Sixth Amendment applicable to the states. It should not go unnoticed that John P. Frank, the lead counsel in the *Miranda* case, was, in 1942, Justice Hugo Black's law clerk and likely participated in the drafting of his mentor's dissent in *Betts*.

The Supreme Court reversed its position on *Betts* three years before the Court was to hear the *Miranda* case. The reversal came as a consequence of an appeal filed by one Clarence Earl Gideon, who had been convicted of five felonies and had spent most of his life in prison. His fifth conviction,[14] on charges of robbery, had led him to compose, in longhand, one of the most famous letters ever written to the United States Supreme Court. In this January 8, 1962, letter, Gideon wrote, "When at the time of petitioner's trial he ask [sic] the lower court for the aid of counsel, the court refused this aid." In deciding *Gideon v. Wainwright* in 1963, the Warren Court essentially adopted the dissenting position urged by Justice Black. It rejected the conclusion that the Sixth Amendment's guarantee of counsel was not a fundamental right of all citizens. Thus, the Court set the stage for *Miranda* by holding in *Gideon* that "Reason and reflection requires us to recognize that in our adversary system of criminal justice, any person hailed into court, too poor to hire a lawyer, cannot be assured a fair trial unless counsel is provided for him."

The Supreme Court appointed a highly regarded Washington lawyer, Abe Fortas,[15] to represent Gideon. On October 29, 1962, Fortas wrote to Gideon, then still in prison. "I should be very glad to receive from you a careful and detailed biographical description . . . employment, family, arrests, [etc.]."[16] From his prison cell in Florida, Gideon penciled a twenty-two-page reply on lined prison-issue paper, detailing his life, his criminal history, his innocence, and his hope for the future. Blending pragmatism with optimism, he concluded:

> I have no illusions about law and courts or the people who are involved in them. I have read the complete history of law ever since the Romans first started writing them down and before of the laws of religions. I believe that each era finds an improvement in law each year brings something new for the benefit of mankind. Maybe this will be one of those small steps forward, in the past thirty-five years I have seen great advancement in Courts in penal servitude. Thank you for reading all of this. Please try to believe that all I want now from life is the chance for the love of my children the only real love I have ever had.
> Sincerely yours
> Clarence Earl Gideon

Gideon's rationale stemmed from the notion that state and national constitutions had laid great emphasis on procedural and substantive safeguards. Specifically, as an overarching goal, judicial articles in constitutions seek to assure fair trials before impartial tribunals, in which every defendant stands equal before the law. That noble ideal could not be realized if poor, ignorant men or women, charged with crimes, had to face their accusers without the assistance of lawyers. Accordingly, the Warren Court decided that *Betts v. Brady* had been a departure from the sound wisdom upon which the Court's holding in *Powell v. Alabama* rested. In overruling *Betts*, the Court established the right to counsel as fundamental to a fair trial and labeled *Betts* "an anachronism when handed down."

The American Privilege against Self-Incrimination

To incriminate means, literally, to charge with crime. Figuratively, it means to involve oneself in a criminal prosecution. The modern origin of the law regarding self-incrimination lies in *Brown v. Mississippi*.[17] This 1935 case involved the murder trial of three black defendants. Their convictions were based entirely on their confessions, which were admittedly obtained under torture inflicted by white deputy sheriffs. In an opinion authored by Chief Justice Charles Evans Hughes,[18] the Court unanimously reversed *Brown*, noting that while "the State was free to regulate the procedure of its courts with its own perceptions of policy," its policies are "limited by the requirement of due process of law. Because a State may dispense with a jury trial does not mean that it may substitute trial by ordeal. The rack and torture chamber may not be substituted for the witness stand."

After *Brown v. Mississippi*, scores of cases involving convictions based on coerced confessions (most having occurred in Southern states) came to the U.S. Supreme Court. The Court repeatedly recognized that coercion could exist even in the absence of physical compulsion,[19] observing, "There is torture of the mind as well as the body."[20] In one famous case, the Court categorically stated, "A confession by which life becomes forfeit must be the expression of free choice."[21]

Legally, this idea of free choice, or *voluntariness,* is a notion separate from *coercion.* If force, or mere coercion, is applied to extract a confession, then the confessor's voluntariness is immaterial. The question can't be dismissed because the context in which these terms are used is evidentiary, not linguistic. In other words, the law focuses on whether the confession is admissible in evidence, not whether it was given freely. Justice Felix Frankfurter, one of the giants in judicial rhetoric, put the distinction in a psychologically elegant way:

> But whether a confession of a lad of fifteen is "voluntary" and as such admissible, or "coerced" and thus wanting for due process, is not a matter of mathematical determination. Essentially it invites psychological judgment—a psychological judgment that reflects deep, even if inarticulate, feelings in our society.[22]

Two 1958 cases, one from Arkansas[23] and the other from Arizona,[24] gave the Supreme Court the opportunity to discuss the difficulty of assessing voluntariness on a case-by-case basis. The Court's opinion in *Payne v. Arkansas* reversed the lower court's decision on the grounds that the confession was coerced;[25] in *Thomas v. Arizona,* the Court's opinion, handed down the same day, affirmed the lower court's decision, arguing that the confession was voluntary.

Affirming or reversing a lower court, easy when the evidence is fundamentally flawed, becomes more difficult when the factual nuances in the case are disputed. In the *Thomas* case, local ranchers had twice lassoed the defendant Thomas on the day of his arrest; however, the local sheriff had, upon arriving to arrest the suspect, immediately removed the ropes and waited until the following day to obtain a confession.[26] The defense argued that the ranchers' abuse of the suspect invalidated his confession. But the Court ruled that the confession was voluntary notwithstanding the lassoing the previous day.

The tricky issue in determining voluntariness concerns the allocation of function between judge and jury. The 1964 case of *Jackson v. Denno*[27] serves as perhaps the best example of an unconstitutional allocation. This case required the Supreme Court to analyze the constitutional validity of the procedure used in New York to assess voluntariness. The state required the trial judge to make a preliminary determination regarding a confession. He or she could exclude a confession if "in no circumstances could the confession be deemed voluntary." If the evidence presented a fair question as to its voluntariness, however, the judge was required to receive the confession and allow the jury to determine its voluntary character as well as its truthfulness. A divided Court[28] concluded that the New York procedure violated due process because it did not afford a reliable determination of the voluntariness of a confession.

The year 1964 was a seminal one for the Fifth Amendment's privilege against self-incrimination. Two cases handed down in June 1964, *Malloy v. Hogan* and *Murphy v. Waterfront Commission,* summarily discarded doctrines that were cemented into the wall of prior self-incrimination cases, decided in 1908,[29] 1931,[30] 1944,[31] 1947,[32] and 1958.[33] In *Malloy,* the petitioner was held in contempt of court for refusing to answer questions in a Connecticut gambling inquiry.[34] The Supreme Court reversed his conviction, holding that the petitioner was entitled to the protection of the Fifth Amendment's privilege against self-incrimination. In *Murphy,* the question was more complicated. The Court decided that a witness who had been granted immunity in one state court could not be compelled to give incriminating testimony that might then be used to convict him of a crime in some other state.[35]

Historical constitutional analysis of cases involving the privilege against self-incrimination provides an important context in which to view the birth of America's right to remain silent. That context begins in 1896 with *Brown v. Walker*,[36] which was largely ignored until 1956, when the Court handed down *Ullmann v. United States*.[37] In this infamous case, the Court sustained the constitutionality of the Federal Immunity Act of 1950, believing "it was sufficiently broad to *displace* the protection afforded by the privilege against self-incrimination." In so holding, Justice Felix Frankfurter cited the 1896 case of *Brown v. Walker*.

That prompted Justice William O. Douglas to dissent, insisting that the Federal Immunity Act left a witness subject to "penalties affixed to criminal acts."[38] Justice Douglas went on to say, somewhat prophetically, that *Brown v. Walker* should be overruled because "The Fifth Amendment was designed to protect the accused against infamy as well as prosecution . . . [and] places the *right of silence* beyond the reach of the government."

Escobedo

The saga of *Escobedo v. Illinois*[39] began on January 19, 1960, when Manuel Valtierra was shot and killed. It was a typical clueless crime—no gun, no witnesses. Knowing that statistically 80 percent of all murders involve friends or family, the police arrested two family members, Danny Escobedo, who was the victim's brother-in-law, and Danny's sister, Grace Valtierra. They also arrested Danny's two best friends, seventeen-year-old Bobby Chan, and eighteen-year-old Benedict DiGerlando.

The police questioned the four young people for fourteen hours. During the interrogation, Chan's mother called Warren Wolfson, a lawyer who had previously represented Escobedo on a minor matter. Around 5:00 P.M. that day, Wolfson arranged to have all four released. No one had made any incriminating statements; the police, however, now had a theory: Escobedo murdered Valtierra to do his sister a favor, as Valtierra had stabbed Grace more than a dozen times a year before the arrest. Valtierra had been arrested but not prosecuted for this attack.[40]

Eleven days later, police again arrested DiGerlando, who was later indicted for the murder of Valtierra. DiGerlando told police that it was Escobedo who fired the fatal shots.[41]

Later that evening, Escobedo and his sister were arrested again, then taken to police headquarters and interrogated. Escobedo later testified, without contradiction, that "the detectives said they had us pretty well, up pretty tight, and we might as well admit to this crime."[42] Escobedo replied,

"I am sorry but I would like to have advice from my lawyer. A police officer testified that although petitioner was not formally charged 'he was in custody' and 'couldn't walk out the door.'"[43]

Shortly after Escobedo and his sister reached police headquarters, Wolfson returned to the Chicago police station and insisted that he be allowed to see his client. The detectives and the chief of police told him he could not see Escobedo until they "completed questioning [him]."

Wolfson later testified that when he went to the detective bureau he was told he could not see his client. Then he went to the homicide bureau and was refused a second time. He tried a third time, then went to the chief detective's office. Chief Flynn flatly refused him permission to see Escobedo. Meanwhile, Escobedo repeatedly asked to talk to Wolfson. The police ignored him and continued their questioning of Escobedo throughout the day while Wolfson waited in the building for permission to intercede.

Eventually, the detectives confronted Escobedo with DiGerlando, and Escobedo broke down and made a statement implicating himself in the murder plot, although he emphatically told DiGerlando, in the presence of the police, "I didn't shoot Manuel. You did it." No one advised Escobedo of his rights during the interrogation.

During the trial, the judge denied Escobedo's multiple motions to suppress the incriminating statement. The jury convicted him of first-degree murder, and the judge sentenced him to twenty years in the Statesville Penitentiary for killing Manuel Valtierra. Afterward, the State of Illinois appointed Chicago lawyer Eugene Farrug to handle the case at no fee. Farrug enlisted Barry Kroll, who, although only twenty-eight at the time, had already handled over three hundred appeals while a member of the Army's Judge Advocate General Corps. In an argument that at times bordered on brilliance, Kroll argued successfully that Escobedo's incriminating statement was entirely the product of false promises made to him by police. The Illinois Supreme Court reversed the trial court's conviction and held Escobedo's statement inadmissible.

On rehearing, prosecutor James R. Thompson (who went on to become governor of Illinois) urged the court to reconsider and change its ruling. The higher court did so, confirming the lower court's ruling that the police officer had denied Escobedo's claim of false promises, and thus finding no reason to disturb the trial court's ruling that the confession was voluntary.

In 1964, Kroll took the case up to the United States Supreme Court, where he argued that Escobedo's incriminating statement became *ipso facto* involuntary and therefore inadmissible when the police turned away his lawyer. On a five-to-four decision authored by Justice Arthur Goldberg, the justices reversed the conviction and remanded the case for a new trial.[44] Justice Goldberg wrote, "When petitioner requested, and was denied, an opportunity to consult with his lawyer, the investigation had ceased to be a general investigation of 'an unsolved crime.' Petitioner had become the accused, and the purpose of interrogation was to 'get him' to confess his guilt despite his constitutional right not to do so."

In retrospect, it is clear that, while the police interrogations of Clarence Gideon in Florida, Danny Escobedo in Illinois, and Ernesto Miranda in Arizona were all conducted while the suspects were in custody in a police station and without the benefit of counsel, Escobedo was the only one of the three to ask for a lawyer.[45] In reversing Escobedo's case, the Supreme Court said, "At the time of his arrest and throughout the course of the interrogation, the police told petitioner that they had convincing evidence that he had fired the fatal shots. Without informing him of *his absolute right to remain silent* in the face of this accusation, the police urged him to make a statement."

As a layman, Escobedo was likely unaware that, under Illinois law, an admission of "mere" complicity in a murder plot was legally as damaging as an admission of firing the fatal shots. Had the police honored his request to talk to his lawyer, Escobedo would likely have known just how damaging his admission of mere complicity could be in a court of law. The Supreme Court sent a message to all lower courts in America when it declared "[the] guiding hand of counsel to be essential in advising Escobedo of his rights in what was certainly a delicate situation. This was the stage when legal aid and advice were most critical to petitioner."

The holding of an appellate decision is the real key to our justice system. When used in a legal sense, the term *holding* describes *what* an appellate court did. It is not used to describe *how* the court arrived at its decision. In essence, a holding is a determination as a matter of law that is pivotal to the judicial decision.

It should be noted, too, that the Court, in its holding in the *Escobedo* case, listed several criteria to be met in order to conclude that a suspect has been denied the assistance of counsel:

(1) the investigation is no longer a general inquiry into an unsolved crime but has begun to focus on a particular suspect; (2) the suspect has been taken into police custody; (3) the police carry out a process of interrogations that lends itself to eliciting incriminating statements; (4)

the suspect has requested and been denied an opportunity to consult with his lawyer; and (5) the police have not effectively warned him of his absolute constitutional right to remain silent.

Unless these criteria are met, the Court held, "no statement elicited by the police during the interrogation may be used against him at a criminal trial." In reversing and remanding *Escobedo,* the Court emphasized, "Nothing we have said here today affects the powers of the police to investigate 'an unsolved crime' [. . .] by gathering information from witnesses and by other 'proper investigative efforts.'" The Court held "only that when the process shifts from investigatory to accusatory—when its focus is on the accused and its purpose is to elicit a confession—our adversary system begins to operate" and "the accused must be permitted to consult with his lawyer."

A year later, in *People v. Dorado,*[46] the California Supreme Court handed down a decision holding that *Escobedo* compelled the furnishing of counsel regardless of whether the accused demands it. In this pivotal precursor to *Miranda,* the California Supreme Court said, "The defendant who does not ask for counsel is the very defendant who most needs counsel."

In April 1966, most constitutional law scholars were aware of Danny Escobedo and his case, but to the rest of America he was unknown. A *Time* magazine article on April 29 changed that. Danny Escobedo made the cover, under the banner headline: "Moving the Constitution into the Police Station." The seven-page article contained three photos of Escobedo,[47] one of the nine justices of the Supreme Court of the United States,[48] a photo depicting a burglary suspect in Atlanta, one of a prowl-car interrogation in Houston, another of a street arrest in Chicago,[49] a photo of Justice Arthur Goldberg,[50] and a photo of three men convicted of murder awaiting execution in New Jersey.[51] The final photograph, of Escobedo and Kroll,[52] carried the caption, "A nobody for everybody."[53] *Time*'s editors had elected to highlight the nation's "concern about confessions" by profiling Escobedo and the vital issues at stake in his case. They also profiled Justice Goldberg and, most significantly, publicized the provocative discussion resulting from the *Escobedo* decision:

> Across the country, many lower courts echoed the dissenter's fears by ruling that *Escobedo* voids a confession only if, as in Danny Escobedo's case, the suspect had retained a lawyer and was not allowed to consult him. By contrast, the California Supreme Court went beyond *Escobedo* and ruled last year that a constitutional right to counsel exists even if a

suspect does not ask to exercise it. In California, police failure to warn a suspect of his rights to silence and to counsel now voids his confession even though he makes no request for a lawyer.[54]

The *Time* article also recognized the significance of the yet-to-be-decided *Miranda* case by reporting:

> Ernesto Miranda, 23, an "emotionally ill" truck driver, received 25-and-30-year sentences in 1963 for robbing a woman and kidnapping and raping an 18-year old girl. Miranda was picked up on suspicion: both victims identified him in a lineup. He talked freely, was neither told, nor knew of his right to counsel. The Arizona Supreme Court took the "hard" Escobedo line, upheld his conviction.[55]

By December 1966, the die was cast. Two federal appellate courts had handed down diametrically opposing interpretations of *Escobedo*. Following longstanding policy, the United States Supreme Court searched its docket for a case that could be used to resolve the federal conflict and answer *Time*'s question: "Do you get a lawyer even if you don't ask for one?" The Court found five cases that involved confession issues. One of the five was *Miranda*.

The five-justice majority in *Escobedo* lost a member when Justice Goldberg departed the Court for the United Nations in 1965. That left the court split four-to-four on the issue of the right to a lawyer during custodial interrogation in a police station. Goldberg's replacement on the Court was none other than Clarence Earl Gideon's lawyer, Abe Fortas. After winning Gideon's case in the Supreme Court, Fortas had himself been appointed to the Court.[56]

The Fortas confirmation hearing in the U.S. Senate produced a prophetic exchange between Fortas and his inquisitor, Senator John L. McClellan (D–AR). After Senator McCellan made his opposition to the *Gideon* case known, nominee Fortas defended his position. After acknowledging that the police depended on "an adequate opportunity [. . .] to interrogate persons who are accused of crime or who are suspected that they might have been involved," he continued, asserting that "At the same time I recognize that there comes a point at which persons should be brought before a judicial officer, such as a magistrate, for the purpose of ascertaining whether there is probable cause for their continued detention, and the great difficulty . . . which I confess I would not be able to suggest a solution to. . . is where to draw the line."

Understanding exactly how *Escobedo* expanded *Gideon* requires a re-examination of Justice Arthur Goldberg's opinion for the Court, which read in part, "When petitioner requested, and was denied, an opportunity to consult with his lawyer, the investigation had ceased to be a general investigation of an unsolved crime."

This critical point, often lost in the media's reaction to the *Gideon* decision, recognized the fact that a person who was the subject of a "general investigation" was not considered a "suspect" and was therefore not entitled to all of the protections of the Bill of Rights. This category would include witnesses, potential witnesses, and sources of information or investigative leads. However, once the "general investigation" ceased and the witness became the focus of the investigation, he was then entitled to the full protection of the Bill of Rights.

Nevertheless, the law protecting our privilege against self-incrimination and our right to counsel did not spring forth fully formed, like Athena from the forehead of Zeus, for constitutional rights, like genetic codes, take time to evolve. The case law developed slowly, gaining nuance and substance, case by case. *Powell* had disclosed the constitutional DNA that would eventually extend to suspects in police stations; then, in sequence, the Supreme Court had handed down *Gideon* and *Betts,* decisions that wove together the Fifth and Sixth Amendments, forming the helix of legal code, which gave birth to *Escobedo*. It would be another year, however, before *Escobedo* produced *Miranda*. In 1966, we were given a truly new species of law that protects our right to counsel and our right to remain silent.

Miranda and the Arizona Supreme Court

Alvin Moore could not have anticipated the June 1964 decision in *Escobedo* when he filed his August 1963 notice of appeal on *Miranda*'s convictions with the Arizona Supreme Court. But he may have read the opinion before he delivered the oral argument to the Arizona Supreme Court in early 1965—perhaps he had even read the *Time* magazine article in July of 1964. In any event, he apparently had read something that rekindled his interest in the case and sparked his argument that several important legal errors had been made during Miranda's first trial.

Nevertheless, the court affirmed the conviction, holding that the errors claimed by Moore could not have affected the outcome of the case. The court also disagreed with Moore's contention that the sentence handed down by Judge McFate was excessive. The court rejected Moore's contention, in light of the record showing Miranda was committed to the custody of juvenile authorities on various charges, including burglary, attempted rape, and assault. His record further shows that he was arrested in California on suspicions of armed robbery and that he had a conviction for violation of the Dyer Act."[57] Confronted with Miranda's history, the Arizona Supreme Court declared itself "loath to disturb the trial court's judgment under these circumstances." Speaking for the court, Justice Fred Struckmeyer said the court also affirmed Miranda's robbery conviction because the evidence established that "The defendant forcibly entered the complaining witness's car at night with the intent to commit rape and at knifepoint compelled her to accompany him to an alley where, after a struggle, she gave him what money she had because she was placed in fear. Judgment affirmed."[58]

Moore also appealed Miranda's conviction on the rape and robbery of Patricia Doe. The Arizona Supreme Court took twenty-one pages to reject all of the claims of error. The only constitutional issue preserved by Moore for appeal was the core issue in the case: Miranda's confession.[59] Justice Ernest McFarland wrote the opinion summarily rejecting Miranda's claim that his confession was improperly received in evidence. Detectives Young and Cooley had testified that "they had informed him of his legal rights and that any statement he made might be used against him,"[60] McFarland argued.

Justice McFarland noted that Moore's only objection to the admission of the written confession had been, "We are objecting because the Supreme Court of the United States says the man is entitled to an attorney at the time of his arrest." There was no objection on the proper ground, which was that Miranda's statement was not made voluntarily, and Moore had not requested that the trial judge determine the voluntariness of the statement. Since the voluntariness and the truth of the confession were not in question, the Arizona Supreme Court saw the sole question before it as "Whether there was a violation of the Sixth and Fourteenth Amendments to the Constitution by the admission of the voluntary statement made without an attorney."

In passing on constitutional provisions, the Arizona Supreme Court is bound to follow the interpretations of the United States Supreme Court. Accordingly, it duly examined the recent decisions in *Massiah v. United States* and *Escobedo v. Illinois.*[61] The court noted that *Massiah,* which involved a wiretap between two codefendants, was not on point. It had more trouble dismissing *Escobedo* but ultimately found it inapplicable as well, because, unlike Danny Escobedo, Ernesto Miranda had been advised of his rights. "He had not requested counsel," the court noted, "and had not been denied assistance of counsel. We further call attention to the fact that, as pointed out in the companion case here on appeal, *State v. Miranda,* No. 1397 [the robbery case] defendant Miranda had a record, which indicated he was not without courtroom experience."

In working its way to its holding in Miranda's appeal, the Arizona Supreme Court also queried rhetorically, "What is the purpose of the right to counsel? What is the purpose of the Sixth and Fourteenth Amendments?" Observing that California had just extended *Escobedo* to cases in which the defendant had not asked for a lawyer, the court asserted that state courts are not bound to follow one another, and the Arizona court "did not choose to follow" California's lead.

The Arizona Supreme Court's holding was a masterpiece of directness: "We hold that a confession may be admissible when made without an attorney if it is voluntary and does not violate the constitutional rights of defendant." This direct holding was to prove helpful to Miranda at the next level of appeal.

Robert J. Corcoran—The Birth of the *Miranda* Warnings

In a real sense, Robert Corcoran stands at the nexus between *Escobedo* and *Miranda,* for it was he who, as Arizona counsel to the American Civil Liberties Union, "found" the *Miranda* case. Upon reading the Arizona Supreme Court's decision, which affirmed Ernesto Miranda's conviction based largely on his stationhouse confession, Corcoran saw a rare opportunity, at least in Arizona, to advance the cause of justice for all—the guilty as well as the innocent.

A former Arizona state prosecutor, Corcoran had, in a sense, changed camps by 1965 and become very active in the Phoenix chapter of the ACLU. His interest in civil liberties, which had taken root at Fordham University, where he had studied law, had also been nourished when he moved to Phoenix to join the law firm Lewis, Roca, Scoville, Beauchamp, and Linton. And it was thriving by the time he left Lewis and Roca[62] in 1964 to join the small firm practice of Jay Dushoff and Sy Sacks. While with Lewis and Roca, Corcoran had worked with John P. Frank, John J. Flynn, and James Moeller—the three men who would eventually form the "Miranda Team."[63] Corcoran became interested in Miranda's case in the summer of 1965.

There were, of course, several *Miranda* cases, including the two trials before Judge McFate and the customary appeals before the Arizona Supreme Court. However, the *Miranda* case referred to by legal scholars and historians is the *writ of certiorari* issued by the United States Supreme Court. This "cert" case is the intellectual birth of the decision that made Ernesto Miranda and his appellate lawyers famous.

What first made Corcoran believe the case might be reviewed by the United States Supreme Court was that the Arizona Supreme Court had declined to apply *Escobedo*'s holding, which had established the Sixth Amendment right to counsel during interrogations. Specifically, the Arizona Supreme Court reasoned that Miranda had not asked for an attorney before he confessed to Detectives Cooley and Young. Because *California v. Dorado* had just expanded *Escobedo* by holding that the right to counsel existed at the stationhouse even if the suspect did not ask for a lawyer, the court had also specifically mentioned the California Supreme Court, saying that it did "not choose to follow Dorado in the extension of the rule announced in Escobedo."[64]

Corcoran, like many others, viewed *Escobedo* as another incremental change, consistent with past standards, and so he became hopeful that *Miranda* might be the next step in the effort to further expand the *Escobedo* doctrine to include cases wherein the suspect had *not* asked for a lawyer. The timing of the U.S. Supreme Court's confession decisions also sparked Corcoran's interest. The Warren Court had recently ruled to prohibit *de jure* segregation—a measure against elements of the McCarthy era's tirades—and to involve itself in the individual rights of suspected criminals.

Also, while the Warren Court had seemed to go out of its way to avoid establishing an absolute right to counsel in *Escobedo,* it had set stringent standards for police officials for the first time. Unlike his former colleagues in the Maricopa County Attorney's office, who viewed *Escobedo* as a threat to the use of crucial police procedures, Corcoran saw a legitimate need for restraint on interrogation behavior and believed the role of lawyers in police interrogations was critical to the Sixth Amendment's guarantee of the effective assistance of counsel in criminal cases.

Finally, in reading the Arizona Supreme Court's summary treatment of the confession issue in Miranda's case, Corcoran realized that the court's handling of the right to counsel issue was "directly opposed" to California's and therefore amounted to a direct constitutional conflict. "[W]hen the investigation reaches the accusatory stage," the California court had held, "the defendant must be advised that he does have the right to counsel and that anything he does say may be used against him."[65] Perhaps sensing the historic opportunity, on June 15, 1965, Corcoran wrote to Alvin Moore and made him an offer of representation. "As counsel for the Arizona Civil Liberties Union, it appears to me that the civil liberties issues may be involved in this case which we would be interested in making and aiding you in presenting to the Supreme Court of the United States." Corcoran, like many in the legal profession in the sixties, felt that the Arizona Supreme Court viewed the Warren Court's expansionist cases too narrowly. Consequently, he told Moore, "Our Supreme Court is limiting *Escobedo* to its facts and will only apply it when Danny Escobedo comes to Arizona and kills his bother-in-law."

Presuming that Moore might not be up to the task of preparing a writ of certiorari to the United States Supreme Court, Corcoran also offered, "If you would like assistance . . . please contact me and I will try to have one of our abler cooperating attorneys assist you."

When Moore responded favorably, Corcoran arranged a meeting, at which he explained that he believed the Arizona Supreme Court erroneously felt if a person "has been bad and put in jail before" that person must be familiar with criminal law and procedure. If this view were true, he told Moore, then, "[You] would have defended and I certainly would have prosecuted people who would have been entitled to receive an LL.D."[66]

Predictably, Moore declined to take the case any further and turned his files over to Corcoran. Corcoran's first thought about a suitable lawyer to handle the new appeal was the then up-and-coming Rex E. Lee[67] of the Phoenix law firm Jennings, Strouss, Salmon, and Trask. Lee had been Justice Byron White's law clerk in 1964, the year the *Escobedo* case was handed down. However, when Corcoran discussed the case with Lee he learned that Lee could not take the case because Lee was still under a sort of Supreme Court "embargo." Given their unique role in the American justice system, Supreme Court clerks cannot appear before the High Court for two years following the end of their clerkship. Lee also told Corcoran that he was "unenthusiastic" about the rules-of-law approach because he did not believe it made sound constitutional law.

Corcoran then turned to Lewis and Roca's nationally renowned constitutional scholar, John P. Frank. Corcoran assumed that Frank would enlist the aid of Lewis and Roca's most well-known courtroom warrior, John Flynn. Flynn was hardly a constitutional scholar and had no Supreme Court experience, but that part of the case would be handled by Mr. Frank. The combination of Flynn's courtroom skills and Frank's constitutional scholarship encouraged Corcoran to write directly to Ernesto Miranda on June 24, 1965. In this proposal letter he told Miranda that while Moore's representation as an "appointed attorney" would not permit him to bear the expense or spare the time to take the case to the United States Supreme Court, Lewis and Roca, however, "would be happy to take your case to the Supreme Court and will bear the expenses."

Corcoran also provided Miranda with a typed letter for his use should he choose to retain Lewis and Roca. On the same date, Corcoran delivered all the case files to Lewis and Roca, telling the firm to expect a retention letter from Miranda, and in his transmittal letter to the law firm, Corcoran offered the aid of the "national office of the American Civil Liberties Union," indicating that either he or another lawyer would petition the United States Supreme Court to "come in as *Amicus Curiae* (friend of the court) on the case." *Amici,* or, persons not parties to the case, are given latitude at the discretion of the Court to introduce arguments, authorities, or evidence to protect any of their interests that might be impacted by the Court's decision in the case.

In his letter of June 27, 1965, Alvin Moore likewise encouraged Miranda to retain Lewis and Roca, and Miranda officially retained Lewis and Roca at the beginning of July 1965. "Your letter which I recently received has made me very happy," Miranda wrote. "To know that someone has taken interest in my case has increased my moral [sic] enormously."

John P. Frank and the *Miranda* Briefs

In American legal practice, a brief is a printed document that serves as the basis for an argument in an appellate court. Filed for the information of the court, it embodies the points of law that counsel desires to establish, together with the arguments and authorities upon which he rests his contentions. The task of writing a brief is never simple, and the composing of such an important document as the *Miranda* brief demanded special skill. It would require not only someone well versed in the pertinent laws and previous case files, but also someone with the stature to carry such an argument before the highest court in the land. Fortunately—although neither Robert Corcoran nor Ernesto Miranda knew it at the time that Miranda retained the law firm of Lewis and Roca—John P. Frank had already begun the historic trek to make Miranda a household name.

For several reasons, Frank was perhaps the perfect man for the job and, ultimately, more than any other individual, responsible for the line of reasoning that was to become known as the *Miranda* doctrine. A specialist in constitutional law by the time he joined the Yale law faculty in 1949, Frank had published work in the prestigious *University of Chicago Law Review* and had just completed the leading biographical sketch of Justice Hugo Black, for whom he had clerked during the October 1942 Supreme Court term. At the time of the *Miranda* appeals, he was working to finish his definitive study of the Warren Court. His extensive scholarship, his impressive faculty appointments, his relationship with sitting justices, and his annual reports on the Supreme Court's published opinions put the Court well within his personal horizon. As Professor John Q. Barrett of St. John's University School of Law had said of Frank, "It was a realm in which he, as citizen, lawyer, thinker, and scholar, comfortably traveled and operated."

When Frank began to formulate the *Miranda* brief, he was well aware that the argument in favor of privilege against self-incrimination, as guaranteed by the Fifth Amendment, might be important. Likewise, he knew of scores of cases suggesting a due-process connection to the Fourteenth Amendment. *Johnson v. Zerbst*,[68] for example, had come down the same year, 1938, that Frank passed the bar. Also, there was *Mallory v. United States*,[69] which had been decided soon after Frank's move to Arizona. And *Escobedo* had given hope just two years earlier than *Miranda*.

But Frank saw every one of these as primarily "Sixth Amendment cases," which was how he expected all the amici briefs to argue. After all, the Warren Court had charted this course with its *Gideon* case ruling three years previously, and in response to the *Gideon* ruling, Congress had modified Federal Criminal Rules 5 and 44, thereby requiring everyone in the criminal justice system to participate in the process of swiftly informing defendants of their right to counsel upon their arrest. As Frank saw it, everyone involved in the appeals would do well to remember that *Gideon* was responsible for the creation of the public defender system in America.

Thus, although in the petitioner's brief (a document that begins with a succinct statement of the issue in the case) Frank wrote that the issue involved both the Sixth and Fourteenth Amendments, his opening brief cites only the Sixth, and consequently, his argument for *Miranda*'s reversal was entirely predicated on what he called the "full meaning of the Sixth Amendment." As a matter of constitutional theory, he contended, a defendant cannot "unwittingly" waive his right to a lawyer during his trial; ergo, even as a suspect, he cannot "unwittingly" waive it in the police station. Furthermore, he reasoned that, as a matter of practicality, one cannot know the precise effect of providing counsel at the beginning of a case. The precise effect will depend on the case, the lawyer, the client, and the situation. What one *can* know is that it makes little sense to establish an elaborate and costly system of appointed counsel, only to see that nothing happens until it is too late to be effective.

With these basic assumptions firmly in mind, Frank built the brief's line of reasoning on the central question of "Whether the confession of a poorly educated, mentally abnormal, indigent defendant, not told of his right to counsel, taken while he is in police custody and without the assistance of counsel, which was not requested, can be admitted into evidence over specific objection based on the absence of counsel?"

In his own brief, Arizona Assistant Attorney General Gary Nelson accepted Frank's assertion that only the Sixth Amendment applied to the case, but he answered with a statement that shifted the argument slightly: "While your respondent accepts the legal substance of the Question Presented as posed by the petitioner, serious issue is taken with the descriptive phrases, 'poorly educated' [and] 'mentally abnormal.'" Also, he went on to note, "The propriety of this description, insofar as it may enhance the question presented for review, is no doubt one of the key issues to be decided by the Court and respondent reserves the right to present argument, *infra,* concerning the description's accuracy and impact."[70] In other words, Nelson was loathe to suggest that the eminent John P. Frank was misstating the factual record; however, he had more to say on the subject but would hold his peace for the moment.

For their part, the fourteen amici briefs filed at the invitation of the United States Supreme Court followed suit. Each cited the Sixth Amendment as the only constitutional issue in the case,[71] and since, technically, amici briefs are not filed in support of either affirmance or reversal of the case itself, in *Miranda,* only the issues are blandly stated:

1. Whether an arrested suspect's lack of the assistance of counsel at the time he makes a pre-arraignment statement renders the statement constitutionally inadmissible at trial.

2. Whether rules presently or hereafter established within the ambit of the first question should be retroactively applied.[72]

It bears repeating that there were actually four other cases joined with *Miranda* for briefing and argument.[73] However, a fifth case[74] was likewise predicated on the Sixth Amendment, and its amici brief, written by Samuel Hirshowitz[75] and filed on behalf of twenty-nine states, one commonwealth, and one American territory, is the *only* one to describe the issue in terms of a "right to be silent."[76]

Hirshowitz also included an implied warning to the Supreme Court, first asking what might happen if the Court were to rule that lawyers should be present during the interrogation of suspects, then answering the question by citing a 1949 Supreme Court opinion:

> To bring in a lawyer means a real peril to solution of the crime because, under our adversary system, he deems that his sole duty is to protect his client—guilty or innocent—and that in such capacity he owes no duty whatever to help society solve its crime problem. Under this conception of criminal procedure, any lawyer worth his salt will tell the suspect in no uncertain terms to make no statement to police under any circumstances.[77]

Stated another way, suspects who know their rights to remain silent and ask for a lawyer will always remain silent *except* to ask for a lawyer. "Virtually the only function of stationhouse counsel," argued Hirshowitz, "will be to paste adhesive tape over his new client's mouth. It is at best dubious whether such a practice would attract the cream of the bar."[78]

In their brief, the lawyers for defendant Vignera, using language straight out of the Supreme Court's opinion in *Escobedo,* argued, in effect, that the field be leveled by requiring the police to inform all suspects:

> When the proceeding has become accusatory, the police or prosecutor *will be obliged* to warn the accused of his absolute constitutional right to silence and of his right to consult before talking any further with the police. If the accused thereupon intelligently and effectively waives his right to silence and his right to immediate consultation with counsel, the interrogation can continue. [Emphasis supplied][79]

By the time the *Miranda* case was argued to the United States Supreme Court, only three states had adopted rules regarding the admissibility of prearraignment statements, and those rules were conditioned on proof that the defendant had been informed of his right to remain silent and to consult counsel.[80] As of 1966, no state had established a system that mandated providing counsel for an indigent defendant at the prearraignment stage of a case. However, the novelty of the right to remain silent as a concept and the antiquity of its collateral cousin, the right to counsel, had raised enormous practical questions regarding the interrogation process. What if suspects had to be warned that they had a right to remain silent? And if they had to be warned, did they also have to be told they had a right to counsel? Did someone—the police, for example—have to warn suspects that they not only had a right to counsel but also had a right to have that counsel assist them during the interrogation itself? Could a suspect waive his right to counsel without being told that the right to remain silent was paramount to the right to counsel?

In an effort to provide some answer to these questions, the 1964 draft of the American Law Institute's proposed Model Code of Criminal Procedure contemplated an exclusionary rule for confessions based on a variety of requirements. Among them, the drafters suggested that a suspect be informed, "He is under no obligation to talk"[81] to police or investigators. One would suppose that not being obligated to talk is tantamount to being able to remain silent.[82]

Others saw grave dangers ahead if such a suggestion became a requirement. In his 1968 book, *Confessions and Statements*,[83] Bill Schafer,[84] the Pima County attorney in Tucson, Arizona, at the time of the *Miranda* decision, predicted a fundamental and permanent change in practical police procedure. In describing the day the Supreme Court handed down its decision, he wrote:

> On June 13, 1966, five justices of the United States Supreme Court infinitely changed the law of confessions. From that day forward, no "confession" is admissible in any court of law, for any purpose, unless the suspect was first "warned" and "advised" of certain basic constitutional rights and procedures under the Fifth Amendment. The case, of course is *Miranda*.[85]

Arguably, no other cases in American legal history had a greater political impact than the trilogy of *Gideon, Escobedo,* and *Miranda*. The "*Escobedo-Miranda* Revolution," as political scientist Otis Stephens termed it in his treatise entitled *The Supreme Court and Confessions of Guilt*,[86] was political because, while the Supreme Court's "law-making" function is peripheral to the central task of legal interpretation, its major implications are of a political character. In a real sense, the Court's involvement in the political process is thus indistinguishable from that of Congress or the president. And John P. Frank understood this as well as anyone. Because of its political ramifications, the case he would present in his brief—in the literal and specialized legal language of the courts—would not sway the Supreme Court justices on its own merit. Therefore, well before he finished and signed the final copy of the petitioner's brief and filed it with the clerk of the

Supreme Court in Washington, D.C., Frank had decided that the oral argument should be delivered by someone with the presence, passion, and oratory skill to put blood into the rational but as-yet-altogether-inert body of facts and assertions he had so carefully fashioned. Luckily, he did not have to look far. No one was better suited to the task than John J. Flynn, his own partner.

Chapter 3

THE ORAL ARGUMENTS

In 1788, Thomas Jefferson said, "[The Constitution] is a good canvas, on which some strokes only want retouching."[1] His occasional friend, Alexander Hamilton, quipped in response, "Constitutions should consist only of general provisions; the reason is that they must necessarily be permanent, and that they cannot calculate for the possible change of things."[2] While Jefferson and Hamilton spoke to the majesty of the Constitution, Justice Felix Frankfurter spoke to the immense power of the court in interpreting the Constitution: "A court which yields to the popular will thereby license itself to practice despotism, for there can be no assurance that it will not on another occasion indulge its own will."[3] Collectively, Jefferson, Hamilton, and Frankfurter set the tone for the historic oral arguments that were about to begin in Washington, D.C., in February of 1966.

The Supreme Court of the United States convenes three days a week in thirty-day periods, three times a year. It hears cases that have been judged of sufficient import to the nation that the final decision handed down can fairly apply to every state. Each of the nine justices has been nominated by the executive branch, vetted by the American Bar Association, and confirmed by the Senate. Each sits on the bench for a term that ends when he or she dies or steps down.[4] These supreme adjudicators have been drawn from the best of both the bar and the courts, and while, in principle, there should be no court in the land subject to less political influence, in fact, the nine sitting Supreme Court justices at any one time are under enormous pressure from the body politic. After all, each was handpicked by the chief political officer of one or the other of the country's two major political parties; each was required to run a gauntlet of popularly elected officials before being permitted to assume a seat on the bench; and once on the bench, each is constantly petitioned by advocates representing individuals whose cases invariably stand in proxy to special political interests. The justices of the Supreme Court are wise men and women—wise in the laws of the land but also wise in the will of the people. Each understands that a law, if unpopular enough, will not stand. Each also understands that popular laws can receive no special standing merely because they are popular.

The Supreme Court building in Washington, D.C., built in 1932, was best defined by Chief Justice Charles Hughes: "The Republic endures and this is the symbol of its faith."[5] Built in the classical Corinthian architectural style to harmonize with nearby congressional buildings, it is built on a scale in keeping with the dignity of the Court and the judiciary as a coequal, independent branch of the United States government. The four-story building was constructed principally of Vermont marble (on the exterior walls), Georgia marble (in the interior courtyards), and creamy Alabama marble (on the floors). American quartered white oak was used for doors, trim, paneling, and some floors. Its main corridor, the Great Hall, opens into the Court Chamber, a massive 7,500-square-foot room with a 44-foot ceiling. Its twenty-four marble columns surround citizens, justices, and lawyers as arguments are presented in the most momentous cases in America.

In basic arrangement, the chamber is not unlike the courtrooms one finds in nearly any county or state courthouse in the country, save that there is no jury box. As one enters, through tall double oak doors emblazoned with the emblem of the Supreme Court, one sees straight ahead the long bench and curved row of nine high-backed chairs where the justices sit. Facing the bench on the left is the table for the petitioner. On the right stands the table for the defense. Between them, facing the bench, stands the advocate's podium of dark mahogany, equipped with a microphone and, mounted just ahead of the reading surface, two small lights—a white one to signal to counsel that he has five minutes of his allotted time left, and a red one to declare that he is out of time. The advocate standing at this podium, with a packed gallery behind him, the nine stern visages ranked above his eye level in front, is automatically at a distinct psychological disadvantage. To add to the weight bearing down, he knows full well that he stands in the harsh limelight of national attention, and under the still harsher scrutiny of his peers. Some relish the moment; others quail. Few can speak and act with unaffected aplomb, yet all know that even a hint of theatrical display or rhetorical posturing will be looked upon with suspicion. Neither does pomposity nor arrogance become that rare lawyer given the chance to argue to the Supreme Court of the United States. And levity is for the justices to initiate. An advocate speaking before the highest court in the land does not play to a jury or the gallery; he does not *play* at all.

A case selected for oral argument invariably involves interpretations of the U.S. Constitution or federal law. At least four justices have selected the case as being of such importance that the Supreme Court must resolve the legal issues. A lawyer for each side of a case will have an opportunity to make a presentation to the Court and answer questions posed by the justices. Prior to the argument, each side has submitted a legal brief—a written legal argument outlining each party's points of law. The justices have always read these briefs prior to argument and are thoroughly familiar with the case, its facts, and the legal positions asserted by each party.

Oral Argument in *Miranda v. Arizona*

The oral arguments delivered by all ten lawyers in the *Miranda* case lasted more than seven hours, spread out over three days, and resulted in a 280-page transcript. Several of America's most capable constitutional advocates[6] answered hundreds of pointed questions asked by all of the nine justices[7] who heard and decided the case. Fourteen briefs were filed in the case that would become known as *Miranda*. In total, they contained over seven hundred pages of argument, advocacy, and legal philosophy. Contrary to popular belief, *Miranda v. Arizona*, Case No. 759, did *not* have the lowest docket number listed on the hearing calendar of the U.S. Supreme Court's October Term for 1965–66. *California v. Stewart* was docketed as Case No. 584; however, *Miranda* had the most compelling facts and arguably the strongest brief and the most persuasive oral argument.

John J. Flynn

John Flynn, John Frank's choice to deliver the oral argument for *Miranda*, was not widely known outside Arizona in 1966. He would become much admired within his profession, for though he argued with earnest passion in the courtroom, in a style of speaking that at times could be candidly assertive and was not easily deposed, he was a man of impeccable sincerity and humility. The combination of Frank's written brief and Flynn's oral advocacy produced a lucid yet wholly extemporaneous quality, as if he were merely speaking his mind and heart honestly, without forethought. In later years, whenever he was in trial, the courtroom would usually fill with journalists, trial buffs, and law students. His closing arguments drew standing audiences who were routinely swept away by the force and persuasiveness of his oratory. Indeed, his influence on the Supreme Court during the oral argument phase of the *Miranda* case was so great that in 1994, American Heritage's *Our Times* magazine, in profiling the previous four decades, gave Flynn the credit for "winning" the case, naming him on its list of "ten people who changed the way you live but you have never heard of any of them."

The records cannot show how well he presented himself at ten o'clock in the morning on February 28, 1966. There are no videotapes of the proceedings; however, anyone familiar with Flynn's style can easily imagine him, uncomfortably restricted to a position behind the podium but nevertheless conveying to the court his passion for his argument. He had but two objectives, which he was determined to obtain. First, he wanted to frame the central argument in such a way that all nine justices could take the first step toward abstracting his central premise: Most American citizens were at a legal disadvantage as soon as they came under police scrutiny. Second, he wanted to make sure the issue from that day forward was not *whether* to warn but *when* to warn. For, as both he and Frank saw it, this was the sticking point. Despite *Gideon, Escobedo,* and subsequent changes requiring police to tell suspects of their right to counsel, those opposed to the whole notion of warning were continuing to argue against the requirement on practical grounds, contending that even if a law mandated a warning, the law simply could not be applied fairly and consistently. If the question of timing could be resolved, both Frank and Flynn believed the one last real obstacle to an American right to remain silent would be removed.

With these goals in mind, and knowing that his time was strictly limited, and that the justices would surely interrupt him at any moment with a question or observation that would sidetrack his formal presentation, Flynn went quickly through the obligatory phase of his argument—the traditional statement of the facts of the case. Without elaboration he explained that the issue before the Court concerned the admission in evidence of the defendant's confession and then finished by simply emphasizing that the confession "had been given in the absence of counsel."

Then, without pausing, he went on, easing into his argument, implying why this absence was so, stressing—as he recounted the facts of Miranda's arrest and interrogation—that the suspect was twenty-three and of Spanish-American extraction. He did not have to say that Miranda thus represented a particular segment of the American population—the poor and uneducated—and it also went without saying that the defendant most assuredly had had no inkling of his constitutional rights.

In closing the opening phase, Flynn also emphasized that the swiftness with which police processed suspects was a factor, and thereby brought into the light a first glimpse of the second fundamental premise of his argument. After telling the Court that on the morning of March 13, 1963, the defendant had been contacted for the first time, arrested, taken straight to the police station, and "immediately placed in a lineup," Flynn then told of how the defendant had been identified and then "immediately" taken into the police confessional. "At approximately 11:30 A.M.," he noted, "and by 1:30 they had obtained from him an oral confession." To make a special note of the time span, he went back over it, this time saying, "He had denied his guilt, according to the officers, at the commencement of the interrogation; by 1:30 he had confessed." Lest the main point be over-looked, Flynn then added, "I believe the record indicates that at no time during the interrogation and prior to the confession—his oral confession—was he advised of his right to remain silent, of his right to counsel, or of his right to consult with counsel."

As John Frank recalled many years later, Flynn paused briefly at this point to examine the faces of the justices, perhaps expecting a question, perhaps even inviting one. None was offered, however, and so he resumed, now with the intention of distinguishing *Miranda* from *Escobedo*. First, he told the court that the defendant had been asked to sign a confession, then handed a typed statement that the officers had had to read to him. Then, with particular emphasis, Flynn declared, "Throughout the interrogation the defendant did not request counsel at any time."

Again, he might have expected a pointed question at this time; again, however, he received none, and so continued presenting facts laced with argument. Not until he reminded the Court that the police had not arrested or interrogated anyone else, and then asserted that Miranda was thus the "focus" of the investigation—that Ernesto Miranda and Detective Cooley had, in a sense, become opposing "advocates,"—did one of the justices finally interrupt.

"What do you think is the result of the adversary process coming into being when this focusing takes place?" Justice Potter Stewart asked. "What follows from that? Is there then, what, a right to a lawyer?"

It was not the question Flynn most wanted to answer, of course, for it led directly toward the issue he wanted to dispense with. But he was not surprised by it, nor would he be deterred by it. Yes, he thought a man could have a lawyer at this time, he told Justice Stewart, "*If the man knew his rights.*" Then, before Justice Stewart could respond, he added, "if he's rich enough, and if he's educated enough to assert his Fifth Amendment Right, and if he *recognizes* that he has a Fifth Amendment Right to request counsel." And there it was: a bold assertion that the *Fifth* Amendment, not the Sixth, made *Miranda* different from its predecessors—*Powell, Gideon,* and

Escobedo. Historically, the right to counsel was addressed, granted, or with-held under the umbrella of the Sixth Amendment, which was exactly what the written briefs in *Miranda* espoused. Flynn's bold assertion to Justice Stewart may have been the spark that generated the firestorm.

It is one of the most curious things about John Flynn that outside the courtroom he was invariably a rather shy and self-effacing man, while in the courtroom he seemed neither. Lawyers of lesser fortitude, after such pointed remarks, and wary of overreaching, might have waited to speak; Flynn simply kept going. Again, before Justice Stewart could deflect the argument, he pressed his point, contending that at that stage of the interrogation, "under the facts and circumstances in *Miranda*—*of a man of limited education, of a man who certainly is mentally abnormal, who is certainly an indigent*—that when that adversary process came into being that the police, at the very least, had an *obligation* to extend to this man not only his clear Fifth Amendment Right, to afford to him the right of counsel."

Justice Stewart's response this time—a third attempt to turn the issue away from Flynn's target—also suggests he reacted at least partially to Flynn's forthright tone, or perhaps merely to the rapid yet lucid tumble of his words, but it is interesting to note how deferential he was. "Again, I don't mean to quibble," he replied, "and I apologize, but I think it's first important to define what those rights are—what his rights under the Constitution are at that point. He can't be advised of his rights unless somebody knows what those rights are."

The "somebody" in question, was, of course, vague, and while Justice Stewart might have meant to suggest that the police could not be expected to act as lawyers, Flynn saw the opening he wanted. "Precisely my point," he told Justice Stewart. "And the only person that can adequately advise Ernesto Miranda is a lawyer."

Whether or not Justice Stewart saw this as a no-win situation isn't clear. One *can* surmise that he knew full well that lawyers were unwelcome in police station interrogations. Still, his next question was simply, "And what would the lawyer advise him that his rights then were?"

Again, where other counsel might have equivocated, Flynn would not. That the suspect had a right not to incriminate himself, he answered promptly, and a right not to make any statement at all. And furthermore, he had "the right to be free from questioning by the police department; that he had the right to ask, at an *ultimate* time, to be represented adequately by counsel in court; and that if he was indigent, too poor to employ counsel, that the state would furnish him counsel."

In retrospect, it was indeed a historic moment. No one before Flynn had come this close in open court to spelling out the contents of what was to become known as the "*Miranda* warning." By the time *Gideon v. Wainwright* was decided, most states, except those in the South, had already begun to consider the right to counsel a fundamental right in criminal cases. *Gideon* ensured that right in every state, and by its 1964 holding in *Escobedo*, the right to counsel had become available to anyone who asked for a lawyer at the interrogation stage. But it was not until John Flynn took the podium on February 28, 1966, that anyone catalogued the rights of mere suspects in police custody.

Whether Justice Stewart, or anyone in the room that day, realized the gravity of Flynn's answer was not recorded. Justice Stewart, for his part, seemed not to have taken notice, for he merely asked if there was any claim that the confession was involuntary. It seemed a throwaway question, completely rhetorical, and intended only to focus the argument on the rightness or wrongness of admitting the confession; if Flynn had taken the question seriously, he no doubt would have shifted the entire discussion to the matter of what, exactly, constituted coercion—and he would have likely lost a substantial portion of his valuable time at the podium.

But once again he refused to be drawn away from his point; instead he actually accomplished a masterstroke of sorts. No, there was no coercion, he told the Court. "None at all," just as John Frank's written brief had indicated. The conundrum he thus posed was obvious. If Miranda had not been "compelled" to incriminate himself, why was the Supreme Court of the United States even considering this case?

The first attempt to answer, fortuitously, came not from Flynn but from Justice Hugo Black. "He doesn't have to have a gun pointed at his head, does he?" Black asked, somewhat facetiously, not so much of Flynn as of the Court, intentionally moving the debate from the advocate's podium to the bench itself. Sitting at counsel table, John Frank likely beamed at his former boss. It was Justice Byron White who first took issue. "Of course he doesn't," he responded. Then he turned back down to the pit of the courtroom and addressed Flynn. "So he *was* compelled to do it, wasn't he, according to your theory?"

"Not by gunpoint," Flynn answered, as if to underscore the hyperbole of Black's rhetorical question. Then he made an assertion that was elegant in its understatement: "He was called upon to surrender a right he didn't fully realize and appreciate that he had," Flynn stated flatly.

Whether or not this answer registered with Justice White cannot be told, for at this point Chief Justice Warren entered the argument. "I suppose, Mr. Flynn, you would say that if the police had said to this young man, 'Now, you're a nice young man, and we don't want to hurt you, and so forth; we're your friends and if you'll just tell us how you committed this crime, we'll let you go home and we won't prosecute you,' that that would be a violation of the Fifth Amendment, and that, technically speaking, would not be 'compelling' him to do it. It would be an inducement, wouldn't it?"

The podium's white light had come on several minutes earlier. Knowing he had but a minute or two left, and perhaps realizing he had a willing ear in the chief justice, Flynn simply said that the chief justice was correct, and immediately Chief Justice Warren asked the question that needed asking: "I suppose you would argue that that is still within the Fifth Amendment, wouldn't you?"

"It's an abdication of the Fifth Amendment right," Flynn answered, and meant to continue quickly, but was interrupted by Justice Black, asking whether the Constitution protected "all" Americans. A gift, to be sure; with his time just about to run out, Flynn had wanted to return to the underlying theme with which he had begun—the inequality he was there to rectify. "It certainly does protect the rich, the educated, and the strong," he declared now, "those rich enough to hire counsel, those who are educated enough to know what their rights are, and those who are strong enough to withstand police interrogation and assert those rights."

The red light had begun to flash. His time was up. But Flynn left the podium satisfied. He had accomplished what he had set out to do. He had brought the Court face-to-face with the central question, the reason they were all there that day, of not simply whether a suspect must be told of his right to counsel, but also of *when* he must be told. And he had provided the key to the answer: When the police began to focus on him as a suspect and not merely as a witness or bystander. Flynn left the podium with one more important message delivered: The right to counsel under the *Fifth* Amendment is the key to both inequality and coercion in America's police stations.

Gary K. Nelson

Gary Nelson, the assistant attorney general of the State of Arizona, took the podium next in order to explain the state's views. Without doubt, he wondered to what extent the argument would now focus on this issue. He didn't have to wait long to find out. He had scarcely begun his recitation of the constitutional rights "in place" at the time of Miranda's confession, when he was interrupted by Justice Abe Fortas, apparently quite interested in bringing the argument to bear once more on Flynn's main contention. "Let us assume that he was advised of these rights," Justice Fortas began. "In your opinion, does it make any difference *when* he was advised? That is, whether he was advised at the commencement of the interrogation or at an early stage of the interrogation, or whether he was advised only when he was ready to sign the written confession?"

Nelson certainly understood the danger of accepting Justice Fortas's assumption, but he also knew, just as Flynn had known, that to quibble about hypotheticals would eat up valuable time. Therefore, he responded straightforwardly. Yes, he told the Court, *if one were to assume,* as Fortas had suggested, that some warning was required, or should have been given, then to be of any effect the warning must be given before the suspect made any statement.

Probably he at least hoped this answer would satisfy Fortas and allow him to continue with his own statement, but immediately Justice Fortas pressed him to expand the point, asking if he believed then that a suspect had to have been warned first—before he confessed in the absence of counsel—for the confession to be admissible at trial.

No, Nelson answered quickly, but Justice Fortas pressed him yet again, asking that he explain his position further.

At this point, Nelson fervently wanted to retain the "totality of the circumstances" doctrine, which held that the specific circumstances of every case dictated whether a denial of fundamental fairness had occurred, and thus, that a confession was admissible in evidence if all of the specific circumstances indicated that it was freely and voluntarily given. So Nelson responded that his position assumed that each case would present a factual situation in which the court or a judge, or prosecutor at some level, would have to make a determination as to whether or not a defendant had been denied a specific right, "whether it be right of counsel, the right not to be compelled to testify against himself—and that the warning, or age or literacy, the circumstances, the length of the questioning, all these factors would be important," he concluded.

It was, essentially the crux of state's argument—this belief that individual courts should decide—and Justice Fortas probably had expected to hear it. "I suppose it's quite arguable that Miranda, the petitioner here, was entitled to a warning," he said. "Would you agree to that?"

Nelson admitted that it was arguable, but then added, "I have extensively argued the facts that he wasn't of such a nature as an individual—because of his mental condition or his educational background—as to require any more than he got. . . . I'm saying he got every warning except . . . the specific warning of the right to counsel. He didn't have counsel. Counsel wasn't specifically denied to him, because of a request to retain counsel. The only possible thing that happened to Mr. Miranda that, in my light—assuming that he had the capability of understanding at all—is the fact that he did not get the specific warning of his right to counsel."

While these remarks might have seemed useful to the prosecution at the time, in retrospect, they were quite damaging. As a representative of Arizona, Nelson had just officially accepted the possibility that Miranda might have given an unwarned confession without being told he had a right to counsel and at a point in time when he might not have been capable of understanding his rights.

As it was, Nelson seemed to intend these remarks to allow him to shift the focus of the argument back to the point Flynn had so successfully pushed aside. If the Court adopted such an "extreme position," he went on to contend—that a suspect must have counsel at such a stage of his detainment—then "a serious problem in the enforcement of our criminal law will occur. First of all, let us make one thing certain," he declared. "We need no empirical data as to one factor: At least among lawyers there can be no doubt about what counsel for the defendant is to do. He is to represent him 100 percent, win, lose, or draw, guilty or innocent. That's our system. When counsel is introduced at interrogation, interrogation ceases."

Nelson's time was up, but he could leave the podium with the feeling that he had accomplished something. This final remark, a succinct statement of the opposition's basic objection, was the single most important part of his script. And it would serve as the launching pad for the next speaker, Duane Nedrud of the National District Attorneys Association, appearing at the invitation of the Court to argue for his fellow prosecutors.

Duane R. Nedrud

Like Flynn and Nelson, Nedrud wasted no time getting through the preliminaries, and then, quite effectively it would seem, he dispensed with Flynn's first theme. "If we are talking about equality between the rich and the poor, we are striving for a worthy objective," he conceded. "If we are talking about equality between the policeman and the criminal, we are on dangerous ground. I would remind this Court that we are not talking about the *police* versus the defendant.[8] We are talking about the *people* versus the defendant. In the same way that we would not talk about the Marine Corps versus the Viet Cong, but we would talk about the United States versus the Viet Cong."

If Nedrud intended to position the police in the same category as the Marine Corps, it was a nice touch, because even though the Vietnam conflict was becoming more controversial at home, patriotic fervor was on the rise; also, the comparison could then extend naturally in the minds of the justices, as Nedrud went on to argue that a suspect with a lawyer at the outset would cost the police their advantage. "If this is to be our objective," he insisted, "to limit the use of the confession in criminal cases, then you are taking from the police the most important piece of evidence in every case that they bring before a court of justice."

He then went on to try to dispel the notion that the police would abuse this advantage. They were public servants, he argued. They weren't bent on putting innocent people in jail. They wanted to follow the law, and they would do so to the best of their ability. They were human, he added, conceding a practical imperfection, but they had the experience and knowledge to investigate crime. "We have not, as lawyers, paid attention to their problems," he concluded. "We have seldom been down to the police station and asked, 'What can we do to assist you in your problem?'"

Chief Justice Warren, certainly mindful of the briefs in the case detailing the interrogation techniques in common use, posed the first question to Nedrud. What would Nedrud say to the man who did not have a lawyer but who said he wanted a lawyer before he would talk?

"If he asked for a lawyer, and he does not waive his right to counsel, I think he should have a lawyer," Nedrud responded. "I would go so far as to say, I think the state should appoint him a lawyer. . . . I do not think, however, that we should in effect encourage him to have a lawyer."

To his credit, Chief Justice Warren was not at all ready to accept this patently ideological assertion. "And why do you say that we should not encourage him to have a lawyer?" he asked. "Are lawyers a menace?"

Nedrud did not answer directly; nevertheless, he stepped into a trap, noting, rather wryly it would seem, that a defense counsel "must—in our system of justice—must attempt to free the defendant. That is his job."

That he and the great majority of his fellow prosecutors felt this to be the truth, and a fundamentally unfair contention, especially in pretrial investigations, seems obviously irrational when removed from the context of the law and culture of the time. But the forces of law and order during the sixties were facing an increasing opposition from the left, and were becoming more ideological, losing sight of the basis of the system—that the government, not the defendant, is required to meet the high burden of proof in criminal cases, that the job of the defense attorney is not to "free" anyone but to protect those accused of crime from a denial of their fundamental constitutional rights. In short, their job then, as it is today, was to defend the system from the admittedly few police, prosecutors, judges, and juries who would abuse it. Thus, Nedrud's answer pointed to the single most important difference between prosecutors and defense lawyers in the sixties. The former assumed guilt at the custodial interrogation stage; the latter assumed that the state had yet to meet its high burden of proof in criminal cases, giving the "suspect" a presumption of innocence.

Chief Justice Warren, although he must have been fully aware of the shaky ground Nedrud stood upon, proceeded delicately, perhaps because he had been a career prosecutor himself. "Because it's his professional duty to raise any defenses the man has?" he asked.

"Yes, sir," Nedrud responded.

"Do you think, in doing that, he's a menace to our administration of justice?"

Once again, most likely seeing where the justice was headed, Nedrud responded indirectly, saying he thought the defense lawyer was not a menace at the trial level. "He is not a menace *per se,* but he is—in doing his duty—is going to prevent a confession from being obtained."

"When does he cease being a menace?" Chief Justice Warren asked then.

"Mr. Chief Justice, I did not say he was a menace," Nedrud promptly responded.

Justice Warren disagreed, contending that Nedrud had implied as much, "if he [the defense attorney] injected himself into it before the trial level."

"I merely said that he in effect will prevent a confession from being obtained," Nedrud argued. Then he made a remark that from his perspective no doubt seemed patently ridiculous but in fact led right back to the very crux of the matter: "And if this is what we are looking for," he said, "then we should appoint a counsel even *before* the arrest stage, because the moment that a murder takes place the government is out looking for the criminal."

It must be said that the justice who spoke now, William O. Douglas, must have been fully ready for the moment, for his question was incisive and interrogative in its inflexion only: "Very important rights can be lost many days, many weeks prior to trial?" he asked.

Nedrud's halting answer, while perhaps belying an agitated state, seems actually patronizing, though more likely—his time running out—he only meant to reassert forcefully his premise: "Mr. Justice Douglas," he said, "We come down to the question as to, dealing with the Constitution, that concededly—I think we'd say 'concededly'—everyone is entitled to a lawyer at the trial, and also at some point anterior to a trial. The question comes, I think, Mr. Justice Douglas, whether or not we are going to allow the trial court to determine the guilt or innocence, or the defense counsel. If the defense counsel comes in at the arrest stage, he will, as he should, prevent the defendant from confessing to his crime, and you will have fewer convictions. If this is what is wanted, this is what will occur."

In the light of present statistical evidence, Nedrud's dire prediction seems easy enough to disregard. If one were to discard his contention on principle, none of this mattered. However, even if any or all of the justices had by this time decided to let principle rule practice, publicly, all were bound by their dogma to remain impartial in regard to the overall issue, for there were two more days of oral argument ahead—four more cases joined with *Miranda* in the quest for a resolution of the pivotal questions: whether or not a defense counsel's involvement at the arrest stage would prevent confessions, and, more important, whether or not this was what was most wanted.

Oral Argument in *Vignera v. New York*

On March 1, 1966, the day after the Supreme Court heard the oral arguments in *Miranda,* Chief Justice Warren welcomed Victor M. Earle III to the advocate's podium in the well of the United States Supreme Court.

Victor M. Earle III

There to make oral argument in defense of Michael Vignera, Earle, an experienced criminal defense lawyer from New York, was making his first appearance before the Supreme Court. In his argument in defense of Michael Vignera, he intended to make a connection between his case and John Flynn's contention that timing was of the essence—his client having been convicted on the basis of a confession made at the police station. Earle felt the connection could be made primarily because there was no evidence that anyone had given Vignera any information about his constitutional rights.

On the other hand, there was no hard evidence to prove Vignera hadn't been warned, and Earle conceded this in his opening statement but quickly added that it was not the practice in New York to give such a warning. "I think it is entirely fair to assume no such warning was given," he concluded.

And in doing so stepped into quicksand. Appellate courts are never comfortable with assumptions that extend to core issues, and Justice Stewart in particular could not let it pass. "When you say he was never advised of his right to counsel," he interrupted, "aren't you begging the question and giving up a good deal of your position? The question here is: Does he have a right?"

"He had a right to counsel the moment when the state proceeded against him," Earle responded, in an effort to extricate himself from the quagmire. "When that moment rose," he continued, "it was not earlier or no later than 3:00 P.M. on the date when the police formally arrested him. . . . The burden is on the police to show waiver of the right. . . . *Escobedo* . . . said that the right to silence and the right to counsel can be waived. . . . I would think the beginning would be to warn him of his rights in a very meaningful way or perhaps to record them."

Justice Stewart seemed willing to let Earle's assumption stand, but not so willing to accept this new point about a "moment" when the warning should become imperative. Wouldn't it be better, he wanted to know, if the police simply provided him with a lawyer at the beginning?

"That would be an easy way of handling it," Earle responded, with no discernable trace of sarcasm.

"The only way of satisfying *Gideon?*" asked Justice Stewart.

"No, I don't think it is—again, because of the waiver point," Earle said, and then went on to explain, needlessly it would seem, that the police didn't want to assign counsel and weren't well equipped to do so anyway. "They *want* to get him to waive it," he said, and then added that of course such a waiver should be regarded with suspicion, and that it should not entitle the police to hold a defendant in custody indefinitely. "It would be a very limited waiver concept, in the sense of the principle of *McNabb*[9] and *Mallory.*"[10]

McNabb (1943) and Mallory (1957) were cases in which convictions were reversed because confessions were improperly admitted in evidence. Justice Black would have been intimately familiar with the *McNabb* and *Mallory* cases, having concurred with Justice Frankfurter's opinion in both cases. Interestingly, McNabb came down in 1942, while John P. Frank was serving as Justice Black's law clerk at the Supreme Court. "Wouldn't you have to have a counsel," he asked, "if the confession is obtained, to put him [the counsel] in charge, and to see that he [the suspect] is left alone and asked no questions?"

"I don't think so, sir," Earle responded.

"If he says anything voluntarily, it might be one thing," Justice Stewart continued, "but . . . unless they interrogate him, he wouldn't need a lawyer."

Finally Earle conceded the point, but contended, "A critical stage can occur prior to arraignment and prior to trial."

In effect, the comment brought the argument back to the matter of when a warning should be issued, and on this point, Justice Abe Fortas apparently wanted it to remain. Asking now for Earle's "help," he said, "Let's suppose that this conversation, which, as I recall, took place in the police car going from point A to point B—in which Vignera said something or other about the weapon—let's suppose that had been the first statement that Vignera had made, and in short, assume with me that the police picked up Vignera, and [while in] the police car going to the police station Vignera said he did it—did the holdup and used a knife—would that be inadmissible because of the absence of a warning or absence of counsel?"

It was essentially the same question Fortas had asked the day before, the question of whether arrest and focus came at the same time. Noting this, Earle said that he thought that, in the hypothetical, the statement might well be admissible. "Certainly, the laying on of hands is arrest," he said. "The probable cause requirements are probably not the same if the state has charged him and begun proceedings against him."

How was this to be applied, though, Fortas wanted to know, seemingly perplexed. "I am really soliciting your help," he said. "I think this is the problem . . . the problem of finding in a set of procedures as this, as is possible and advisable, the point at which the warning has to be given or counsel provided, or both."

Earle proceeded then to outline quickly his ideas on how and when constitutional warnings should be given, and when he finished, Justice Stewart promptly brought up a new and, as it turned out, pivotal issue. "What should this warning contain?" he asked. "What should this warning be?"

The question did not catch Earle off guard, however, for he had already done his homework. As he explained to the Court, the chief of police in the District of Columbia had last August formulated a warning, which, as he understood it, was now being issued to detainees by all police officials in the District. Thereupon, as well as he could recall it, he recited the warning: "You have been placed under arrest. You are not required to say anything to us any time or to answer any questions. Anything you say may be used against you as evidence in court. You may call a lawyer, a relative, or a friend. Your lawyer may be present here, and you may talk with him. If you cannot obtain a lawyer, one will be appointed for you when your case first goes to court."

Upon finishing, Earle added that he might have "a little quibble" with the third point because it suggested that the detainee might not be able to get a lawyer until after questioning.

Justice Fortas was clearly surprised by such an important concession. That is to say, the words "a little quibble" provoked a rather sharp rejoinder, Fortas remarking that it would seem Earle should have much more than a little bit of quibble, given what he had argued thus far, which was that the detainee had an absolute right for a lawyer to be appointed for him at the time of the warning, unless he waived the right.

"Yes, sir, unless he waives it," Earle readily agreed. The question might come up, he added, of "what do the police do when the fellow says, 'Thanks, I would like a lawyer now that you mention it, but I don't happen to have any money.'" They would have a choice, Earle quickly contended in answer to his own question. "They can give him ten cents and the number of a legal aid society" or they could "just stop interrogating."

"It seems to follow that he needs a lawyer before he can waive his right to a lawyer," said Justice Stewart now, clearly wishing to remind Earle that such was neither practical nor realistic.

"I wouldn't be happy to have the lawyers in the police station," Earle conceded, no doubt surprising any prosecutors present. As for the justices on the bench, while it can't be known who among them also welcomed this counterintuitive concession from a defense lawyer, Justice Stewart must not have been pleased, for he answered that it followed "naturally" that lawyers should be allowed into interrogation rooms.

Whereupon, Earle, knowing that his time at the podium had nearly run out—and undoubtedly surprising everyone again—responded, "It *doesn't* follow naturally, because the majority of the Court in *Escobedo* says these rights can be waived." Then he immediately launched into his ending comment, an articulation of the basic point of contention: "I think we do have to reorganize some of the realities of law enforcement," he said. "They [defense lawyers] do have to investigate. They do have the public duty of— if crimes are being committed by the minute—they do have to operate out of the police station." He might have continued, but his time was up, and so he relinquished the podium to the next counsel, New York's lead prosecutor, William Siegel.

William I. Siegel

As a law-and-order man, Siegel was strongly opposed to any ruling that would take away what he saw as law enforcement's most potent weapon, and above all else, he wanted to make that clear; hence, he wasted no time bringing the argument back to the question of just what kind of damage any legal counsel during interrogation would cause. "I think there has been too much talk of the police on the one side and the right of the defendant on the other side, and not enough reference to the rights of the community," he said. "We have thousands of cases, I suppose, where convictions are based in whole, or in part, on confessions."

His reference to an actual number, as approximate and speculative as he made it, might have passed unnoticed in the minds of the general public, but judges in general, and certainly those who have risen to the Supreme Court, know full well to mistrust such conclusive numerical assumptions offered without verifiable statistical support. Which was exactly what Justice White immediately called for; asking if Siegel could make any estimation of how many cases would have to be thrown out if the confession were inadmissible.

Siegel could not and, after conceding as much, tried to move beyond this sticking point, saying that he based his argument on "the importance of confessions on human nature and human evaluation." It was a principle of conduct, he went on, that people didn't, as a rule, confess to crimes they hadn't committed, and it was for this reason the courts had always said a true, honest, freely given confession was the highest type of evidence. Then, likely sensing a possible disagreement—since he knew well enough that more than a few confessions were owed to the interrogator's skill as much as the suspect's need to unburden his guilt—he added, "The problem that is before this Court, it seems to me, is just how to keep the balance between the ultimate necessity of the civilized, peaceful society and the constitutional rights of a specific defendant."

Thus, he seemed to have headed off one possible objection, but in doing so, he invited a more serious one from Justice Black, who tended to give the benefit of the doubt to the individual rather than to society. "Don't you think that the Bill of Rights has something to do with making that balance?" Black asked. "There is no doubt, is there, that *no* person should be convicted on evidence he has been compelled to give? Why do we have to get into a discussion of society or the beauties of the ideal civilization when that [coercion] is the issue before us?"

"Because the Bill of Rights only says that it shall not be *compelled*," Siegel argued, "but the word 'compelled' is not self-defining. What compelled means comes from this vantage [the Supreme Court]. We, for many, many years, were told by Your Honor's predecessors, and I would say by a great many of Your Honor's predecessors, that compelled meant that which couldn't make a man talk by the exercise of process. . . . You couldn't subpoena him into a court and, under pain of punishment, make him talk."

While it does not show in the text of Justice Black's immediate retort, one can surmise, from the subsequent exchange, that he resented the oblique slighting of his ability to remember past holdings of the Supreme Court. On the other hand, it can also be inferred that he was one step ahead of Siegel on this point, for he next asked, "Can it be determined, whether, if a man is interrogated while he is in a police station, that is compulsion?"

To answer Siegel, once again seeming to challenge Justice Black's legal memory, referenced *Escobedo,* the most recent Supreme Court decision on the issue, pointing out that the Court had already decided that compulsion occurred if the police ignored a suspect's request for a lawyer, or a lawyer's request to see his client. "If I get Your Honor's point of view," he then remarked, "it is that you don't have to wait until he is in the accusatorial stage."

At this point, Justice Fortas, diplomatically it would seem, defused the impending confrontation. "Mr. Siegel," he said, "may I ask you this question, in view of your long experience: There have been references many times and some made by members of this Court, to the effect that if lawyers were brought in at the early stage or pretrial stage, they would always advise the person under custody not to say anything. There are instances, however, where lawyers are representing persons under arrest or during custody, and they tell their clients they should plead guilty. Is that your experience? Has that occurred quite frequently, or do most of the people plead guilty? Are most of the people who plead guilty not represented by counsel?"

Either Siegel missed the point of the question or did not want to answer directly, for he merely observed that the State of New York upheld the right to counsel and had been upholding it long before it became a question.

"So the guilty pleas are entered against them after consultation with counsel?" Justice Fortas asked again. "Are guilty pleas rather frequent in your experience?"

Once again, however, Siegel failed to answer directly, saying only that the state "couldn't dispose of the volume of our business if we didn't have 85 to 90 percent convictions." It was possibly a deliberate confusion. Certainly, Siegel would have known at this point that to avoid having to make a potentially damaging concession he only needed to stall for another minute—the white light having come on several minutes earlier.

And now his red light did begin to flash. Accordingly, Chief Justice Warren ended the *Vignera* arguments, thanking the advocates and formally advising them that "the Court will take this matter under advisement."

Oral Argument in *Westover v. United States*

Later that same day, the Court resumed the bench and took up the arguments in the case of *Carl Calvin Westover versus the United States*. Unlike the other three cases consolidated in the *Miranda* oral argument schedule, *Westover* involved two different right-to-counsel issues. The first centered on the length of Westover's detention by the FBI. The second focused on the lack of counsel during that protracted interrogation. Westover's conviction for robbery of a federally insured bank was, it should be remembered, based on his confessions to FBI agents while he was in state custody concerning an unrelated state crime. The federal exclusionary rule did not bar admission of his confession *because* he was in state custody at the time of his interrogation.

F. Conger Fawcett

Fawcett, a San Francisco lawyer privately retained to represent Westover at the Supreme Court, delivered his oral argument. Noting first that four of the five cases before the Court at that time indicated that the police routinely held suspects for long periods during interrogation, Fawcett contended that it was "precisely because of this detention" that measures such as the presence of counsel were needed to safeguard the suspect's rights. "The fundamental philosophy of *Escobedo* seems to be the right against self-incrimination," he asserted and then added, "The fundamental force of *Escobedo* seems to be the understanding—the realization—that the right to counsel is necessary to remedy that situation." In other words, the Court had affirmed "in loud tones" that individual right outweighed the needs of the police. And when police interfered with constitutional rights, the "totality of the circumstances" test did not work and so there should be an automatic exception to the test.

Although Fawcett gave no specifics on how or even when exceptions were constitutionally mandated, he did assert that the "starting place" for an exception "would be the individual's constitutional rights versus self-incrimination, as protected by the right to counsel." He then concluded his argument by contending that there was a definite need for an exception for Westover because, as the prosecuting attorney himself had stated, the confessions were superfluous. Fawcett ended his remarks with time to spare, thus reserving a few minutes for a rebuttal he anticipated he would want to make.

Possibly, for similar reasons, the Court had allowed his entire argument to progress largely without interruption, for it is certain that every justice on the bench foresaw the debate coming to a head as the next lawyer approached the podium.

Solicitor General Thurgood Marshall

The Honorable Thurgood Marshall, there to argue for the United States, was the United States solicitor general and was undoubtedly the best known of the fifty-eight lawyers from fourteen states whose names were on the appellate briefs in the *Miranda* cases. The country knew him as the man who had argued and won the most important civil rights case in history— *Brown v. Board of Education*. He would, in time, take his own seat on the United States Supreme Court. Until then, his admirers on the high bench knew him as a consummate advocate for individual rights. This, plus the fact that *Westover* was a federal case involving the FBI (ostensibly a police force that took pride in its professionalism), promised a confrontation over one of the key issues of the whole proceeding: the practicality of warning a suspect and the equality of the present system.

Marshall, for his part, seemed ready to close the battle, although it must be said that he might not have foreseen what was to come, for he began with a statement clearly intended to dispense with any question of the suspect's competence. "There is testimony," he stated, ". . . that, when the FBI began to question [Westover] he was mentally alert and appeared to know exactly what he was doing." Moreover, Marshall went on to point out, there was no evidence that the interrogation had been held late at night or that Westover had been kept awake, and, furthermore, the FBI agent leading the investigation had testified from the witness stand that Westover had been fully advised of his rights.

All well and good in and of itself, but the set of questions that followed, coming from several justices, indicates how uninterested the Court was in any of these points. Justice Fortas, for example, the first to take a turn, immediately asked, "At what stage was the statement made?"

And after Marshall had stated that the time range was between 12:00 and 2:00 or 2:30, Justice Fortas asked if the advisement was standard FBI warning.

"Yes sir," Marshall answered. " . . . this is the practice of the FBI."

Justice White then stepped in and began, methodically, to paint Marshall into a corner. "Suppose," he said, " . . . the person being interrogated is given such a warning and the person being interrogated says, 'I want a lawyer.'"

To this Marshall responded with the standard, FBI-policy answer: "This statement says that if he wants to see an attorney he can do it before he talks."

"If he says, 'I don't know anyone, I don't know a lawyer, I can't afford one but I still want to talk to one,' what happens then?" Justice White asked.

To which Marshall answered, "If he says he still wants to talk to one it would be my position the agent has to say, 'We do not have a lawyer and we have no means of furnishing a lawyer.'"

"Will the agent then go on and interrogate him?"

"The agent would then say, 'In view of the fact that we can't give you a lawyer and we can't pay for a lawyer for you do you still want to talk?' [H]e is then in a position I think to say, 'If I don't get a lawyer I don't talk,' and that is the end of it."

"What if he says, 'No, I don't want to talk.' Is the interrogation over?"

"Yes, your Honor, I think so," Marshall responded. This was an admission that would not likely have come from any of the other government lawyers in the case, but it is entirely consistent with Marshall's view of individual rights.

Justice Black spoke up now. "As I understand you to say, of course, any person that has a lawyer or has the money to get a lawyer could get one immediately. This man has no lawyer and has no money to get one. The only reason he doesn't have a lawyer is for that reason. Does that raise any principles as to what an indigent is entitled to? He is certainly not going to get treated like a man that has the money to get a lawyer."

Marshall, however, disagreed with Justice Black's premise. "He is not being denied anything," Marshall insisted. "The state is not affirmatively denying him anything. The state is just not furnishing him anything."

Whereupon, Justice Black, doubtless recognizing a distinction without a difference, did what he was well known for: He called on the Constitution, noting that it granted the government power to detain a man and question him. Justice Black's point, that the power to detain and the power to question have to be balanced by the obligation of fairness to the person being detained and questioned, was not lost on Marshall. Justice Black was probing for the specific place in the Constitution where the power to detain and question is explicit. Marshall candidly admitted, "I have been unable to find one that grants it as such." Then he provided a weak defense, saying, "It is inherent in the investigatory process. . . . I don't think it has ever been questioned."

"It has with me," Justice Black countered.

Perhaps to lighten the mood for his good friend, Chief Justice Warren now stepped in to ask facetiously if Marshall meant to suggest the Court overrule *Escobedo*.

"No, sir," Marshall answered promptly. "I think *Escobedo* can fit into this case under the Fifth Amendment. I don't want to give support to the theory that . . . *Escobedo* requires a lawyer be appointed for an indigent at the police precinct or on arrest."

This suggestion—made, it should be remembered, by the government's chief oral advocate—that the Fifth Amendment, rather than the Sixth Amendment, applied in this case, might not have been then appreciated by the audience, for it was an audience focused on the Sixth Amendment's right to counsel at the accusatory stage, not the yet-to-emerge right to remain silent in the police station. The idea wasn't lost on Chief Justice Warren, however. "You wouldn't ask us to weaken *Escobedo*," he suggested, "to the point of saying a man could be interrogated if [he] didn't have a lawyer but he said that he wanted a lawyer and he could not raise one at the particular time either because of lack of money or couldn't get him on the telephone?"

Marshall did not answer directly. Instead, he described the conditions under which he thought the suspect's statement would not be valid. For instance, he said, if it appeared to the trial judge that he wasn't going to talk and after that was cajoled, or, as in *Escobedo*, was handcuffed, then the statement shouldn't be admitted in evidence.

When Marshall finished, Justice John Harlan spoke for the first time, and since Justice Harlan was well known for his reticence during oral argument, one can imagine the gallery taking special notice while he cited the Constitution as requiring "neither a warning of counsel or a warning of the right to remain silent." But without either one of those warnings, he then asserted, "those are factors to be taken into account as bearing on voluntariness, and the ultimate constitutional issue is whether or not the statement or confession is voluntary."

It was a good point, which was to be expected, since Justice Harlan, as everyone was aware, knew his Constitution. And Marshall was only too glad to have it made. "That is our position exactly, sir," he said. "We also say the warning is better to be given but not required."

With that, Marshall stepped down and Fawcett returned to the podium for his rebuttal. He meant to take Marshall to task for contradicting the Federal Bureau of Investigation's standard warning, claiming he couldn't understand why the federal government was "talking out of both sides of its mouth at the same time," but he got no further before Justice Fortas tried to subtly warn him that in doing so he was wading into constitutional waters. "Do you agree," Justice Fortas asked, "that the issue here should be considered Fifth Amendment and not the right to counsel?"

Fawcett didn't seem to get the hint. "As I interpret *Escobedo*, I think it makes sense," he responded, then went on to say he thought *Escobedo* had devised a means of protecting the right to counsel.

"What about a third approach—due process?" asked Justice Harlan. "Would you be troubled with that especially?"

Fawcett answered that he wouldn't be troubled about putting it in due process. "I think all of these other rights ultimately come down to due process in any case," he offered.

Chief Justice Warren apparently wasn't comfortable with this, and for good reason; it could lead to the Court's deciding all five cases on all the questions before the Court—an all or nothing proposition. If the Court elected to resolve the myriad confession issues in these cases on the basis of the Fourteenth Amendment's guarantee of due process, then it would have to find that the Fourteenth Amendment guaranteed all of the specific rights under consideration in the *Miranda* cases—i.e., the right to a lawyer, the right to remain silent, the right to have a lawyer present at interrogation, and the right to be told the consequences of any statement made in the absence of counsel.

When Chief Justice Warren tried to point this out, however, Fawcett again seemed not to understand, for he answered by saying that he rejected "the totality of the circumstances and thought that *Escobedo* rejected them as well, when it held that there must be access to counsel at the time an interrogation became 'focused.'" It "wasn't that important," he asserted, whether the reason was due process or a specific provision in the Sixth Amendment.

Not only the chief justice but also at least four other justices must have wondered how anyone could reject the core premise in a due process analysis (the totality of the circumstances) while accepting the core premise of the Sixth Amendment (the right to counsel) and still say the difference was "not that important."

Fawcett's rebuttal time had ended, however, and so the Court let matters stand, adjourning until the next morning, when it took up the next case in the *Miranda* foursome.

Oral Argument in *California v. Stewart*

Roy Allen Stewart, it should be remembered, had been convicted of robbery and murder based on confessions he'd given in the course of being interrogated nine times over a six-day period, and while two of his confessions were tape-recorded, no record had been made of any warnings, nor had he been represented by counsel at the time he confessed.

Gordon Ringer

Gordon Ringer knew that his case was primarily different from the other cases in that the prosecution was actually the petitioner, since Stewart's conviction had been overturned as part of the *Dorado* doctrine in California. Otherwise, the argument made by Gordon Ringer, the California assistant attorney general, while lucid and eloquent, added little by way of new theory or old law. Calling the case "a grandchild of *Escobedo* and a child of *Dorado*," Ringer posited that the central question had to do with whether "antecedently" to the giving of his confession, the police were constitutionally obliged to advise Stewart of his right to remain silent and right to consult counsel. In his opinion, it came down to how the California Supreme Court had interpreted *Escobedo*, and apparently that court had decided that it was compelled by federal constitutional law to hold, on the basis of the *Escobedo* case, that warnings must be given, and rights must be waived, or the statement, no matter how free and voluntary it might otherwise be, could not be received in evidence.

In other words, the California Supreme Court had held [in *Dorado*] that there is a general Sixth Amendment right to counsel, which emanated from circumstances occurring either at or after the arrest of the accused. "We believe that the true interpretation of *Escobedo* is the interpretation, which was suggested . . . by Mr. Justice Stewart and Mr. Justice Harlan," Ringer asserted, and then on the basis of that concluded that it was a totality of circumstances case. Only by looking back at the real message of *Miranda* can we see the incredible change in emphasis from the Sixth Amendment's explicit right of counsel to the Fifth Amendment's implicit right of counsel. Both rights exist in custodial interrogation of suspects, but it is the Fifth Amendment privilege against self-incrimination that is lost if counsel is not available. This would, in time, become the core of a new American right to remain silent.

William A. Norris

Norris, arguing for the defendant Stewart, ran into a bit of trouble with a question from Justice Stewart. After reminding the Court that his client had been arrested, along with his wife and three other persons who just happened to be at his house, Justice Stewart interjected, almost casually, "Of course the house was full of stolen goods, was it not?"

"It was, Mr. Justice Stewart," Norris answered. He was trying to get back on track when Justice Fortas interrupted: "I hope you'll forgive me for interrupting the order of your argument, but I'd like to get back to what you were talking about a few moments ago. . . . Does the distinction between this case and *Escobedo* turn solely on the request [for a lawyer] that was made in *Escobedo* and the lack of a request here?"

Norris changed the question somewhat by answering, "If the question is whether we adopted the *prima facie* test—when we would reach an accusatory stage in this case, as well as in *Escobedo*—I would say clearly 'yes,' and without regard to the request because here I believe the police had much more evidence against him by the time of the confession certainly and even at the time of the arrest than against Escobedo."

Justice Black picked up the thread: "You are not arguing, I'm sure, that every time a man gets arrested, he's got to have a lawyer appointed at that moment—that we should establish such a rule?"

Norris, not wanting to ask too much, wisely said, "I would not want to argue that, Mr. Justice Black, and I think that is not required by *Escobedo*. I think that's a false argument." Norris, however, continued the point by addressing Justice Black and hoping to catch the attention of the rest of the Court: "My position is that the only effective way to protect the right to remain silent, the right not to testify against yourself, is to make sure that he has a lawyer. It is counsel that is the vehicle for protection of all of these other rights. I was interested that the American Civil Liberties Union argued [in its brief] that this is primarily a Fifth Amendment case, on the ground that there may be some other way of protecting the right to remain silent. But when it is all said and done, they agreed that the only one they could really think of was the right to counsel."

Oral Argument in *Johnson and Cassidy v. New Jersey*

On March 2, 1966, the Court heard the final oral argument, that of Stanley Johnson and Sylvester Cassidy against the State of New Jersey. In the appeal to the New Jersey Supreme Court, Johnson's and Cassidy's lawyers had portrayed the police interrogations as secret and protracted and had argued that not only were the two men denied counsel, but also their confessions were unwarned. The New Jersey prosecutors, on the other hand, had characterized the confessions as free and voluntary, given by suspects who had not requested counsel, and had made intelligent decisions when they had waived the right to remain silent. It was this latter point that the defense counsel, Stanford Shmukler, meant to argue first.

Stanford Shmukler

Stanford Shmukler felt that his clients had been coerced because neither was capable of making an intelligent decision. Consequently, during his statement of the facts, when Justice Black asked if the confessions were coerced, unlike those advocates before him, Shmukler answered in the affirmative, reminding the justices that his clients were held "illegally . . . incommunicado . . . not told of their rights . . . and confronted with confessions of *other* defendants, which were later held to be coerced." Then he went on to explain that Cassidy, twenty-five when he was arrested, had an eighth-grade education and had never been in contact with police. Moreover, his psychological profile indicated that he was "a highly conflicted, immature individual with deep feelings of incompetentcy [sic] and inadequate personality, and who needed narcotics to alleviate his anxiety and was a very passive and repentant [sic] individual."

Johnson's history wasn't any better. Twenty-one at the time of his arrest, with only a seventh-grade education and one prior criminal conviction, he was said to have "tense feelings of insecurity and inadequacy." Also, he was diagnosed as grossly inadequate with a schizoid personality and his ability and judgment "would go to pieces under strain."

Thus, by holding "these individuals under threatening, coercive circumstances," Shmukler then argued, " . . . [and telling] them they just want a statement . . . [makes them] sign their own doom without knowing the significance of it . . . admitting to a robbery would have seemed to them a small matter compared to admitting to a homicide."

In answer to a question from Justice Fortas as to whether the police had known of Cassidy's emotional profile when they interrogated him, Shmukler noted that there was no admission on record by the police, but he admitted that it should have been obvious to them, especially because Cassidy, in his motion to suppress his confession, had testified that he was under the influence of narcotics at the time of his arrest.

This answer satisfied Justice Fortas. In answer to further series of questions from the bench, Shmukler then reported the rest of the pertinent facts. Yes, there was other evidence besides the confessions. An informant had testified against them, and the fingerprint of one of the defendants had been found on one of the items in the store they had robbed. Also, there was evidence he believed was adequate to sustain the homicide conviction. And the arrest was valid, he agreed. As to the question of what had happened to Cassidy during the five hours that he was held, Shmukler answered that his five-hour interrogation had been "practically" continual. Also, he had been warned only when the formal recording of the confession took place, and neither defendant had been advised of his right to remain silent.

The bench then moved on to the policy issues, Justice Black wanting to know what Shmukler thought would be the practical effect on "universal practice in the United States," if the Court held that counsel must be appointed when the man was detained and held for questioning.

Shmukler didn't think the policy would necessarily apply universally. "Perhaps the ruling should be only an exclusionary one, that the evidence obtained in the absence of counsel would not be admissible," he asserted, explaining that the state did not have an absolute duty to appoint an attorney at such a stage of the investigation. But on the other hand, he said, if the state didn't appoint—if the suspect had no counsel—then any confession obtained would not be admissible.

Norman Heine

New Jersey's response was given by Norman Heine, the Camden County prosecutor who later assumed the bench of the New Jersey Superior Court. As soon as he began his explanation of how Cassidy was "picked up, not arrested," he was interrupted by the chief justice, who wanted to know the circumstances under which he was "picked up."

No warrant was issued, Heine explained. The police officers had gone to his home and, while there, they had asked him to accompany them to police headquarters to be questioned about an alleged robbery-murder. Yes, he could have declined to go, Heine stated in response to a question from Justice Black.

The chief justice then brought up what he termed "a very important factor," the number of police officers present at Cassidy's home when he was asked to go to the station.

"I think . . . there were five or seven," Heine said. "They were looking at this time and questioning people in connection with a robbery-murder."

"Are we to assume they went because they wanted to?" asked Justice Black.

"They had some information that led them to this suspect so they wanted to question him about it," responded Heine.

Probably as much as to Heine, Justice Black commented to his fellow justices, "That *would* be a very important factor as far as I am concerned."

"May I ask in what form he was advised of his rights?" Chief Justice Warren asked.

"He was given a warning," answered Heine and then went on to quote the warning: "'I am going to ask you some questions as to what you know about the holdup but before I ask you these questions it is my duty to warn you that everything you tell me must be of your own free will, must be the truth, without any promise or threats having been made to you or any other persons at some future time. Do you understand what I have said to you?'" Upon finishing, Heine also added that Cassidy had answered that he did understand what had just been said to him.

But Justice Black retorted, "Why did they not tell him he didn't have to answer or could go home if he wanted to? Did they tell him that?"

It was implied, Heine tried to argue, in the phrase advising the suspect that his answers had to be of his own free will. But Justice Black seemed not the least satisfied with this answer. "There would be a difference," he said, "in telling a man who is under arrest or in jail or in custody, 'If you don't have anything to say to us of your own free will' or telling a man on the street, 'We would like to have you come down to the place and talk to us if you want to.'"

When Heine responded that he thought the questioning of suspects should be done at the convenience of the police and at the police station, Justice Black asked, "Is it your position that you have a right to take a man and compel him . . . to go to the station . . . and be interrogated?"

"That's right," Heine said. "We think we have a right."

"Where does it stem from, the law?" the chief justice then asked him.

"There is an inherent right in the police power of the state," Heine answered.

However, when the chief justice asked if the police had the power to "compel" suspects to go to the police station, Heine admitted that he would not go as far as to say "compelling" but he did think they had the right to ask a suspect to "accompany" them. Whereupon the chief justice observed that there were seven officers involved in this case, to which Heine responded, "That is very compelling." It was an admission that ended his time at the podium.

M. Gene Haeberle

Haeberle, arguing for the defense, moved quickly to emphasize the arrest had taken place at Cassidy's apartment at four o'clock in the morning and the defendants were certainly "not guests at a police social." Haeberle reminded the Court that the suspects were subjected to a very long period of interrogation before they confessed. He closed the entire three-day proceeding with a statement that in its general content could have served to describe all of the defendants:

> [T]hey took these . . . people of limited intelligence and poor background, and got confessions from them. They didn't know the difference, of [sic] the felony murder rule. When those confessions were taken, they were in the death house; and when those confessions were used in the joint trial, they were so incriminating, so completely, so overwhelming, there was very little left to be done."

It could even be said that all of the *Miranda* cases were bound by the facts of each, and the arguments that had been built upon the foundation laid by John Flynn in many ways seemed like one continuous argument, which, apparently, the Court found quite compelling, for it needed but a mere two and one-half months to construct a landmark opinion.

Chapter 4

THE AFTERMATH

The *Miranda* Opinion

An "opinion" from an appellate court such as the U.S. Supreme Court is unlike any other document produced by any other branch of government. Even split-vote opinions are the result of equal, binding, independent, and single-minded debate. They are remarkably collegial, given that they are handed down by a group that has no peers, no superiors, and a chief whose administrative responsibility is greater than the rest but who nevertheless has only one vote.

While individual justices often differ in their social values and philosophy, they share a common discipline of the law and fidelity to the Court. They have no constituency, no party, and no "higher court." Most important, they respect each other's opinions in a way that diminishes pride of authorship and honors deeply held convictions.

The *Miranda* opinion contains inordinately long sentences professing arcane Latin maxims upon which so much of our Anglo-Saxon law is based.[1] It is imbedded in principle,[2] clothed in scholarly material,[3] and limited to a specific brand of custodial interrogation.[4] It is both eloquent and prophetic.[5] It is nevertheless quite specific:

> The Supreme Court of Arizona held that Miranda's constitutional rights were not violated in obtaining the confession and affirmed the conviction [citation omitted]. In reaching its decision, the court emphasized heavily the fact that Miranda did not specifically request counsel. We reverse. From the testimony of the officers and by the admission of respondent, it is clear that Miranda was not in any way apprised of his right to consult with an attorney and to have one present during the interrogation, nor was his right not to be compelled to incriminate himself effectively protected in any other manner. Without these warnings, the statements were inadmissible. The mere fact that he signed a statement, which contained a typed-in clause stating that he had "full knowledge" of his "legal rights," does not approach the knowing and intelligent waiver required to relinquish constitutional rights. [Citations omitted][6]

Thus was the procedural gateway for the Fifth Amendment's privilege against self-incrimination set forth in nonconstitutional terms for the first time. In supporting this opinion, Chief Justice Warren was joined by Justices Black, Douglas, Fortas, and Brennan. Justice Harlan, with whom Justices Stewart and White joined, dissented. Justice White wrote a separate dissenting opinion, as did Justice Clark. Whereas most Supreme Court opinions are simply filed with the clerk of the court and mailed to the parties, in this case, Chief Justice Warren read the full sixty-plus-page opinion aloud in the Supreme Courtroom on Monday, June 13, 1966.[7] In a voice laden with emotion, Chief Justice Warren made clear the connection between the Fifth Amendment privilege and the new right—the right of silence—by saying, "At the outset, if a person in custody is to be subjected to interrogation, he must first be informed in clear and unequivocal terms that he has the right to remain silent."[8]

While the *Miranda* decision is a single United States Supreme Court opinion, it was handed down in four separate cases.[9] In *Vignera*, the Court reversed the conviction because Michael Vignera had not been warned of any of his rights before he was questioned by the detective and the assistant district attorney. The Court said that, since no other steps were taken to protect these rights, he had not been effectively apprised of his Fifth Amendment privilege or of his right to have counsel present and his confession was inadmissible. The Court also made abundantly clear that the responsibility for protecting a suspect's constitutional rights rests with the police and, when involved, the district attorney. And the penalty for failing to have counsel present is indisputable: Unwarned statements are inadmissible—end of argument.

The Court reversed the conviction in *Westover* for similar reasons and also gave specific answer to the key question posed in the case—whether the new standard would require "*actual consultation* [emphasis in original] with, and the continued presence of" an attorney both before and during interrogation.[10] Noting that there was no evidence showing that Carl Calvin Westover had knowingly and intelligently waived his right to counsel before he made his confession, the Court argued that even though FBI agents had issued a warning before they questioned him, those warnings had come after fourteen hours of interrogation by local police. "Thus," the Court concluded, "in obtaining a confession from Westover the federal authorities were the beneficiaries of the pressure applied by the local in-custody interrogation."[11]

The case of *California v. Stewart* differed from the other cases under the

Miranda umbrella partly because the petitioner was the State of California, the prosecutor of the case. Consequently, California posed its certiorari question in familiar terms, asking whether a fair warning mattered in the case of a freely given confession, especially when the suspect had not been refused counsel.[12] Stewart's lawyers, in plain language and relying on the crucial specific of the case, asked simply, "Did the secret police interrogation of Respondent, over a period of five days following his arrest and before he was taken before a magistrate, constitute a denial of his constitutional right to the "Assistance of Counsel" and thereby render inadmissible at trial a confession elicited during the fifth day of interrogation?"[13]

The Supreme Court answered both the State of California and Stewart, the respondent, by affirming the lower court's decision, saying that it would not presume a defendant had been told of his right and privileges when "the record does not show any warnings have been given." The Court also noted that the record did show the defendant's "steadfast denial of the alleged offenses through eight of the nine interrogations" over the five-day period, and concluded, quite easily it would seem today, that Stewart had been "compelled by persistent interrogation to forgo his Fifth Amendment privilege."[14]

The Court's rhetoric in *Stewart* suggests that *any* lengthy interrogation in the absence of counsel might be constitutionally defective. This was the first case in which the Court decided that "persistent" interrogation can "compel" a suspect to "forgo" his Fifth Amendment privilege. That language alone makes the *Miranda* decision unique in its message—sent to the world at large—that police officers are not to be trusted.

The fifth case, *Johnson and Cassidy*, had been argued with the other three cases, but the opinion was delivered separately, on June 20, 1966, because the Court wanted to clarify the important question of retroactive applicability in *Escobedo* and *Miranda*. Notwithstanding the fact that Johnson and Cassidy's original convictions had become final in 1960, their postconviction appeal argued for the admissibility of their confessions under a standard set by *Escobedo* in 1963 (even though *Escobedo* itself held that it was inapplicable to convictions that had become final prior to the date of its release by the Supreme Court). The Supreme Court had in the year immediately preceding the *Johnson and Cassidy* and *Miranda* decisions found it necessary to deal twice with the problem of retroactivity.[15] In handing down a third decision regarding retroactivity in criminal procedure, the Court wanted to reinforce the principle controlling prospective rulings: "In criminal litigation concerning constitutional claims, the Court may in the interest of justice make the rule prospective . . . where the exigencies of the situation require such an application. . . . These cases also delineate criteria by which such an issue may be resolved."[16]

Thus, on this issue, Chief Justice Warren, the author of this particular *Miranda* opinion, duly wrote that *Escobedo* affected only those cases in which the trial had begun after June 24, 1964 (the date of the *Escobedo* decision). *Miranda,* on the other hand, applied only to trials beginning after the date of the Court's decision on *Miranda* (one week previously, on June 13, 1966).[17] Having found the *Johnson and Cassidy* petitioners' other grounds for overturning also without merit, the Court consequently affirmed the lower court's decision in the case.

Constitutional scholars, prosecutors, and defense lawyers understand and generally agree that the doctrine of retroactivity must be applied sparingly. In particular, cases that establish new law and new standards or announce new applications of constitutional amendments cannot be fairly applied retroactively without reducing the judicial system to utter chaos. That said, it is worth remembering that of the five cases collected under the *Miranda* umbrella, Johnson and Cassidy were the only petitioners whose unwarned confessions resulted in the death penalty. Miranda and his four copetitioners got reversals but not much help with their prison time.

The *Miranda* Warnings

The *Miranda* doctrine came down in installments. The first, the June 13, 1966, sixty-plus page opinion, contained the police procedures that are now known as the *Miranda* warnings.

The second installment, handed down a week later in the *Johnson* case, created arbitrary deadlines for the application of the *Miranda* doctrine. In effect, *Johnson* allowed a discriminatory remedy for some suspects whose fortunes were cast in the gatehouse but made it to the main house on time. Those suspects who became defendants and had their cases actually tried after Miranda's own original trial in Arizona could use the *Miranda* doctrine to their benefit. Those tried "between" Escobedo and Miranda were stuck with *Escobedo*'s doctrine, which held that a suspect must ask for a lawyer before the police were required to provide one. Those tried before *Escobedo* were stuck with the "old days" doctrine, that is, whether the confession was "voluntary" irrespective of warnings given by police.

As Sam Dash, the director of the American Institute of Criminal Law and Procedure put it, "It is ironic that for four people *alone* the Court applied *Miranda* retrospectively."[18] Those four were Ernesto Miranda himself and Vignera, Westover, and Stewart. As for Johnson and Cassidy, to put it plainly, their timing was poor.

Application guidelines aside, the *Miranda* warning itself, as stipulated in the first installment, must include all of four separate warnings: (1) The suspect must be warned *prior to questioning* that he has the right to remain silent; (2) He must be warned that anything he says can be used against him in a court of law; (3) He has the right to the presence of an attorney; and (4) If he cannot afford an attorney one will be appointed for him *prior to any questioning* if he so desires.

In judicial circles, warnings are euphemistically called admonitions. What, then, was the Warren Court's intention in crafting these four particular admonitions? Were all four considered of equal importance? Is the order of their presentation meaningful?

And then there is the question of whether or not this set of four explicit warnings is constitutional. Many constitutional scholars worried about the exact constitutional predicate for holding that the police must give these four explicit warnings to suspects. Justice Black, the senior member of the *Miranda* majority, was famous for carrying around a frayed vest-pocket-sized copy of the Constitution, produced by the U.S. Printing Office. At the slightest provocation during an oral argument, he would reach for his little dog-eared book, wave it toward the advocate's podium, and ask, "Where exactly in the Constitution does it say *that?*"

For constitutional scholars, at least, the answer begins with marking the boundaries of due process. Even the due process clause of the Fourteenth Amendment contains no description of limits, and over the last two hundred years, the Supreme Court has repeatedly attempted to articulate the general procedural guidelines to which those governing as well as those governed should adhere. In a "settled usages and modes of proceeding" case in 1921, for example, the Court said, "[a] process of law is due process within the meaning of constitutional limitations if it can show the sanction of settled usage both in this country and in England."[19] Judge Cardozo said, "Not lightly to be vacated is the verdict of quiescent years."[20] After his transition from the New York Court of Appeals to the United States Supreme Court, Justice Cardozo expanded his subtle view of the matter by saying, "We do not find it profitable to mark the precise limits of [due process]."[21]

Justice Douglas, a member of the *Miranda* majority, in considering the legal mechanism by which some words not found in the Constitution or the Bill of Rights become constitutional mandates, once said, "The right to educate one's children as one chooses is made applicable to the States by the force of the First and Fourteenth Amendments." He then added:

> The state may not, consistently with the *spirit* of the First Amendment, contract the spectrum of available knowledge. The right of freedom of speech and press includes not only the right to utter or to print, but also the right to distribute, the right to receive, to read, and freedom of inquiry, freedom of thought, and freedom to teach. . . . Without those *peripheral* [emphasis supplied] rights, the specific rights would be less secure.[22]

Perhaps the most apt explanation of whence came *Miranda*'s explicit warnings occurs in the opinion handed down in *Griswold v. Connecticut*.[23] This, another watershed Supreme Court case, preceding *Miranda* by a year, established the right of privacy. Thus, in leading inexorably to *Roe v. Wade*,[24] it accomplished for the right of privacy what *Miranda* accomplished for the right to remain silent. The case concerned Dr. Griswold, a physician who gave information and medical advice to married couples on how to prevent conception. He was arrested, charged, and convicted of violating a state statute that criminalized those who engaged in such "ungodly" conduct. The Supreme Court used the First and Fourteenth Amendments as the basis to reverse Griswold's conviction. Using a 1958[25] case involving completely different facts and an entirely different issue, the Court held that the freedom of speech and expression guaranteed by the First Amendment had a "penumbra" where privacy was protected from governmental intrusion. Justice Douglas cited *NAACP v. Alabama*'s rhetoric as follows: "[the] freedom to associate and privacy in one's association [is] a peripheral First Amendment Right."[26]

Griswold's relevance to *Miranda* is limited to the discussion of the implicit inclusion of the right to remain silent as part of the *letter, penumbra,* or *spirit* of, and *peripheral* to, the Fifth Amendment. *Griswold* came down the year before *Miranda* and was authored by a member of the *Miranda* majority. In other words, *Griswold* is to *Roe* what *Escobedo* is to *Miranda*.

The Right to Remain Silent

The sixty-plus page *Miranda* opinion is most explicit in detailing the requirements, purpose, and reach of each of the four warnings,[27] as well as the order in which the warnings should be given. The Court asserted that "such a warning" was an "absolute prerequisite in overcoming" the pressures inherent to the interrogation room.[28] "For those unaware of the privilege," the Court wrote, "the warning is needed simply to make them aware of it—the threshold requirement for an intelligent decision as to its exercise.[29]

The same reasoning was used to apply this notion of criticality irrespective of the priority of the first warning's placement in the broader scheme of the four warnings. Consequently, it cannot be limited to "Just the subnormal or woefully ignorant who succumb to an interrogator's imprecation [because] the interrogation will continue until a confession is obtained or silence, in the face of an accusation, [becomes in] itself damning [which] will bode ill when presented to a jury."[30]

Silence at the custodial stage is also critical because, as stated in the opinion, "the warning will show the individual that his interrogators are prepared to recognize his privilege should he choose to exercise it."[31] The opinion also carefully establishes the legal justification for the right to remain silent, with the Court contending that "The Fifth Amendment privilege is so fundamental to our system of constitutional rule and the expedient of giving an adequate warning as to the availability of the privilege is so simple, we will not pause to inquire in individual cases whether the defendant was aware of his rights without a warning being given."[32]

And finally, the opinion holds that the lower courts need not bother inquiring into the idiosyncratic variations among suspects:

Assessments of the knowledge the defendant possessed, based on information as to his age, education, intelligence, or prior contact with authorities, can never be more than speculation; a warning is a clear-cut fact. More important, whatever the background of the person interrogated, a warning at the time of the interrogation is indispensable to overcome its pressures and to insure that the individual knows he is free to exercise the privilege at that point in time.[33]

The Second Warning

That a suspect must be told that anything he says can be used against him in a court of law follows the first warning because, in the Court's opinion, it is a natural, and necessary, extension of the first warning. An individual must know that his words can and will be used against him in court in order to make him aware not only of the privilege, but also of the consequences of forgoing his right to silence. The Court further asserted that only through an awareness of these consequences can there be any assurance of real understanding and intelligent exercise of the privilege.[34]

Thus, while early Fifth Amendment cases had focused on the more formal and easily recognizable stages of criminal prosecution, like arraignment and trial, the inclusion of *Miranda*'s second warning, as the Court was well aware, moved custodial interrogation up the uncertain steps of criminal justice. "[T]his warning," the Court speculated, "may serve to make the individual more acutely aware that he is faced with a phase of the adversary system—that he is not in the presence of persons acting solely in his interest."[35]

The Right to the "Presence" of an Attorney

Miranda's third warning, that the suspect has a right to counsel, results from the grafting of the Sixth Amendment onto the Fifth Amendment, an action that adds strength and flexibility to both. In plain terms, it allows for what TV detectives prejudicially refer to as "lawyering up," meaning the suspect's right to have a lawyer present during interrogation. While often enough nothing infuriates TV detectives more, in reality, modern professional police accept as part of their daily challenge the silence that usually follows when a "perp" says he wants to lawyer up. Those who toil in the interrogation room also can easily understand why the Court explained the inclusion of this warning in these terms:

> The circumstances surrounding in-custody interrogation can operate very quickly to overbear the will of one merely made aware of his privilege by his interrogators. Therefore, the right to have counsel present at the interrogation is indispensable to the protection of the Fifth Amendment privilege under the system we delineate today.[36]

The physical setting of the interrogation room on a television studio set, while hardly realistic, nevertheless offers a glimpse of how "circumstances" might overbear a suspect's will. Behind the suspect stands the chain-link cage, noticeably dirty and lacking in furniture. In front of the suspect is the open door that leads back home—as soon as he tells the truth. The interrogation stool has four stout legs to support a confession; they appear unstable enough to be easily knocked from under the suspect if he will not talk or wants to lawyer up. He sees but two equally undesirable alternatives: to talk or to stick by his constitutional privilege to remain silent. The former might well seem easier and offer closure, whereas the latter might result in hard feelings, or something worse, depending on the size and demeanor of the interrogators. In demanding that the suspect be advised that he has a right to the presence of an attorney, the *Miranda* opinion seeks to "assure that the individual's right to choose between silence and speech remains unfettered throughout the interrogation process. . . . A mere warning given by interrogators is not alone sufficient to accomplish that end."[37]

The Warren Court also specifically included the prosecutors' inherent connection to the third warning:

> Prosecutors can claim that the admonishment of the right to remain silent without more will benefit only the recidivist and the professional [citing the brief filed by the National District Attorneys Association]. Even preliminary advice given to the accused by his own attorney can be swiftly overcome by the secret interrogation process [citing *Escobedo*]. Thus the need for counsel to protect the Fifth Amendment privilege comprehends not merely a right to consult with counsel prior to questioning but also the right to have counsel present during any questioning if the defendant so desires.[38]

In legal circles, where it is generally believed that polysyllabic, abstract words carry more precise meaning, the standard policy regarding constitutional rights assumes a waiver in most cases unless a right is specifically asserted. In plainer language, this means that if one doesn't ask for a lawyer then the system will assume one doesn't want one. The *Miranda* opinion anticipated that policy and tried to nip it in the bud by stating, "While such a request affirmatively secures [the suspect's] right to have one, his failure to ask for a lawyer does not constitute a waiver. No effective waiver of the right to counsel during interrogation can be recognized unless specifically made after the warnings we here delineate have been given. The accused who does not know his rights and therefore does not make a request may be the person who most needs counsel."[39]

This special articulation of the third warning's intent recognizes the clash between individual liberty and community need and tries to balance the two, although it still gives precedence to individual liberty, calling the third warning "an absolute prerequisite to interrogation." The *Miranda* opinion, in this instance then, is finely focused on the umbilical-like connection between the constitutional demand for warnings and law enforcement's admitted need to interrogate suspects. "No amount of circumstantial evidence that the person may have been aware of this right will suffice to stand in its stead," the Court concluded. "Only through such a warning is there ascertainable assurance that the accused was aware of this right."[40]

The Right to Counsel, Free of Charge

The fourth component of the *Miranda* warning, "If you cannot afford an attorney, one will be appointed for you," is actually more a promise than a warning, and while the first three parts are cut from common stock, this fourth leg is surely carved from exotic wood. Even in 1966 dollars, providing competent counsel to every indigent suspect would have been fiscally impossible. The Court, and everyone else involved, knew that the price tag attached to the fourth warning was never going to be paid. Nevertheless, the Court, in its desire to adhere to the fundamental principle upon which its opinion was based, recognized the need to remove financial concerns from the suspect's mind. Consequently, the Court, explaining its inclusion of the right to counsel free of charge, stated:

> If an individual indicates that he wishes the assistance of counsel before any interrogation occurs, the authorities cannot rationally ignore or deny his request on the basis that the individual does not have or cannot afford a retained attorney. The financial ability of the individual has no relationship to the scope of the rights involved here. . . . The need for counsel in order to protect the privilege exists for the indigent as well as the affluent.[41]

The Court justified this opinion by stating simply:

> In fact, were we to limit these constitutional rights to those who can retain an attorney, our decisions today would be of little significance. . . . Denial of counsel to the indigent at the time of interrogation while allowing an attorney to those who can afford one would be no more supportable by reason or logic than the similar situation at trial and on appeal struck down in *Gideon v. Wainwright.*[42]

By reminding the lower courts, the prosecutors, and police investigators that the "vast majority of confession cases" involve "those unable to retain counsel," the Court offered a partial explanation for why some suspects confess and others do not: Some have money and others do not. Those who have money hire lawyers and go to trial. Those who do not have money confess and go to jail. While simplistic, this explanation is supported by statistical evidence: Poor suspects confess to crimes in vastly greater numbers than do affluent ones. Even more simplistically, but following logically, it explains why our prisons are full of poor people.

Finally, two aspects of the *Miranda* warnings should be emphasized: All four warnings must be given *prior* to questioning, and giving the warnings is an *absolute* requirement. The burden thus falls squarely on the prosecution, which must establish beyond a reasonable doubt that the warnings were in fact given. Also, the trial judge must come to believe that the accused was made unmistakably aware of all four of these specific rights. Then the trial judge must make a specific finding on the record that the warnings were given at the right time and under the right circumstances. Most important, the trial judge must make a specific finding of fact that the accused understood his rights before any waiver could be entered on the record. And last, the defense lawyer can insist on ritualistic compliance with the absolute letter of the warnings.

Waiving *Miranda* Rights

What does *Miranda* say about what happens *after* the four warnings have been timely given and clearly understood? The accused may waive the protection afforded him by the Fifth and Sixth Amendments. He may elect to continue the interrogation, believing, as he might, that his words of innocence will not only be accepted but also that the police will thank him for his time and wave goodbye—an occurrence that probably takes place once or twice a day somewhere in America.

More likely, if a suspect is in custodial interrogation rather than a mere witness interview, detectives already believe they have the right man sitting at the table in front of them. In that case, an interrogation often produces incriminating statements that do not sound like a confession but are detailed enough for the police to put the "waiver" man in a cell.

Reading a signed custodial confession can be like looking into a mountain lake. The surface might be clear while the depths are murky and therefore debatable. At face value, in other words, the suspect's statement might well be a confession, a substantial acknowledgement of guilt. In that case, little or nothing remains to be proved. Also, in its subtext, the statement might seem an admission, needing only corroborating evidence to prove guilt. A deeper plumbing of the suspect's words, however, often produces what lawyers call an "exculpatory statement," that is, an assertion intending to prove innocence but which, in the context of *Miranda,* might be offered as some evidence of guilt. Consequently, prosecutors often think the statement a clear admission of guilt, while defense lawyers squint and shake their heads, seeing otherwise.

As far back as 1938, the Supreme Court had demanded a high standard of proof by the prosecution for the waiver of constitutional rights.[43] "If the interrogation continues without the presence of an attorney and a statement is taken, a heavy burden rests on the Government to demonstrate that the defendant knowingly and intelligently waived his privilege against self-incrimination and his right to retain or be appointed counsel."[44]

Why place such a heavy burden on the state? *Miranda* answers this way: "Since the State is responsible for establishing the isolated circumstances under which the interrogation takes place and has the only means of making available corroborated evidence of warnings given during incommunicado interrogation; the burden is rightly on its shoulders."[45]

Hence, *Miranda* excludes confessions on the basis that "police action" results in a violation of constitutional rights. The rule is simple: no police action, no violation. Lengthy or incommunicado incarceration before a statement is given is strong evidence that a waiver is invalid. Making a statement under such circumstances is consistent with the conclusion that the compelling influence of the interrogation finally forced the confession. Moreover, evidence tending to show that the accused was threatened, tricked, or cajoled into a waiver will show that a waiver was not voluntary.[46] A suspect can confess to an airline stewardess,[47] a TV camera,[48] a spouse,[49] a fellow inmate,[50] or a newspaper reporter[51] *without* any warning of any kind, and the confession can be admitted in evidence. However, such "unwarned confessions" often raise the issue of primary taint, a question of what, specifically, is admissible and what is not. The doctrine of primary taint rests on the concept lawyers and lawmakers often refer to as "the fruit of the poisonous tree."

The legendary Supreme Court justice Felix Frankfurter was probably the first to use the phrase—long before it rose to the level of a legal cliché. Importantly, Justice Frankfurter employed it in talking about a confession, noting that a confession may be either the "fruit" or the "poisonous tree."[52]

A "fruitful" confession is excluded from evidence because it derives from prior, unconstitutional police conduct—not because of any primary taint in the confession itself. Thus, as a technical matter, *Miranda* is not the case of choice to suppress this kind of confession.

Sometimes, however, the confession is actually the poisonous tree itself. In that case, it is suppressed because the methods used in obtaining the confession were unconstitutional. That, as a technical matter, is where

Miranda is used to support the suppression motion. Some unconstitutional confessions lead to derivative evidence. For example, a suspect might give an unwarned statement revealing the type and model of the gun used in a crime. The confession would be suppressed because the proper *Miranda* warnings had not been given, and the gun would be suppressed because it is derivative (the fruit) of the tainted confession (the tree).

The *Miranda* doctrine, in barring the use of all unwarned confessions, makes those confessions poisonous trees, which in turn taint any derivative fruit, such as guns, tapes, drugs, or dirty socks, that might be mentioned in the confession.

Miranda's Retrials

Ernesto Miranda's victory in the United States Supreme Court entitled him to a new trial in Arizona on his rape conviction involving Patricia Doe. However, since his robbery conviction involving Barbara Doe had not been appealed to the Supreme Court, he was not automatically entitled to a retrial on that case. Nevertheless, John Flynn obtained a new trial on the robbery case, and as a result, Miranda was retried for rape in 1967[53] and for robbery in 1971[54]. Because his robbery case had not been reversed by the United States Supreme Court, Miranda remained in the Arizona State Prison pending retrials in both cases. His retrial on the robbery charge was conducted before Judge William Gooding of the Maricopa County Superior Court in September 1971. Robert Storrs[55] prosecuted the case. John Flynn and Tom Thinnes[56] represented Miranda. Because Miranda had by then become a national figure, Judge Gooding did not think he could get a fair trial in Phoenix if he were tried under his real name.

Accordingly, the jury was told that the defendant's name was "Jose Gomez." As Gomez, he projected a demeanor that at least one jury member described as a "bland personality who never smiled, moved, or drew attention to himself in any way." Apparently, throughout the retrial he did precisely as he was told by either the judge or his lawyers, showing no emotion as the victim of the crime testified, as she had in the original 1965 trial, identifying Miranda as her attacker on the night of February 27, 1962. She also gave essentially the same account of the details of the robbery. This time, however, Miranda's oral confession to Detective Carroll Cooley was *not* offered in evidence, and Judge Gooding also excluded any reference to the interrogation room confrontation between Miranda and Barbara Doe, contending that this evidence was so unnecessarily suggestive that to admit it would be to deny Miranda due process of law. For the same reason, he excluded evidence of Cooley's morning lineup in the police station.

Consequently, the new jury, in 1971, heard no confession, nothing of the lineup, nothing about the interrogation room identification, and no testimony from either Cooley or Miranda. The *only* evidence of the crime came from the victim, in open court. Nevertheless, in short order, the jury convicted Miranda of robbery once again.

Miranda's appeal to the Arizona Supreme Court was handled by the public defender's office. The appeal was based on a single claim, an assertion that Judge Gooding had erred in ruling that the in-court identification was based on the victim's contact with Miranda on February 27, 1962, rather than on her contact with him in jail on March 13, 1963. The Arizona Supreme Court devoted a scant two pages to the facts and unanimously affirmed the conviction.[57]

The legal history of Miranda's rape case is more complicated; he had been convicted in the first trial of raping Patricia on June 20, 1963, but that conviction was reversed by the United States Supreme Court on June 16, 1966. Accordingly, he was retried in Maricopa County Superior Court in February 1967. Arizona's attorney general at the time, Robert "Bob" Corbin, personally conducted the prosecution, while an out-of-county judge, the Hon. Lawrence Wren, was brought in to conduct the trial. John Flynn personally conducted the defense.

Technically, the retrial was a model of compliance with the Supreme Court's remand. No mention was made of Miranda's custodial confession, and Miranda did not testify. Patricia Doe recounted the same facts as in the first trial; however, because of the Supreme Court rulings, she was not permitted to offer identifying evidence against Miranda, her identification being the product of the inadmissible confession. Since no one identified him, he did not testify, and his confession was suppressed, it appeared that Miranda would win this time around. Certainly Judge Wren thought he would go "bone free."[58] Prosecutor Bob Corbin also sensed that the state would lose but insisted on "going down fighting," perhaps because there was one enormous difference this time: Twila Hoffman, the woman Miranda had been living with when the police arrested him on March 13, 1963.

Miranda had met Twila Hoffman in California shortly after his release from Lompoc Prison, in 1961. A year later, Hoffman, twenty-nine at the time and the mother of two children, returned with Miranda to his home in Mesa, Arizona. Although she was still living with Miranda when he was taken into custody, and very likely could have provided incriminating evidence at that time, she did not testify at Miranda's original trial before Judge McFate.

Her reason for doing so during the retrial is fairly evident. Miranda, no doubt anticipating an acquittal in the retrial, had complained to welfare authorities about his common-law wife shortly before the retrial began. Hoffman, obviously angered by this, had taken her "story" to Corbin just before the retrial started in late February 1967. What Hoffman told the prosecutor prompted Corbin to contact the recently promoted Lt. Carroll Cooley and ask him to interview the woman. Hoffman repeated her story to Cooley. When she had visited Miranda in jail on March 16, 1963, three days *after* his arrest on the original rape charge, they had talked about the written confession he had given to Detective Cooley. Miranda had repeated it to her, Hoffman said, and admitted to robbing and raping Patricia Doe. Hoffman also claimed that Miranda had asked her to visit his accuser and give her his promise to marry her—if she dropped the charges against him.

In the courtroom, Corbin surprised Flynn with Hoffman's testimony about *another* confession by Miranda—one that the Supreme Court had *not* reversed and that Cooley had *not* extracted. As his first response, Flynn argued that the common-law marriage precluded Hoffman's testimony. When Judge Wren disagreed, holding that the marital privilege was applicable only to statutory marriages, Flynn then argued that her testimony was the fruit of the poisonous tree, but again Judge Wren disagreed and allowed Hoffman to testify. The jury took just over an hour to reach a unanimous jury verdict of guilty. Miranda's retrial resulted in a reconviction, which netted him a resentence of twenty to thirty years on each of the two original counts.

As expected, Flynn engaged John Frank to write the appeal brief to the Arizona Supreme Court. In his brief, filed in October 1967, Frank reminded the state court of an ironic twist of timing. "The claimed confession to Twila was made three days after the original and now clearly declared illegal confession, with no intervening change of circumstance," Frank noted. "[Miranda] was still under arrest, still in prison, still had no counsel, and still had no knowledge of his rights. Every element of which had been involved in the original confession also inhered in its successor. Under the *Miranda* decision, the second confession was no more valid than the first."[59]

In essence, Frank argued, had it not been for the illegally obtained confession by the police, Miranda would not have "confessed his guilt to this woman."[60] The reasoning seemed plain and irrefutable; nevertheless, the

Arizona Supreme Court dismissed his argument, saying, "We believe it to be conclusively established here that Mrs. Hoffman was in no way acting for the police when she visited the defendant with whom she was living and to whom she referred as 'husband' on occasion." In affirming the conviction, the court contended that "Certainly, the nature of the illegality which gives rise to the 'fruits' must be considered in determining whether the evidence obtained is 'tainted,' [but] here, the violation was a failure to warn of constitutional rights which did not exist until sometime subsequent to the conduct. Certainly, such a 'taint' should be more easily 'attenuated' than conduct more clearly proscribed by our Constitution." Therefore, the court held "that there was a sufficient 'break in the stream of events' between the confession to the police and the confession to Mrs. Hoffman, to justify the court in admitting this testimony."[61]

Miranda's initial brush with Arizona law enforcement had occurred in March 1963. Over the course of the next four years, he had gone through four jury trials, five appeals, and more than a dozen hearings. He confessed to rape and robbery at least twice, and those confessions sent him to jail for almost nineteen years. One wonders whether he *ever* knew when to keep silent and when to ask for a lawyer.

Miranda's Death

Ernesto Miranda's parole applications were rejected four times. Thus he remained in the Arizona State Penitentiary from March 1963 until December 1972. Finally, on his fifth attempt at parole, six months before the Arizona Supreme Court opinion affirmed his conviction for robbery and three years after his second rape conviction was affirmed, the parole board relented and released him.

For a time he became a minor celebrity of sorts, selling autographed, preprinted *Miranda* warning cards for $1.50 apiece in downtown Phoenix. However, after eighteen months of freedom, during which time he collected several misdemeanor arrests (and several readings of "his" *Miranda* rights), his parole was deemed violated and he returned to prison for an additional five and one-half years. Upon completing the mandatory one-third (ten years) of his original sentence in mid-December of 1975, he was released once more and returned to Phoenix. Scarcely more than a month later, he was stabbed to death in a barroom fight.

The ironic and unresolved circumstances of Ernesto Miranda's death befit the man's shabby life. The facts, as best they can be established, are these: On January 31, a Tuesday, Miranda went to a bar named La Ampola, one of the several run-down taverns in the area of Phoenix known as "The Deuce" because it extended along Second Street. He spent the last afternoon of his life there, at some point joined by two acquaintances, one a part-time field hand named Fernando Rodriguez, who was an occasional resident of the Hayes Hotel, a nearby flophouse; the other, a man known only as Moreno, also worked sometimes as a field hand and apparently spoke little or no English. All three men were Hispanic, and from their dress and appearance, all three were existing near the bottom of the social ladder with little hope of ever rising in the world.

During most of the time they spent together at La Ampola that afternoon they apparently drank beer, played cards, and got along well enough, but toward dusk an argument arose over some perceived unfairness. Punches were thrown and bottles were knocked over. Miranda left the table and went to the men's room. When he returned, Rodriguez was gone, and Moreno had a knife. A scuffle ensued, during which Miranda was stabbed in the chest and neck and collapsed, dying within a few minutes.

As might be expected, the several people questioned by the police soon afterward gave differing accounts. Fernando Rodriguez, apprehended and brought in later that night, admitted to being with Moreno at La Ampola but denied having anything to do with the murder. He had started drinking at the Tivoli Bar at around eleven, he told Police Detective Ron Quaife, then moved on to the Nogales Bar, accompanied by a woman he said was his girlfriend. There they had met up with Moreno, whom he did not know by name but only from having seen him in the area and in the fields.

Soon after, he said, a friend of his girlfriend arrived, and the four of them went to La Ampola. There, they began playing cards with the victim. An argument broke out when Rodriguez passed on a hand and "threw his cards in on a 2-dollar bet."[62] Rodriguez said that he didn't know why, but at this point the victim, whom he said he knew only as "Ernie," began to throw punches at him. Rodriguez claimed that he did not try to fight back but only put up his hands and arms to protect himself. The police record shows that Rodriguez did, indeed, bear on his forehead and cheeks marks consistent with this claim.

Rodriguez went on to explain that, after Miranda quit attacking him, he and his girlfriend left La Ampola and went back to the Nogales Bar, which was where the arresting officer had found him. When Detective Quaife asked if the other man involved had been staying with Rodriguez at the Hayes Hotel, Rodriguez vehemently denied it. In answer to questions about why he had left La Ampola, he said that he had gotten blood on his shirt and wanted to change it, and also that he had not wanted to get involved in "whatever happened."

Quaife interviewed Rodriguez's girlfriend next, a woman identified only as "Cruz." Cruz confirmed that Fernando "had gotten into the argument with Ernie," but she claimed that the victim had started the fight and that Rodriguez did not fight back. She confirmed Rodriguez's assertion that the first fight was over with when they left the bar. When she and Rodriguez saw Phoenix Fire Department trucks roar up to the entrance of La Ampola, she told Rodriguez, "We're not going to hide, 'cause we got nothing to hide about." She also corroborated Rodriguez's statement about changing his bloodstained shirt.

About an hour after Rodriguez's interview ended[63] Moreno was apprehended at the Hayes. When he arrived at Interrogation Room Number Two, Detective Quaife immediately noticed a "partially scabbed-over" injury to the bridge of Moreno's nose. A cut on the third finger of his right hand appeared to be several days old.[64]

Speaking in Spanish, Moreno, as had Rodriguez before him, waived his rights, saying that he did understand his rights and would answer questions, that he had no need for an attorney, as he had done nothing wrong."[65] He had been living in the cot room at the Salt River Hotel, he claimed. He admitted that he spent part of the previous day at the Nogales Bar but denied going to any other bar in The Deuce area that afternoon. Instead, he had been drinking in his room and did not wish to drink in any of the downtown bars. In answer to questions about his injuries, he explained that he had injured his nose a few days earlier on the work bus and hurt his finger while working in the fields. He looked at a photo of Rodriguez and said he did not know him.

After Moreno was photographed and fingerprinted, he was escorted back to his hotel.[66] Detective Quaife then submitted his reports to Maricopa Deputy County Attorney James Rizer, requesting that Fernando Rodriguez be charged with Ernesto Miranda's murder. However, Rizer noted several discrepancies in the various officers' reports and "declined to issue a complaint"[67] at that time.

In response, Quaife reinterviewed one of La Ampola's employees, a barmaid identified as "Mary Ann."[68] In this interview, Mary Ann told Quaife that Miranda had arrived at La Ampola Bar about 3:00 P.M. on January 31, 1976. She confirmed the other details of her earlier statement. Rodriguez had taken a knife from the old man who was drunk at the end of the bar.

The men had argued over three dollars. This time, however, Mary Ann said that Rodriguez had taken three dollars of Moreno's money and had thrown it at "Ernie," saying, "There's your money."

Mary Ann also recalled Ernie saying something to the effect of, "No, it won't be done that way," and that the three of them—Ernie, Rodriguez, and Moreno—then "got into it." She repeated her earlier story that Ernie proceeded to fight both Rodriguez and Moreno, knocking Moreno to the floor. After Ernie had struck Rodriguez several times, the fight stopped. Because he had blood on his hand, she said, Ernie then went into the men's room to wash it off. While he was gone, Moreno said, in Spanish, to Rodriguez, "Pass me the knife." Whereupon Rodriguez took the knife out of his pocket and handed it to Moreno, saying, "Here, you can finish it." Then he and Cruz left the bar.

When Ernie came out of the men's room, Mary Ann then told Quaife, Moreno waved the knife at him in a "threatening manner." And when Ernie grabbed him and attempted to wrestle the knife away, Moreno stabbed him in the chest.

Quaife then reinterviewed another La Ampola witness, a patron known as "Indio," who confirmed Many Ann's version of the events, then added a few accusations of his own.[69] Indio said Moreno had begun to taunt Ernie with dirty names as he came out of the men's room. And Moreno had stabbed Ernie twice, once in the lower abdomen and once in the upper chest. Indio also corrected his first interview to say that the fight between Moreno and Ernie took place near the men's room and not on the west side of the bar as he had previously said.

Quaife's partner, Detective C. Lash, also reported new information, collected from his downtown sources. For instance, after being released in the early morning hours of February 1, 1976, Moreno had bragged to other field laborers staying at the Hayes Hotel, telling them that the police had had him in custody but "let him go." Moreno's roommate, a man named Torrez, told Officer Bueno that Moreno had admitted to being in a knife fight in the La Ampola Bar and then boasted that the cops still "let him go."

The next day Mary Ann was interviewed again, this time by Detective Lash. He showed her the photographs taken of Moreno when he had been in custody. Lash's report indicates that she cried out in a "loud excitable voice, 'That's him! Oh yeah, that's him.'"[70]

Quaife immediately ordered Moreno picked up for homicide, and he was "blue booked and broadcast and the Border Patrol and Immigration was [sic] notified."[71] Follow-up contacts with the Border Patrol established that it had had two prior contacts with Moreno, one in 1971 and the other in 1974. On both occasions, Moreno had used the name "Perez," which Quaife learned was Moreno's mother's name. Knowing that Mexicans normally use the mother's name as a middle name, Quaife realized that the name on the hotel records, Perez, was the same man, Moreno, who had been in custody a few hours after Miranda's murder.

Quaife's final report notes, somewhat apologetically, that while Miranda was the aggressor on the first altercation over three dollars in the card game, he was later assaulted and killed by Moreno, also known as Perez. Consequently, Quaife, in an effort to close his file, asked Maricopa County to issue murder complaints.[72]

The Maricopa County attorney's office issued formal homicide complaints against both "Fernando Rodriguez and Eseziquel Moreno" on February 3, 1976.[73] The police file confirms that arrest warrant Number 9320(E-1) was duly issued, but "neither man could be found."

The investigation of Miranda's murder had obviously been conducted in full compliance with *Miranda* warnings. Both suspects had voluntarily waived their rights and told police their stories without benefit of counsel's presence. However, unlike the 1963 police investigation of Miranda himself, no confessions were extracted and no one went to jail for the crime. Fernando Rodriguez and Eseziquel Moreno, released pending further investigation, both disappeared and were never seen again.[74]

Chapter 5

THE ONGOING DEBATE

The most frequent criticism of *Miranda,* in the years after it was handed down, has been that the ruling makes law enforcement more difficult because the primary advantage of the "old world of criminal procedure" has been lost: Police can no longer interrogate a suspect quickly, before the suspect has a chance to concoct an alibi or reflect at length on the legal consequences of truthful confession. Some even go so far as to say this has had "a devastating effect on enforcement of criminal law, for it would effectively preclude police questioning—fair as well as unfair."[1] Perhaps the most radical and foolish attack in this vein came from former Attorney General Edwin Meese III[2], who, when asked whether "suspects" should have the right to have a lawyer present before police questioning, replied, "Suspects who are innocent of a crime should. But the thing is you don't have many suspects who are innocent of a crime. That's contradictory. If a person is innocent of a crime, then he is not a suspect."[3]

Such a patently ridiculous assertion of course deserves no serious answer; John Frank's response, that Meese was "a dangerous buffoon in a high place," serves best to dispense with this entire line of irrational overreaction, which has tainted the argument against *Miranda.* The far better argument, one deserving a reasoned response, is that *Miranda* has created the possibility that even confessions given freely, prior to any police questioning of any kind, might well be inadmissible in a courtroom, and thus dangerous criminals, relieved of their confessions, can and do walk away unprosecuted.

It simply cannot be denied that this has happened, just as it cannot be denied that the job of the arresting officer has been made more difficult, for he is now required to advise the suspect of his rights "without word games, lies, or qualifiers," as Peter Baird wrote in a *Wall Street Journal* counterpoint editorial, published on the twenty-fifth anniversary of the *Miranda* ruling.[4] Baird, who had written portions of the appellate briefs in Miranda's retrials and appeals, further conceded that if the arresting officer failed to warn, and "if the only evidence is the unwarned suspect's confession," then the prosecutor's case would be "stillborn."[5]

However, Baird then put this difficulty in perspective, reminding critics of the obvious: In the twenty-five years since becoming law, *Miranda* has had no effect on police methods of *prearrest* investigation and detection because the Court's decision applied only to suspects *in custody.* There was no legal requirement to read *Miranda* warnings to suspects until they were actually placed under arrest. Also, six years after *Miranda,* in a case that raised the question of what to do with confessions made before the warning could be issued, the Supreme Court contended that if the police failed to warn a suspect of his constitutional rights and the suspect did confess, the unwarned confession could be "cured," that is, presented at trial to contradict a subsequent denial.[6]

In his anniversary editorial, Baird also made one of the most compelling arguments in answer to the charge that *Miranda* hampered law enforcement. First pointing out that the educated and the affluent, as well as the organized criminal, are almost always aware of their constitutional rights, he insisted that "More than anything else, *Miranda v. Arizona* means that information about our constitutional guarantees is no longer rationed on the basis of wealth, experience, or education."

Some of *Miranda*'s earliest, most vocal, and most respected critics, including former Supreme Court Justice Tom Clark and Chief Justice Warren Burger, had by 1989 changed their views regarding *Miranda*'s effect on law enforcement, no doubt giving way to the statistical evidence, which showed that, as of 1988, less than 1 percent of all American criminal cases had been dismissed because of "unwarned" confessions.[7] And only a fraction of that 1 percent was dismissed for noncompliance with *Miranda.* In fact, most law teachers, academic lawyers, professional prosecutors, and managerial level police officers see increased professionalism rather than decreased prosecutions as a consequence of the *Miranda* doctrine.[8]

Nevertheless, opposition has remained strong. Chief among the critics of late has been Professor Paul G. Cassell, who was appointed to the United States District Court for the district of Utah in the summer of 2002. In his confirmation hearing in the U.S. Senate, although he vowed to uphold *Miranda,* saying, "It is the law of the land and that's the law I will follow," clearly he meant to imply that, could he do otherwise, he would.[9] In his 1996 law review article chronicling "Miranda's Social Costs," he argued that the ruling would "return a killer, a rapist, or other criminal to the streets and to the environment which produced him, to repeat his crime whenever it pleases him."[10] This reasoning, however, by the very nature of its logic was hardly worth refuting; Prof. Cassell, in this instance anyway, simply stated the obvious in order to conclude that exceptional abuses should be cause enough to overturn *Miranda.*

Cassell, has, however, in continuing to actively oppose *Miranda,* made one point worth debating: The *Miranda* decision has blocked the search for superior approaches to custodial interrogation.[11] Professor Welsh White, in his recent, definitive book, *Miranda's Waning Protections: Police Interrogation Practices after Dickerson,*[12] mentions many of those blocked approaches and perhaps rightly contends that during the post-Miranda era the Court has not struck an appropriate balance between protecting the interests of law enforcement and safeguarding the constitutional rights of criminal suspects. However, White goes on to note that "Contrary to Cassell and other conservative scholars who have criticized Miranda, my position is not that Miranda has unnecessarily impaired law enforcement's ability to obtain confessions. Rather, I believe that during the post-Miranda era, the Court has provided suspects with insufficient protection against pernicious interrogation practices."[13]

This intriguing contention has not been overlooked by those engaged in the debate, but over the last decade, the majority of *Miranda* combatants, more interested in the basic issues of rightness or wrongness, has concerned itself with the question of *Miranda's* constitutional validity. Leading the opposition on this issue is Professor Joseph D. Grano, one of America's foremost legal scholars. In 1993, in his largest work on the subject, *Confessions, Truth, and the Law,* Grano argued that, among other harms, *Miranda* exacerbated the abuses of plea bargaining (the system by which defendants can plead guilty to lesser charges and thus go unpunished for other, greater crimes they truly did commit). Therefore, *Miranda* was constitutionally in error because it undermined what Grano believes to be the justice system's fundamental role. The Warren Court "seemed to forget," he wrote, "that the search for truth is the primary goal of American criminal procedure." In Grano's opinion, an overruling of *Miranda* would, "restore the Fifth Amendment's correct meaning, help to reinstate the discovery of truth as the primary goal of the criminal justice system, and reestablish police interrogation as a legitimate and important means of ascertaining truth."

Grano's wish to return to the pre-Warren Court system of criminal procedure drew support from former Supreme Court Justice John Marshall Harlan, who had written in his dissent to the majority opinion in *Miranda,*

"Society has always paid a stiff price for law and order, and peaceful interrogation is not one of the dark moments of the law."[14] That view is not shared by many others, however, including Yale Kamisar, the Clarence Darrow Distinguished University Professor of Law at the University of Michigan. Stating that he, unlike Grano, did not look back fondly on the "Old World of criminal procedure," Kamisar drew a distinction between the right to remain silent and the right to confidential communication with an attorney. "If truth may be obstructed in the name of an attorney-client or marital relationship," he went on to conclude, "what is so odd about doing so in the name of constitutional guarantees?" To answer this question, he poses a hypothetical: Assume that five suspects are brought to a police station for questioning. Each is held incommunicado and subjected to intensive questioning. Two confess, but only one confession "checks out." In answer to the question of how to handle these suspects, Kamisar then suggests that the court should admit the verifiable confession and remand the defendant—along with those who were mistreated but never confessed—and the one who did confess but was released when his confession did not check out. The "remand" should be to the remedies of private action, says Kamisar. That would result in such protection as the internal discipline of the police, under the eyes of an alert public opinion, may afford. And finally, in the conclusion to his essay, Kamisar asks the pivotal question: If *Miranda* is not adversely affecting law enforcement, if the police have learned to live with it, if the opinion has not been given an expansive reading, and if the Court now views the decision as a serious effort to strike a proper balance between the need for police questioning and the importance of protecting a suspect against impermissible compulsion, then why overrule it?[15]

Today, *Miranda* appears to have more proponents than detractors; nevertheless, the complexity of criminal procedure, constitutional compliance, and the law enforcement community's inherent resistance to change all keep the debate going. Perplexing questions remain about whether the Fifth Amendment belongs in the station house or only in the courtroom. There are questions about how to encourage police to refrain from trickery. And there are cultural and demographic questions about the relationships between authoritarian police agencies and disadvantaged, often minority, suspects. In the final analysis, "[The debate] involves transcendent questions of American values as we approach the twenty-first century," noted Professors Richard Leo and George Thomas in their 1998 book, *The Miranda Debate: Law, Justice, and Policing*. Perhaps these two authors also drive to the heart of the matter when they observe that the debate often comes down to those who see nothing wrong with persuading *guilty* suspects to confess as opposed to those who see an enormous distinction between the guilty suspects who are uneducated, uninformed, and poor, and those who have both education and financial resources.[16]

To be sure, *Miranda* can claim the high ground as a symbol of government's appreciation of the dignity of the individual, "[E]ven where police have probable cause to believe that he has committed a serious crime."[17] John Frank probably said it best, in a speech he made in 1985 when he returned to his hometown of Madison, Wisconsin, to accept an honorary Ph.D. (one of many such honors) from Lawrence University. "We speak today about two provisions of [the] Bill of Rights," he told his audience. "The Sixth Amendment provides, among other things, that '[i]n all criminal prosecutions the accused shall enjoy the right . . . to have the assistance of counsel for his defense.' The Fifth Amendment provides that 'No person . . . shall be compelled in any criminal case to be a witness against himself.'" He spoke then of how forced or coerced confessions were commonplace in rural America and usually the product of unprofessional police conduct, which by definition, was often difficult to prove,[18] and even when such could be proved, it took a lawyer to prove it. "I believe," he concluded, "that the right to counsel and the freedom not to be a witness against oneself are a shield by which our Constitution protects persons in our society from suffering the broken bodies, not merely of distant centuries but of today, broken bodies of persons whom some government seeks to compel to testify against themselves. The minimal safeguard against such abuses, a safeguard that has been demonstrably necessary in our own country, is to declare that no confession may be used unless it is clear that it was made by a person who knew his constitutional rights and chose to waive them."

PART TWO
Miranda in the Twenty-First Century

Chapter 6

THE DICKERSON CASE

Miranda Revisited

Two witnesses saw a man, later identified as James "Jimmy" Rochester, leave the First Virginia Bank in Alexandria, Virginia, in a hurry on the morning of January 24, 1997. One of the witnesses, Stephen DeWitt, always paid attention to such things because he was a probation officer for the Alexandria Juvenile Court. This day, because the bank had recently been robbed of $876, he took special note. When the man got into a white Oldsmobile Ciera parked at the curb, DeWitt jotted down the car's District of Columbia license plate, D5286. He gave the number to the FBI, who identified the car as being registered to Charles Thomas Dickerson of Takoma Park, Maryland.

The FBI and the Alexandria police arrived at Dickerson's apartment three days later, on January 27, at about 5:30 in the evening. They saw a white Oldsmobile Ciera with D.C. plate number D5286 parked on the street in front of the apartment. They waited for just over an hour. Around 6:30 P.M., ten FBI agents and several local police officers knocked on Dickerson's door, guns drawn. Three FBI agents, including Special Agent Christopher Lawlor, entered the apartment without a warrant and without Dickerson's consent. Agent Lawlor told Dickerson that they were investigating a bank robbery.

The agents asked Dickerson to accompany them to the FBI field office in Washington, D.C. Dickerson later testified that he did not feel he had a choice about whether to accompany the agents to the field office.[1] He asked the agents if he could get his coat from his bedroom. While he was doing so, Agent Lawlor noticed a large amount of cash on the bed. Dickerson put the money in his pocket and told Lawlor that he had won it gambling in Atlantic City. As they were leaving the apartment, Lawlor asked Dickerson for permission to search the apartment. Dickerson refused.

Upon reaching the FBI field office, Agent Lawlor and Detective Thomas Durkin, of the Alexandria Police Department, interviewed Dickerson. They did not advise him of his *Miranda* rights prior to the interrogation. Dickerson admitted to driving his Oldsmobile Ciera in the general vicinity of the bank on the morning of January 24 but denied any knowledge of a bank robbery.

Agent Lawlor left the interview room to call United States Magistrate James E. Kenkel in Maryland to obtain a search warrant for Dickerson's apartment. He told the magistrate what he had learned from Dickerson. Kenkel issued the search warrant at 8:50 P.M. Lawlor then returned to the interrogation room and told Dickerson that his apartment was being searched. Dickerson decided to make a supplemental statement concerning his involvement with Jimmy Rochester. He had gone to Alexandria on January 24, 1997, with a man named Jimmy, he said. He knew Jimmy because Jimmy was married to his cousin. The rest of Dickerson's statement reads as follows:

> While in Alexandria, I parked my car and went into a bagel shop. Initially, Jimmy waited in the car, but as I walked away, Jimmy got out of the car. When I returned to the car, Jimmy was already back in it. When I began to drive away, Jimmy told me to pull over. I complied, thinking Jimmy had to use the bathroom. Jimmy got out and returned after a few minutes. When I stopped at a stop sign, Jimmy got out of the car and put something in the trunk. When I stopped again at a red light a short distance down the street, Jimmy told me to run it. It was at this point that I suspected that Jimmy might have committed a robbery. I knew that Jimmy had come to the Washington, D.C. area after committing a number of robberies in Georgia.[2]

After receiving this written statement, Agent Lawlor advised Dickerson of his *Miranda* rights. Dickerson signed a standard FBI rights waiver form. He was then placed under formal arrest.

The published opinion of the United States Court of Appeals for the Fourth Circuit notes as a "factual" matter that Dickerson had confessed to "robbing a series of banks in Maryland and Virginia." This differs from Dickerson's actual statement. The confusion may stem from the information Agent Lawlor got from the other defendant, Rochester.[3]

The court record also indicates Dickerson told Lawlor that Rochester gave him a silver handgun and some dye-stained money that Rochester feared the police might find in his apartment.

The agents searching Dickerson's apartment found a silver .45-caliber handgun, dye-stained money, and a bait bill from another robbery, as well as ammunition, masks, and latex gloves. They also found a small quantity of illegal drugs. A subsequent search of Dickerson's Oldsmobile Ciera produced a black leather bag and solvent used to clean dye-stained money.[4] Dickerson's landlord told the FBI that Dickerson had been three months behind in his rent until January 27, when he paid in full by handing the landlord $1,350 in cash.

The FBI agents took Dickerson to Rochester's apartment in Oxon Hill, Maryland, where they arrested Rochester for bank robbery. Rochester eventually admitted to robbing eleven banks in Georgia, three banks in Virginia, four banks in Maryland, and an armored car in Maryland. He identified Dickerson as his getaway driver in each of the Maryland and Virginia bank robberies.[5]

After Dickerson was charged with one count of conspiracy to rob a bank and three counts of using a gun during a bank robbery, Dickerson's lawyers filed a motion to suppress the confession he had made shortly after his arrest. Agent Lawlor testified in federal district court that when he informed Dickerson about the search warrant, Dickerson said he wanted to add to his statement. The agent's testimony concerning the time of the search did not correspond to the time logged on the warrant, issued at 8:50 P.M., and the waiver form, signed at 9:41 P.M.

On July 1, 1997, the district court issued an Order and Memorandum Opinion suppressing Dickerson's statements because he had not been advised of his *Miranda* rights until after he had completed his statement.

The brief filed by Dickerson's lawyers quotes the trial judge as finding that Agent Lawlor's testimony at the suppression hearing was impeached by the government's own documents and that his demeanor lacked credibility. Lawlor had apparently "dodged questions" about whether the officers had their guns drawn while at Dickerson's apartment. He also asserted that Dickerson had not been under arrest when they took him from Maryland to the D.C. field office, thus rendering *Miranda* warnings unnecessary. The district judge noted that he had made a "first-hand assessment of witness credibility, based on demeanor, voice inflection and a totality of other factors not well reflected by an inanimate record," for which the district court is uniquely suited. The brief also indicates that Agent Lawlor's testimony was contradicted by Agent Durkin.[6]

Federal prosecutors did *not* argue that Dickerson's statement was admissible under 18 USCA §3501. The federal statute (for ease of reference called "Section 3501") was a political response to the 1966 *Miranda* decision. It had been passed by the U.S. Congress "with the clear intent of restoring voluntariness as a test for admitting confessions in federal court. Although duly enacted by the United States Congress and signed into law by the President of the United States, the United States Department of Justice has steadfastly refused to enforce the provision."[7] Dickerson's defense lawyers at the trial court level did *not* brief or argue 18 USCA §3501 either.

Dickerson was not tried on charges related to robbing the First Virginia Bank. His trial was halted while both sides briefed an appeal to the Fourth Circuit Court of Appeals. Pending appeal, which was limited to the admissibility of Dickerson's statement, he was released on "home arrest."

The fourth circuit reversed the district court based solely on its interpretation and application of Section 3501, notwithstanding the fact that neither side had raised the issue at either the trial or the appellate level. In their brief filed with the U.S. Supreme Court, Dickerson's lawyers said:

> In explaining this unusual exercise of discretion, the court of appeals observed that in recent years "career prosecutors" (but not the Department of Justice), political groups and politicians had repeatedly urged the court of appeals to address §3501. . . . The Washington Legal Foundation and the Safe Streets Coalition . . . took the government to task. . . . As a result, we ordered the Department of Justice to address the effect of §3501. . . . In the instant case, because the DOJ [Department of Justice] had expressed its view that §3501 was unconstitutional, and in order to ensure "the proper administration of the criminal law." The Fourth Circuit determined that it would accede to the urgings of *amici*.[8]

The pivotal section of Section 3501 says, "A confession . . . shall be admissible in evidence if it is *voluntarily* given." No one disputes that Congress enacted Section 3501 as part of the Omnibus Crime Control Act of 1968, with the express purpose of legislatively overruling *Miranda* and restoring voluntariness as the test for admitting confessions in federal courts.

The law was on the books for thirty-two years and six executive branch administrations, during which time the Supreme Court never once considered whether Section 3501 overruled *Miranda*.[9] No one ever pressed the question of whether *Miranda* or Section 3501 governed the admissibility of confessions in federal court. In fact, Justice Antonin Scalia, in 1994, noted that Section 3501 "has been studiously avoided by every Administration . . . since its inception 25 years ago."[10]

Every prosecutor and every court simply ignored Congress's political attempt to overrule a constitutional decision of the United States Supreme Court until Attorney General Janet Reno wrote a letter to Congress in

1997, asserting that Section 3501 was "unconstitutional."[11] Justice Scalia, on the other hand, expressed his concern with the Department of Justice's failure to enforce Section 3501. "In addition to causing the federal judiciary to confront a host of '*Miranda*' issues that might be entirely irrelevant under federal law," he wrote, "the Department of Justice's failure to invoke the provision may have produced—during an era of intense national concern about the problem of run-away crime—the acquittal and the nonprosecution of many dangerous felons."[12]

The connection between law and politics is clear in the Fourth Circuit's eighty-page opinion. After citing Justice Scalia's concern regarding the acquittal and nonprosecution of dangerous felons, the divided Fourth Circuit panel called *Dickerson* "just such a case" and asserted that "Dickerson voluntarily confessed to participating in a series of armed bank robberies. Without his confession it is possible, if not probable, that he will be acquitted."[13]

Setting aside both politics and law for the moment, one might note that Charles Dickerson did *not* confess to either one *or* a series of armed bank robberies. There can also be little argument that without his self-incriminating statements prosecutors would have extreme difficulty convicting him. This outcome seems likely for at least three reasons. First, Dickerson would probably not testify at trial. Second, the prosecution would likely be precluded from offering the incriminating statements because they were unwarned and in violation of *Miranda* standards. Third, the evidence obtained when police searched Dickerson's apartment was suppressed by the federal trial judge.[14]

The constitutional question of whether Section 3501 or *Miranda* controlled the admissibility of confessions in federal courts was raised *sua sponte* ("on the court's own volition") by the Fourth Circuit. The mere fact that this question was raised sua sponte is salient. Neither side had raised any constitutional issue at all, not to mention the question of why a federal statute was never used by state or federal prosecutors.

To make the matter even more unusual, not all constitutional questions are decided by the courts. Certain issues, most notably "political questions," are rarely addressed by the judiciary. A definitional as well as cultural problem arises from the underlying judicial thesis known as "justicability."

Over the last century, lawyers, legislators, and judges have engaged in a lively debate about exactly what makes an issue "justiciable." Obviously, adjudication may have significant political consequences. Article 3 of the

Constitution also plays a role in the debate, as does discretion. Courts have often exercised discretion as a device for declining cases they thought would be more appropriately handled by some other government agency.

As is the case in almost every lawsuit, there are at least two competing views. One side sees the line between political and justiciable questions to be thinner than it need be: that courts can abstain from deciding an issue only when the Constitution has committed the determination of the issue to another agency.[15] The opposing view regarding proper exercise of what is justiciable is broader and more passive. As one legal scholar put it, the political-question doctrine "simply resists being domesticated. There is something different about it, in kind, not in degree, from the general interpretive process; something greatly more flexible, something of prudence, not construction, and principle."[16]

Very few ordinary citizens were aware of the historic battle advancing on the United States Supreme Court as it decided to review the Fourth Circuit's essential overruling of *Miranda*. Law professors, however, watching the battle from a safe distance, opined cautiously.

The National Debate about *Dickerson*'s Chances in the United States Supreme Court

Of the many opinions expressed, those of three constitutional scholars in particular will suffice to frame the intellectual debate about *Miranda*'s chances of survival after the blasting it had taken in the Fourth Circuit. John P. Frank told his friend Richard Orton on the eve of the *Dickerson* arguments that he was "optimistic that *Miranda* would survive." [17] He felt that "the overwhelming majority of the American people believe that every citizen is entitled to know of his constitutional rights."

Professor Donald Dripps[18] called *Miranda* a compromise between a free society's need to protect itself from crime and its abiding respect for individual dignity and autonomy. He nevertheless outlined many potential alternatives, any of which might be better compromises than the one struck in *Miranda*.

Professor Jonathan L. H. Blaine[19] lauded the safeguarding of constitutional rights in *Miranda* and was disappointed in the Fourth Circuit's beloved Section 3501 because it contained no safeguards of any kind save those offered by a congressional political view.

The legal complexity of *Miranda* versus Section 3501 is exceeded only by the volume of rhetoric on both sides. At its core, however, the debate revolves around a simple, quiet question: Are the rules set forth by the Court in *Miranda* "required" by the Constitution? If the Constitution mandates the safeguards inherent in the *Miranda* warnings, then Congress acted outside its authority when it passed Section 3501; consequently, Section 3501 is unconstitutional. Conversely, if the *Miranda* warnings are not vested in the Constitution, then Section 3501 overrules *Miranda,* at least in the federal courts.

Frank conceived another question that created a possible ambiguity in *Miranda.* Was the Supreme Court laying down a constitutional standard or a rule of practice? If a constitutional rule, then Congress could not abrogate or limit it because Congress cannot violate the Constitution. The opposing viewpoint regarded the *Miranda* rule as a directive to the federal courts by the Supreme Court in its capacity as the head of the federal judicial system. That, Frank believed, "is a high policy, not a constitutional requirement."

Rules of court can affect all three branches of government, requiring that a delicate balance be struck among them. The executive branch must faithfully execute the laws according to the Constitution. Congress controls the federal courts by enacting legislation and has the power to propose amendments to the Constitution. The judicial branch has the rhetorical power to say exactly what the law is. When a federal circuit court of appeals appears to defy the Supreme Court and to favor Congress, it can be said to disregard the balance of power deeply embedded in our constitutional form of government.

Congress passed Section 3501 with the clearly expressed intent of overruling *Miranda.*[20] That intent was largely ignored for thirty-two years. Prosecutors, defense lawyers, police officers, and grand juries followed the law, as expressed in the *Miranda* decision, rather than apply Section 3501, because it was almost universally thought to be unconstitutional. The only surprise was that no court even tried to apply it from 1968 until 2000, when the Fourth Circuit took it upon itself to raise the issue. Indeed, the very idea of allowing Congress to "overrule" the Supreme Court on a matter of constitutional law would have set a very dangerous precedent.

Professor Blaine was blunt about the issue: "Given the prudential reasons and *stare decisis* considerations arguing against overruling *Miranda,* the Supreme Court should overturn the Fourth Circuit's opinion." Professor Dripps, on the other hand, was abstruse: "My point is not that the existing case law is ideal, only that it is not dysfunctionally incoherent." And Frank was expansive: "*Miranda* has large consequences. It has created a major new industry in the United States, the public defenders. The overwhelming number of persons who are charged with crime who plead guilty with or without *Miranda;* this is into the ninety percentile. It is no legitimate criticism of *Miranda* to assert that some people exercise their constitutional rights, once they know what they are. This is a step toward civilization and is as it ought to be. I have seen no data suggesting that any great number of the wicked go unwhipped of justice because of *Miranda.*"

Also, while Professors Blaine and Dripps did not predict the outcome of *Dickerson* once it reached the Supreme Court, Frank did. "What will be the outcome?" he asked rhetorically. "It is a safe bet that Justices Stevens, Souter, Breyer, and Ginsburg will vote to uphold *Miranda* and to invalidate the statute. Justices Scalia and Thomas, and quite possibly Rehnquist, will go the other way. This leaves the matter, as it is with most of the important cases, to Justice O'Connor and Justice Kennedy. I think we will win!"

In his original *Miranda* brief, Frank had said that we must look to the future by looking at where we have been. He had accurately predicted the original *Miranda* decision, in 1965, and was confident that the case would withstand judicial review when the Court took up *Dickerson* in 2000.

The *Dickerson* Oral Arguments

On Wednesday, April 19, 2000, three lawyers sat in the majestic courtroom of the United States Supreme Court: James W. Hundley of Fairfax, Virginia, was there to argue for Charles Dickerson and to uphold *Miranda* while the solicitor general of the United States, Seth Waxman, would present the case for neutrality on behalf of the United States. Professor Paul Cassell, by special invitation of the Court, would present an amici argument asking the Court to affirm the Fourth Circuit and overrule *Miranda*. Presiding was Chief Justice William H. Rehnquist, who sat in his customary position in the middle. In order of seniority, the other eight members of the Court were John Paul Stevens, Sandra Day O'Connor, Antonin Scalia, Anthony M. Kennedy, David Souter, Clarence Thomas, Ruth Bader Ginsburg, and Stephen G. Breyer.

All present that day knew the central issue before the Court involved 18 United States Code, Section 3501. The widely ignored but suddenly important law had been enacted by a "conservative" Congress to overrule a "liberal" Supreme Court. In part, the statute provided that in any criminal prosecution brought by the United States or the District of Columbia, a confession would be admissible in evidence if it were given voluntarily.

Before such confession was let in, however, the trial judge would, out of the presence of the jury, determine "any issue as to its voluntariness." If the trial judge determined that the confession was voluntary, he would admit it and permit the jury to hear all relevant evidence on the issue of voluntariness and would also instruct the jury to give such weight to the confession as seemed justified by all the circumstances.

It should be noted that the nine justices and the three lawyers, beyond whatever common political or philosophical opinions they held, shared two perspective qualities on this case: First, none had held his or her present position when *Miranda* was decided in 1966. Chief Justice Rehnquist and Justice Sandra Day O'Connor had been practicing lawyers in Phoenix, Arizona, when *Miranda* was decided by the Warren Court; Justice Stevens was in practice in Chicago; Justice Scalia was in practice in Cleveland; Justice Kennedy was a law professor in California; Justice Souter was in practice in Concord, New Hampshire; Justice Clarence Thomas would not begin his law practice for another eight years; Justice Ruth Bader Ginsburg was a law professor in New Jersey; and Justice Stephen Breyer was a law clerk to Justice Goldberg, the author of the *Escobedo* opinion.

Two of the justices (Rehnquist and O'Connor) were from Miranda's home state, Arizona. Two (Kennedy and Breyer) were from California. Thomas was from Georgia, Stevens from Illinois, Souter from New Hampshire, and Ginsburg from New York. Scalia had been born in New Jersey, practiced in Ohio, taught law in Virginia and Illinois, and worked in Washington, D.C., just prior to his appointment to the Court. Rehnquist had been appointed by Nixon; Stevens by Ford; O'Connor, Scalia, and Kennedy by Reagan; Thomas by Bush; and Ginsburg and Breyer by Clinton.

The second perspective quality all shared was simply that each knew full well the historic implications presented by the case at bar. Each was intimately familiar with the *Miranda* doctrine, as each had sat on numerous challenges, modifications, and affirmations of America's right to remain silent.

James W. Hundley began his argument on behalf of the petitioner by citing *Miranda v. Arizona,* reminding the Court that thirty-four years before then it had held that the Fifth Amendment privilege against self-incrimination required police interrogators to "fully inform" a suspect of his rights and provide him a full opportunity to exercise those rights. "The question before the Court today," Hundley then said, "asks whether Congress has the authority to legislatively overrule and reverse this Court's decision in *Miranda.*" He went on to contend that key to answering this question would be determining whether or not the requirements of *Miranda* were "constitutionally based and therefore immune from legislative modification," or were, as the Fourth Circuit had ruled, a "mere exercise of the Court's power to prescribe rules and procedures for courts."[21]

Justice Scalia interrupted Hundley at this point to ask if the requirements in question were "substantive." Was it a violation of the Fifth Amendment *not* to observe them, he wanted to know.

Hundley believed so, even though the specific warnings articulated in *Miranda* were not constitutionally mandated. As he then put it to Justice Scalia, the "constitutional threshold" represented by those warnings was "constitutionally required."[22]

"I presume," Justice Scalia responded, "that if a policeman should beat someone with a rubber hose and extract a confession, and then introduce that confession in a criminal prosecution, that the policeman would be subject to a civil action not only for assault, but also for a violation of the constitutional right, or Fifth Amendment right?"

When Hundley answered in the affirmative, Justice Scalia probed further. "Now do you think that a policeman who fails to Mirandize the suspect, obtains a confession without having Mirandized them, and then introduces that confession in court, is subject to suit?" Justice Scalia, likely thinking about a "1983" action, asked, "Do you know of any suit that has ever been brought?"[23]

"I am unaware of any," Hundley answered, then changed his mind, saying, "I believe the Ninth Circuit is currently wrestling with the issue of whether or not the intentional disregard of an individual's exercise of his rights under *Miranda* could constitute a civil action."

Justice Scalia disagreed, however, that this example constituted such a suit. He would be very surprised if the issue would prove prosecutable civilly, he said, and went on to note that the right in question might be what he termed "a procedural guarantee that the court instituted, rather than a substantive one."

At this point in the argument, Justice Kennedy inserted himself to ask Hundley if not allowing a confession in evidence wasn't, in effect, an "exclusionary rule" in the criminal process. Before Hundley could answer, the justice went on to assert that in his opinion, regardless of whether a confession had been "technically" extracted in violation of the Constitution, as a matter of criminal procedure, a federal court would not admit it, nor would a state court.

Respectfully disagreeing, Hundley said he believed such a confession would not be admitted because it had been obtained without the requisite protections that the Constitution demanded in an effort to ensure it had been given voluntarily. It would be kept out "to dispel the inherent compulsion," he argued.

Justice Kennedy was not yet satisfied, however. It seemed to him that Hundley was saying the warnings specified in *Miranda* were constitutional requirements. "I thought you said something somewhat different at the very outset," he said.

There was a subtle distinction, Hundley explained, "a distraction, I think, which has led to some confusion in the literature. The constitutional requirement of *Miranda* is that there be protective procedures in place to fully inform a suspect of his rights, so that he knows his rights, so that he knows he can exercise those rights, he knows that his interrogators will honor those rights, and so that the Court will know that any waiver of those rights was made knowingly and intentionally, not just voluntarily."

Justice Scalia chose this time to raise his views on Section 3501, wanting to know how the section was deficient under Hundley's analysis.

Hundley responded by saying that 3501 didn't require the affirmative, objective procedures that provided notice and protections to the defendant. Instead, the section simply reverted the analysis back to the totality-of-circumstances test that courts had wrestled with for many decades until *Miranda* explicitly rejected it as unworkable and inconsistent.

Justice Ginsburg took this answer as an opportunity to point out that, as she understood it, the proponents of *Miranda,* in an effort to prevent suspects from getting "the third degree," had switched from the totality-of-circumstances test to something quite different. "And I'm not sure you're explicit about it," she said. "That is, *Miranda,* for the first time put this right under the First—under the Fifth Amendment, and it became a right to notice and [an] opportunity to exercise your rights." By which she meant the opportunity to exercise the right to silence, she added—that that was an interpretation of what the self-incrimination privilege required, wasn't it?

Hundley had to agree, but added, "The *Miranda* Court had specifically shifted the focus of the analysis from the traditional due-process, totality-of-the-circumstances case to a more objective, concrete, clear-cut procedure whereby procedures had to be in place to ensure that the individual knew his rights, knew his interrogators would honor those rights, and to provide a knowing and intelligent waiver of those rights."

Chief Justice Rehnquist now joined in the fray. "Well, Mr. Hundley, you say 'shifted.' You don't mean superseded, I take it, because I think the voluntariness rule of previous cases is still a constitutional requirement. That a confession that is not voluntarily extracted is nonetheless—is a violation of the Constitution?"

It was, Hundley responded, but went on to explain that he thought an exception should be made for confessions obtained following *Miranda*. In those cases, confessions could still be deemed involuntary, if the police used physical coercion or other forms of coercion that "overbore the will of the individual." However, the benefit of the *Miranda* rule, he asserted, was that in most instances it provided the court with clear-cut evidence that a confession had been given voluntarily.

Apparently, the chief justice was not so certain. Noting that there were approximately fifty cases "construing *Miranda,*" he argued that to say the rule would categorically produce clear-cut evidence "is just a myth."

"I would respectfully disagree, Mr. Chief Justice," retorted Hundley, and then asserted that most of the cases the chief justice was referring to had come down when the *Miranda* requirements were new. The number of such cases had since diminished, and certainly the situation had improved when compared to when the courts operated under the old totality-of-circumstances analysis. During that era, the Supreme Court, he noted, was "consistently wrestling with the issue on almost every term."

The totality-of-circumstances analysis was not a criterion of police conduct, however, Justice Scalia now argued.

"It was a criterion by which this Court evaluated the voluntariness of the confession," Hundley responded, "so are you suggesting that *Miranda* is not a substitute rule governing police conduct, but simply a rule that the Court has adopted for all federal courts as to how federal courts will procedurally determine—for purposes of admitting evidence—whether the confession was voluntary?"[24]

"We can certainly do it for statutory causes of action," Justice Scalia said. Then he explained further that, if Title VII[25] cases, that is, employment discrimination cases, could be brought in state court, the Supreme Court could require the state court to use the prima facie, burden-shifting procedures that the Court had applied in federal court for Title VII. "Why can't we do the same thing with the Constitution?" he asked.

In response, Hundley began to explain that, in the justice's example, the Court would be exercising federal statutory jurisdiction, "but in cases such as *Miranda,*" he said, "unless the Court is interpreting and applying the theory put forth by a court-appointed *amicus* that there is some form of constitutional common law, which this Court to my knowledge has never recognized—"

He got no further; Justice Scalia, barely disguising his disdain, said, "It seems to me you're swallowing the camel and straining out the gnat. You're willing to allow—you're willing to acknowledge—this power of the Court to establish substantive procedures for the states, but you're not willing to acknowledge the much lesser power of this Court to say how constitutional questions in state courts will be adjudicated. It seems to me it's a much lesser power."

Hundley would not back down, however. To interpret the Constitution and to determine the protections required under the Constitution were perhaps the greatest powers of the Supreme Court, he argued, and then cited for support *Marbury v. Madison*,[26] an 1803 case in which the Supreme Court had held that an act of Congress will not be enforced by the courts if what it prescribes violates the Constitution of the United States.

Whether or not this point would have been debated further cannot be said, for Hundley's time at the podium had run out, and his place was taken by the advocate for the United States, Solicitor General Seth Waxman. Waxman, a widely respected constitutional scholar and President Clinton's first choice for solicitor general of the United States, was, if not a particularly animated advocate, an imposing figure. He looked entirely the part of the government's chief advocate before the Supreme Court as he was the only man in the room dressed in the traditional formal morning coat.

"Mr. Chief Justice and May it please the Court," began Waxman. "The position of the United States is based on three propositions, and I'd simply like to state them. First, as this Court's repeated application of *Miranda* to the States reveals, its rule is a constitutional one. Second—"

Justice Sandra Day O'Connor was not inclined to let this major point go unchallenged, however. "Well, in our past *Miranda* cases," she said, "I think the government has taken the position that *Miranda* warnings are not constitutionally required."

Retreating, Solicitor General Waxman agreed with this assertion, then said that it didn't matter how many cases were in question, that where the Court led, the government would follow. But as the Court had explained in *Miranda*, he went on, the warnings themselves were not constitutionally required, and this repeatedly invited legislatures, including the national legislature, to enact constitutionally adequate safeguards.

The government's proposition, he declared, was that, in the absence of systemically adequate safeguards, the rule the Court had announced in

Miranda "must be a constitutional rule because the Court had in dozens of cases applied to the State courts."

Justice O'Connor interrupted again to require the solicitor general to defend his legal assertion. "What's the source of that authority for the Court?" she asked. "And how do you equate it with other exercises of such a right? If it isn't a Fifth Amendment right itself, what is it?"

Miranda's requirements were based on its power to interpret and apply the Constitution, Waxman responded. Also, the Court had held in *Garner v. the United States*[27] that the doctrine was necessary, saying it was impelled to adopt the doctrine in order to protect, in the distinctive context of custodial interrogation, the privilege against self-incrimination. "Now, it is, as the Court said, therefore in the nature of a prophylactic rule, that is, a rule that when it is violated—when the warnings themselves aren't given—it is not true that the statement is thereby as a matter of fact inevitably coerced."

Justice O'Connor apologized now for keeping the solicitor general from making his other two points, but she did not yet understand this first one, she said. "You say the warnings are not constitutionally required, [but] the *Miranda* rule is constitutional?"

Patiently, it would seem, Solicitor General Waxman now explained that the Court had held in *Miranda*—and every post-*Miranda* case that had "tailored and explicated" the doctrine consistent with its principle—that, with the exception of a narrow exigency—such as a public safety exception—the government may not use as evidence of guilt at trial any statement made in response to custodial interrogation, not without either a warning or a "waiver of some other systemically adequate safeguard."

This protracted explanation apparently satisfied Justice O'Connor, for she allowed Waxman to proceed to his other two points, the second being that Section 3501 could not be reconciled with *Miranda* (and therefore could be upheld by the Court only if the Court were prepared to overrule *Miranda*); and the third being that he did not believe the showing made by the petitioner was sufficient to overrule *Miranda*.

In support for this last contention, he offered four reasons. One, stability in the law, always important, was nowhere more important than in this case, given the Court's dissatisfaction with the ambiguities of the totality-of-circumstances rules, as opposed to the certainty that *Miranda* provided. Two, *Miranda* had proven workable, its benefits to the administration of justice repeatedly emphasized and documented by the Supreme Court. Three, in all of its post-*Miranda* cases, the Supreme Court had affirmed *Miranda*'s underlying premise, that custodial interrogation created inherently compelling pressures and thus required some safeguards. And four, any re-evaluation of *Miranda* must take account of the Court's "profoundly unhappy experience," which had impelled it to adopt *Miranda* in the first place. In thirty-six cases over thirty years before 1965, the Court had simply been unable to articulate manageable totality-of-circumstances rules for the lower courts to apply.[28]

Although Waxman had not used his entire time, he had no further points to make, and the Court had no further questions. Professor Paul G. Cassell,[29] the third and final lawyer to argue the *Dickerson* case, took the podium. Cassell may have been invited as amicus curiae because he was a frequent critic[30] of the *Miranda* decision and could be counted on to present an articulate review of the Court's perceived 1966 error and the constitutional ramifications of that error. Although not a practicing lawyer, he was certainly no stranger to Supreme Court litigation; he had clerked for then-Judge Antonin Scalia on the U.S. Court of Appeals for the D.C. Circuit and for Chief Justice Warren Burger on the U.S. Supreme Court.

In opening, Cassell turned immediately to the question that Justice Kennedy had posed earlier. "I think it goes to the heart of this case," he said, and then explained at length but, nevertheless, quite succinctly and clearly:

> You have asked both of our colleagues on the other side of the room whether the *Miranda* rights or the *Miranda* procedures are constitutional requirements, and I think the answer they gave was yes, which is what they have to say to win this case. The difficulty with the answer is, it would require this Court to overrule more than a quarter of a century of jurisprudence. To turn, for example, to this Court's holding in *Oregon v. Elstad,* this Court refused to apply the fruit-of-the-poisonous-tree doctrine, and the reason it gave was that a simple failure to administer *Miranda* warnings is not, in itself, a violation of the Fifth Amendment. Justice O'Connor's opinion for the Court went on to say that the *Miranda* rule may be triggered even in the absence of a Fifth Amendment violation, and it's important to understand what the holding in that case was. The holding there was that there was no reason to suppress the fruit of non-*Mirandized* statement that is derivative evidence, and the reason this Court gave was, and again I am quoting, there was no actual infringement of the suspect's constitutional rights.[31]

At this point Justice Ginsburg finally interrupted, first to say that she thought

Cassell could point to other cases, including one that Chief Justice Rehnquist had authored, *Michigan v. Tucker*,[32] which referred to the rule as a prophylactic. "But here we're kind of faced with a conundrum," Cassell said. "If the rule can be applied to state courts, as it was in *Miranda,* how can it be that it doesn't originate in the Constitution?"

Justice Souter now joined Justice Ginsburg in posing difficult questions to Cassell, and in time, Justice Breyer added his concern with a comment and a summary question. The *Miranda* warnings were known to "2 billion people throughout the world," he said, adding that the *Miranda* decision was "a hallmark of American justice in the last thirty years." "Now, given that phrase and those rights set forth with clarity, what is your response to Justice Ginsburg's question, namely that *Miranda* itself says that the phrase that I read, or the equivalent, is demanded by the Constitution?"[33]

Cassell's attempt to answer this and the questions of the other justices only brought Chief Justice Rehnquist into the discussion. Saying he hated "to complicate" the matter further, he posed what he thought might be the key question: "Do you contend that the statute [18 USCA 3501] complies with the requirement of *Miranda,* that it could be a substitute adequate procedure, or do you think the statute overrules *Miranda?*"

Cassell answered that he thought it provided an adequate substitute and that he simply hadn't had an opportunity to lay out a full version of his position—the way it had been expressed in the prosecution's brief. Unfortunately, for him anyway, he soon thereafter ran out of time, and James Hundley again assumed the podium for two minutes of rebuttal. First reminding the justices that in *Miranda,* the Court had set a constitutional minimum, he contended that Congress hadn't attempted to meet that minimum. Rather, the legislators had attempted to roll the clock back and reimpose the totality-of-the-circumstances rule. Section 3501 failed for that reason, he said, and then closed by stating what he had said before, that if a warned statement was found to be involuntary, it would be excluded—that was the strength and clarity of the *Miranda* rule, "it provides guidance for the police, it provides guidance for the courts, and it protects the individual's rights."[34]

At 11:03 A.M. on Wednesday, April 19, 2000, the chief justice promised the crowded courtroom, "The case is submitted."

The *Dickerson* Opinion

Nearly all of the arguments in opposition to *Miranda* were based on the premise that it was *not* constitutionally required. First and foremost of the factors on the side contending that *Miranda* was a constitutional decision was the observation that both *Miranda* and two of its companion cases had applied the rule in state courts, and since 1966, the Court had consistently applied *Miranda*'s rule to prosecutions arising in state courts. The Rehnquist Court acknowledged that there was language in some of its opinions that could support the opposing argument. However, the Court obviously wished to disabuse all who might continue to foster that notion.

Accordingly, the United States Supreme Court resolved the thirty-four-year debate over *Miranda*'s fate, specifying in its core holding that certain warnings must be given before a suspect's statement made during custodial interrogation could be admitted into evidence. The opinion also dealt with the congressional response to *Miranda* in 18 USC §3501. Chief Justice Rehnquist, joined in the opinion by six other justices, with Justices Scalia and Thomas dissenting, delivered the opinion on June 25, 2000, the crucial holding of which is as follows:[35]

> We hold that *Miranda*, being a constitutional decision of this Court, may not be in effect overruled by an Act of Congress, and we decline to overrule *Miranda* ourselves. We therefore hold that *Miranda* and its progeny in this Court govern the admissibility of statements made during custodial interrogation in both state and federal courts.[36]

The *Dickerson* opinion is a history lesson (citing cases from the King's Bench in England in the sixteenth century[37]), a primer on constitutional law (citing constitutional law precedents from 1884[38] through 1936[39]), and a shining example of judicial rhetoric ("custodial interrogation takes a heavy toll on individual liberty and treads on the weakness of individuals"[40]).

With respect to proceedings in state courts, the Supreme Court's authority is limited to enforcing the commands of the United States Constitution. The *Miranda* opinion itself had begun by stating that the Court granted certiorari to explore some facets of the problems of applying the privilege of self-incrimination to in-custody interrogation and to give concrete constitutional guidelines for law enforcement agencies and courts to follow. Indeed, the Court's conclusion in *Dickerson* was that the unwarned confessions obtained in the four cases before the Court in *Miranda* "were obtained from the defendant under circumstances that did not meet constitutional standards for protection of the privilege."[41]

The most compelling aspect of the *Dickerson* decision, irrespective of judicial ideology or the political persuasion of the moment, is that it relies on the same underlying values as *Miranda,* values that so bitterly separated the civil libertarians from the law enforcement community for three decades. "We need not go farther than *Miranda* to decide this case," the *Dickerson* opinion states. And furthermore:

> In *Miranda,* the Court noted that reliance on the traditional totality-of-the-circumstances test raised a risk of overlooking an involuntary custodial confession. [That is] a risk that the Court found unacceptably great when the confession is offered in the case in chief to prove guilt. The Court therefore concluded that something more than the totality test was necessary. Section 3501 reinstates the totality test as sufficient. Section 3501 therefore cannot be sustained if *Miranda* is to remain law.[42]

"In sum," closed the *Dickerson* opinion, "we conclude that *Miranda* announced a constitutional rule that Congress may not supersede legislatively. Following the rule of *stare decisis,* we decline to overrule *Miranda* ourselves."

Stare decisis, loosely translated, means "to stand by things decided." For simplicity's sake, the phrase need be thought of only as the doctrine of precedent under which courts are obliged to abide by former judicial decisions when the same points arise again in litigation. In constitutional litigation, the doctrine takes on special meaning because of issues of federalism, states' rights, and the vagaries among the states in how confessions were obtained from persons suspected of crimes. Thus, the duality of this ruling cannot be emphasized strongly enough. Because Congress cannot overrule the Court in constitutional matters *and* because of stare decisis, the 1966 decision in *Miranda v. Arizona* will forever be law. The right to remain silent is now as permanently embedded in our law as it is in our culture.

However deeply the Supreme Court embedded the right to remain silent in American law and culture with its landmark decision, Charles Dickerson was still "in the system," remanded back to the trial court. In this and other particulars, Ernesto Miranda and Charles Dickerson share a similar legal consequence after traveling the same legal path. Dickerson's lawyers no longer had to worry about his confession because it had been suppressed and could not be used against him at trial, but just as Ernesto Miranda in his retrial after his Supreme Court victory had had to contend with Twila Hoffman, his former live-in girlfriend, so did Dickerson have to worry about his former friend Jimmy Rochester.

Apprehended by the police based solely on Dickerson's now-suppressed confession, Rochester, in the parlance of the streets, "turned" Dickerson; he told the police that Dickerson had been his getaway driver when he robbed the First Virginia Bank in January 1997. He also fingered him in eight other bank robberies.

Dickerson's legal team argued that Rochester's "he did it" statement was tainted because Dickerson's arrest was unlawful. If not for his unlawful arrest, they contended, Dickerson would not have identified Rochester, and but for Rochester's own arrest, he would not have "turned" Dickerson. The trial judge declined to follow this circular reasoning and denied the motion, exactly what Judge Wren had done in Miranda's case in 1967, and the jury, although they did not hear Dickerson's confession, still convicted him, believing the trial testimony of the man Dickerson had identified in the first place: Jimmy Rochester.

On January 5, 2001, Charles Dickerson was sentenced to 125 months in a federal prison by the same court that had originally suppressed his confession. Once again, Dickerson appealed his conviction to the Fourth Circuit Court of Appeals. In its *per curium,* or, unsigned opinion, the court observed: "Dickerson contends that Rochester's testimony should have been excluded as the 'fruit of the poisonous tree' because the officers were led to Rochester through Dickerson's identification of Rochester, which followed Dickerson's unconstitutional arrest."[43]

Unfortunately for Dickerson, he was in the wrong appellate court once again. Just a few years before, in 1997—about the time Dickerson and Rochester robbed the First Virginia Bank—the Fourth Circuit Court held that the "tainted fruits" doctrine does not apply to derivative evidence discovered because of statements taken in "technical" violation of *Miranda.*[44]

Dickerson also tried to get the Fourth Circuit Court of Appeals to order the trial judge to decrease his sentence because he had already served three and one-half years of "pre-trial home arrest" (Dickerson's case had remained in limbo from July 1, 1997, when his confession was suppressed, until January 5, 2001, when he was convicted without the use of his confession). The federal district trial court had discretion but declined to exercise it in favor of Dickerson. The Fourth Circuit appellate court also had discretion but noted that the three-year-and-eight-month period, while lengthy, was not atypical and did not warrant a downward departure in the sentence.

The Supreme Court, having previously exercised its discretion in Dickerson's favor, now declined and denied his petition for a writ of certiorari. Charles Dickerson, like Miranda, Vignera, Stewart, Westover, Johnson, and Cassidy, notwithstanding their historic victories in the Supreme Court, went to jail. Dickerson began his imprisonment in the spring of 2001.

Continuing Legal Challenges to the *Miranda* Doctrine in the Wake of *Dickerson*

There is a certain cadence to constitutional litigation. Earl Gideon's letter to the Supreme Court had begun a drumbeat that was repeated in Danny Escobedo's plaintive cry for his lawyer and echoed by Ernesto Miranda's silent acceptance of custodial interrogation. The next drum roll might come from the vague but ominous beats emanating from the grant of certiorari on March 10, 2003, to John J. Fellers. [45]

Fellers v. United States, U.S. Supreme Court Docket No. 02-6320, October Term, 2003–2004

Reminiscent of Gideon, Fellers had handwritten a letter to the Court, asking to proceed *in forma pauperis* (on his own behalf) as he did not have a lawyer.

Miranda had been first questioned at his home in Mesa, Arizona, in 1963. Dickerson's initial interrogation had occurred at his apartment in Philadelphia in 1998. The first questions put to Fellers were at his home in Lincoln, Nebraska, on February 24, 2000. In all three cases, the police had focused on the suspect and secured incriminating statements, and had not warned the suspect that he had a right to remain silent.

In Fellers' case, two policemen had gone to his home to arrest him for conspiracy to distribute methamphetamine.[46] He allowed the officers into his home and then was told that they were there to arrest "pursuant to an indictment" and that they wanted to discuss his involvement in the case.[47] They did not advise him of his *Miranda* rights. He consequently admitted using methamphetamine and told the two cops that he had associated with the other persons named in the indictment, and thus he effectively incriminated himself in a criminal conspiracy.

Fellers was taken to jail, finally advised of his *Miranda* rights, and asked further questions. He signed a *Miranda* waiver, reiterated his inculpatory statements, and signed a written confession.

Later, however, he moved to suppress both the inculpatory statements made at his home and those made at the jail. The federal magistrate judge suppressed both sets of statements because Fellers had been in custody when he made them but had not been given his *Miranda* rights. The magistrate judge specifically found that the officers had used deceptive stratagems to prompt Fellers' statements, and that the statements at the jail would not have been made but for the prior "ill-gotten" statements at his home.[48]

In the federal system, since the magistrate judge does not have the last word, Fellers went to trial before a district court judge, who agreed that the statements made at Fellers' home should be suppressed, but he admitted the statements made at the jail. The district court judge specifically found that Fellers had "knowingly and voluntarily waived his Miranda rights before making [the stationhouse] statements."[49]

Fellers appealed his conviction to the Eighth Circuit Court of Appeals. Citing a 1985 Supreme Court decision in affirming Fellers' conviction, the Eighth Circuit made clear its view that striking the statements given at Fellers' home would be an "unwarranted extension" of *Miranda*. As the Eighth Circuit saw it, a simple failure to administer the warnings, unaccompanied by any actual coercion, which might undermine a suspect's ability to exercise free will, does *not* taint the investigatory process. In the court's view, as long as the suspect later executes a valid waiver, the admissibility of the statements should turn solely on whether they were "knowingly and voluntarily" made.

Inexplicably, the Eighth Circuit opinion makes no mention whatsoever of the original *Miranda* decision, although it refers to *Miranda* rights. Curiously, too, the Eighth Circuit opinion does not cite the pivotal opinion—*Dickerson*—that makes the American right to remain silent a "constitutional" decision. Perhaps the Supreme Court noticed these oddities as well because all nine justices agreed to take up *Fellers* and the ominous challenge to *Miranda* it presents.

United States v. Patane, U.S. Supreme Court Docket No. 02-1183, October Term, 2003–2004

Samuel Francis Patane was arrested at his home in Colorado Springs, Colorado, on the night of June 6, 2001. He was out on bail following a previous arrest on June 3, 2001, for threatening his ex-girlfriend, who had secured a restraining order that prohibited Patane from any contact with her. She got a phone call on June 6, and thinking that it was from Patane, called the police. Colorado Springs Police Officer Tracy Fox responded and was told that Patane had a gun in his home. Seemingly by coincidence, a Federal ATF agent notified Colorado Springs Police Detective Josh Benner that Patane had a Glock .40 caliber pistol and that he carried it with him at all times. Detective Benner and Officer Fox conferred and the two arranged to meet at Patane's house. Both knew that possession of a gun would have been a violation of Patane's probation on an old drug charge.

Fox knocked on Patane's front door while Benner covered the back door in case Patane attempted to flee. A woman answered the door and summoned Patane. Fox asked Patane to step outside and engaged Patane in a conversation about the hang-up call to his ex-girlfriend. Patane denied making the call. Nevertheless, Fox told Patane he was under arrest and handcuffed him. With Patane arrested and handcuffed, Detective Benner emerged from the back of the house and began to read *Miranda* warnings to Patane. He only got as far as "you have a right to remain silent" when Patane interrupted to tell Benner and Fox that "he knew his rights." Detective Benner then asked Patane what guns he owned. Patane said, "That .357 is already in police custody." Benner responded that he was more interested in "the Glock." Patane said he wasn't sure he ought to talk about the Glock "because he did not want them to take it away," whereupon Benner said he needed to know about it. Patane then said, "The Glock is in my bedroom, on a shelf, on the wooden shelf." Patane gave Benner permission to go into the house and get the Glock from the bedroom. Benner later testified that he did not intend to arrest Patane for illegal gun possession because he wanted to do more investigation. Fox took Patane to the police station and booked him for violating the restraining order.[50]

Patane was indicted by a federal grand jury for possession of a firearm by a convicted felon. The trial court held a suppression hearing at which the police investigation leading to discovery of the gun was detailed by Officer Fox and Detective Benner. The district court granted the defendant's motion to suppress, holding that Patane's arrest resulted from the intersection of two essentially independent investigations—one by Detective Benner regarding Patane's gun possession, and another by Officer Fox regarding Patane's violation of a domestic violence restraining order. The court concluded that the evidence was insufficient to establish probable cause to arrest Patane. On appeal to the Tenth Circuit Court of Appeals, the court affirmed the trial court's suppression on the "alternative ground that the evidence must be suppressed as the physical fruit of a *Miranda* violation."[51]

The government sought review of the Tenth Circuit's order by way of certiorari to the United States Supreme Court, which granted the petition on April 21, 2003. The sole question presented in the Supreme Court is "whether a failure to give a suspect the warnings prescribed by *Miranda v. Arizona* requires the suppression of physical evidence derived from the suspect's unwarned but voluntary statement?"[52] The oral arguments in *Patane* were held on December 9, 2003. The argument coincides with two other challenges to the *Miranda* doctrine on the same date: *Fellers v. United States* (Supreme Court Docket No. 02-6320) and *Missouri v. Seibert* (Supreme Court Docket No. 02-1371).

Missouri v. Seibert, U.S. Supreme Court Docket No. 02-1371, October Term, 2003–2004

On the morning of February 12, 1977, Patrice Seibert found Jonathan, one of her five sons, dead in her trailer home in Rolla, Mississippi. Jonathan, a twelve-year-old cerebral palsy victim, could not walk, speak, or feed himself. Seibert had been treating her son for bedsores and, upon finding him dead, feared that authorities would think she had neglected her son. Hysterical, she decided not to report the natural death of Jonathan. In her presence, two of her teenaged sons and two of their friends discussed a plan to set the trailer on fire to cover up Jonathan's death. They decided Donald Rector, age seventeen, a friend who lived with the family, should be present in the fire so it would not look as though Jonathan had been left alone. Seibert later testified that she did not agree or disagree with the plan to set fire to the trailer. Seibert gave twenty dollars to her sons, who claimed it was for cigarettes. They used the money to buy gasoline. Seibert sent her two younger sons to church and she left the trailer later that night. Apparently, the two boys started the fire but Rector had a seizure and started convulsing during the fire. He died and Darian Seibert escaped with serious facial burns.

On February 17, 1977, while staying with her son Darian in the hospital, Seibert was awakened at 3:30 A.M. by a St. Louis County police officer, Kerry Clinton. Clinton had been sent to the hospital by Rolla Police Officer Richard Hanrahan to arrest Seibert. Officer Hanrahan specifically instructed Officer Clinton *not* to advise Seibert of her *Miranda* rights. Clinton took Seibert to the police station, put her into a small interrogation room, and gave her twenty minutes to "give her a little time to think about the situation."[53] Clinton followed Hanrahan's instructions, did not warn Seibert of her right to remain silent or to have an attorney present, and extracted a confession from her in twenty to thirty minutes. She told Clinton she knew Donald Rector was to die in his sleep. Then she was given a twenty-minute break for coffee and a cigarette, following which the interview was continued, this time with a tape recorder and after being advised of her *Miranda* rights. Seibert signed a *Miranda* waiver form and Hanrahan began the "second stage" of the interview by referring to the first stage.

Hanrahan testified that he made a conscious decision to withhold *Miranda*, hoping to get an admission of guilt. He said, "An institute, from which he had received interrogation training, has promoted this type of investigation 'numerous times' and that his current department, as well as those he was with previously, all subscribe to this training."[54] Seibert was indicted and convicted of second-degree murder for her role in the death of Donald Rector and sentenced to life imprisonment. She appealed the conviction to the Missouri Court of Appeals, which held that, if a *Miranda* warning preceded an interrogation, it was permissible to extract a confession. However, the Missouri Court of Appeals also concluded that the violation of *Miranda* was a tactic to elicit a confession and was used to weaken Seibert's ability to knowingly and voluntarily exercise her constitutional rights. The Missouri Supreme Court agreed and reversed her conviction and remanded her back to the Circuit Court of Pulaski County for a new trial. In doing so, the Missouri Supreme Court was unequivocal in its condemnation of the two-stage interrogation process:

> Here, Officer Hanrahan candidly admitted that the breach of *Miranda* was intentional and part of a tactic to elicit a confession. . . . Officer Hanrahan's intentional omission of a *Miranda* warning was intended to deprive Seibert of the opportunity knowingly and intelligently to waive her *Miranda* rights. Both stages of the interview formed a nearly continuous interrogation—she was interrogated by the same officials in the same place with only minutes separating the unwarned and warned questioning. There are no circumstances that would seem to dispel the effect of the *Miranda* violation. For these reasons, Seibert's post-*Miranda* waiver and confession was involuntary, and therefore inadmissible.[55]

The State of Missouri sought review in the United States Supreme Court, which granted certiorari on May 19, 2003. Thus, with Fellers, Patane, and Seibert on the Supreme Court's oral argument docket, this trio of cases presents a new challenge for *Miranda* in the wake of *Dickerson*. All three cases involve intentional violations of *Miranda* by police officers intent on securing admissions of guilt or derivative evidence of guilt. The three cases are likely to be litmus tests of *Miranda*'s durability since there is little incentive for police officers to give warnings if they know they can wait and then come back and secure a second warned confession that is admissible notwithstanding the inadmissibility of the first confession.

Chapter 7

THE GLOBAL REACH

Miranda in the Wake of September 11

One of the many unpredictable consequences of *Miranda*'s development is the globalization of America's right to remain silent. It has spread from police stations in America to custodial interrogations of foreign nationals in foreign countries. In 1998, for instance, two non-U.S. citizens were arrested in Kenya and South Africa for their alleged involvement in bombing the U.S. embassies in Kenya and Tanzania. Eventually identified as Saudi Arabian nationals, the suspects were interrogated by FBI agents after they were given printed forms indicating the "possibility" that they lacked the right to counsel during the interrogation. The forms did not contain all of the now customary *Miranda* rights. Both suspects gave oral and written statements incriminating themselves in the embassy bombings, and their statements were evaluated, along with other evidence.

When the investigation was complete, the Saudi suspects were indicted by a federal grand jury and charged with terrorism and related capital crimes in the U.S. District Court in New York. American lawyers were retained to represent the men. As one of their first legal efforts, they filed motions to suppress the incriminating statements made to the FBI while in custody overseas. U.S. District Judge Leonard B. Sand duly suppressed the statement given by the defendant arrested in Kenya because he had confessed to being involved in the bombings before he was advised of his *Miranda* rights. The motion to suppress filed by the suspect interrogated in South Africa, however, was denied because he had been apprised of his *Miranda* rights.

Neither defendant was considered the primary instigator of the destructive bombings. That distinction falls to Osama bin Laden, the primary target of the federal grand jury in 1998 (although he has not as of this writing been arrested and certainly has not confessed).[1] As noted in at least one of the critiques of the *bin Laden* case, the FBI, with understandably increasing frequency, travels to other nations to investigate violations of

American criminal law by non-American citizens who are "suspects" and often in the custody of a foreign law-enforcement agency.[2] Does the Fifth Amendment's privilege against self-incrimination apply to non-American citizens who confess to American authorities abroad and who are later tried in this country? And if the Fifth Amendment does apply, does an FBI inquisitor have to provide *Miranda* warnings to non-American suspects in a foreign country?

No other country in the world requires its police to issue *Miranda* warnings. That fact alone creates a conundrum for the FBI and other American law enforcement agencies, for if a foreign suspect is Mirandized on foreign soil, in a nation that does not recognize the right to remain silent nor provide counsel in pretrial settings, then *Miranda* warnings are inherently misleading.

Largely because of this globalization of *Miranda* in the *bin Laden* case, the United States District Court divided its review into two parts: the right to remain silent and the right to counsel. The court held that a non-American suspect must be told he has the right to remain silent; however, a non-American suspect must be advised that he would have a right to counsel only *if* he were in the United States, and the interrogator must be "clear and candid as to both the existence of the right to counsel in the foreign country and the possible impediments as to its exercise."[3]

The United States Supreme Court will have the final say on these issues because the day will come when a case involving a foreign suspect will reach the Court. Then the *Miranda* doctrine, buttressed by *Dickerson* and tested by *bin Laden*, will face yet more challenges—for one, the reality that for many non-Americans, our notion of individual constitutional rights is counterintuitive, and for another, the reality that those who are already suspicious of the American government will take *Miranda* warnings at something less than face value.

Miranda and the al Qaeda Terror

America's sense of security was seriously shaken on September 11, 2001, when terrorists, using three hijacked commercial airliners as flying bombs, attacked New York City's World Trade Center and the Pentagon in Washington, D.C. The reality of the attack became even more numbing when CNN told the world, in early December, that a young American had been captured among Taliban and al Qaeda fighters in the ensuing armed conflict in Afghanistan.

When John Philip Walker Lindh's bedraggled figure began to appear on television monitors all over the country, it was to the horror of a people who had just come to sense that, despite all their divisiveness, they were truly a society united by common ideals and facing a common foe. And Lindh, in the minds of most Americans, was betraying his country at the very time when patriotism was most needed. It did not seem unjustified when the *Washington Post* headline blared "Walker Charged with Treason," and, in slightly smaller print, noted "He Could Be Sentenced to Life for Fighting Alongside Taliban."[4]

It was also inevitable that Lindh quickly became nearly as hated in the United States as Osama bin Laden, and many were happy to oblige his apparent renunciation of American citizenship. Legally, however, the idea that he was anything other than an American and thus potentially not subject to American justice, on American soil, was equally distasteful. Thus, while other Taliban fighters who may have participated in the reign of terror against America would face military tribunals outside the United States, Lindh, the so-called "American Taliban," would have a chance to exercise his privilege as an American citizen: his right to be tried in an American court, with the aid of counsel and the right to remain silent.

The case at first seemed simple enough. Lindh was charged with conspiracy to kill nationals of the United States overseas, providing material support and resources to designated foreign terrorist organizations, including al Qaeda, and engaging in prohibited transactions with the Taliban. As evidence the prosecution would have Lindh's own confession, given freely to the FBI after he had been informed of his *Miranda* rights, including his right to speak to counsel. Furthermore, he had acknowledged that he understood each of his rights and he had chosen to waive them, both verbally and in a signed document. As Attorney General John Ashcroft told the nation on January 15, 2002, "The charges filed against Walker are based on voluntary statements made by Walker himself."[5]

Soon, however, the print press, as well as broadcast media, had noted that the bulk of the case against Lindh would rely on the admissions he made to FBI agents on December 9 and 10, 2001, days after Lindh had been brought into custody. That fact alone made Lindh's case an obvious challenge to *Dickerson*'s "constitutionalization" of America's right to remain silent. The American public gave scant notice to *Dickerson*'s affirmance of the *Miranda* doctrine in the context of crime, however violent, on American soil. But Lindh, the American Taliban, gave rise to the specter of giving

Miranda warnings on foreign soil to terrorists who also happened to be American citizens.

At first the chief question raised in Lindh's case seemed to be not so much *when* had he been informed of his rights but, more to the point, *when* had he become the focus of a criminal investigation. While a suspect who confesses before he is the focus clearly does not enjoy the protection of *Miranda* and so need not be informed of his rights, Lindh was clearly both in custody *and* the focus of an investigation for a period of time before he was told of his rights; prior to the FBI interviews on December 9 and 10[6] he had been interrogated by a military investigator. Therefore Attorney General John Ashcroft's contention, that the charges filed against Walker were based on voluntary statements made by Walker, seemed moot.[7] Lindh had become the focus of an investigation before he was informed of his rights.

As it turns out, at issue is another ambiguity in the law, having to do with the *intent* of the interrogator. Normally, intent is irrelevant, but since Lindh had been questioned in a war zone, by both military and law enforcement personnel, a number of law scholars considered the question of special importance, believing that *Miranda* warnings must be given only if the interrogator *intended* to elicit information concerning criminal conduct. The intent of the interrogator did not matter, then, if the interrogator sought only intelligence for military purposes.[8] And the military interrogator in question claimed he had sought only the latter, as stipulated in the standard operating instructions for military investigators, which specify that "[Investigators] are not to question regarding any criminal conduct. . . . If you have to ask . . . about matters that will reveal criminal conduct, use rights advisement card."

Lindh's lawyers had apparently received a letter indicating the military investigator who spoke to Lindh "was in the business of collecting [tactical] intel[ligence] information, not in the business of *Mirandizing,* and "never gave Lindh *Miranda* warnings."[9]

This did not deter Lindh's lawyers, however. They asserted that the waiver of his rights was neither "knowing" nor "voluntary." Presumably, he had had no opportunity to talk to anyone not selected by the military or FBI. He was not told that his family had hired a lawyer or that the lawyer had contacted the government regarding his new client on December 3.[10] Arguably, notwithstanding his apparent conversion to militant Islam and his commitment to bin Laden and the al Qaeda network, Lindh had felt pressure to cooperate with U.S. government officials. Attorney General Ashcroft vehemently disagreed with this characterization of the events. "At each step in the process, Walker Lindh's rights, including his rights not to incriminate himself and to be represented by counsel, have been scrupulously honored,"[11] Ashcroft declared.

On July 15, 2002, *USA Today* reported, "The biggest battle in *United States of America vs. John Walker Lindh* begins today as defense attorneys and prosecutors face off over using the American Taliban fighter's incriminating statements to the military, media, and FBI against him."[12]

The path toward suppression of his confessions had been laid down in Lindh's pretrial hearing, on July 11, 2002. Judge T. S. Ellis had held, first, that Lindh retained a Sixth Amendment right to select competent and experienced counsel from another district, but he was not entitled to rely on the exercise of that right to effect a change of venue.[13] Second, Judge Ellis had found that Lindh did not have "lawful combatant" status because the Taliban was not a true military force. It had no internal system of military command or discipline, had no clear hierarchical military structure, and wore no distinctive sign, uniforms, or insignia. Further, the members of Lindh's group had failed to observe the laws and customs of war. Accordingly, Lindh's status as an *un*lawful combatant made him ineligible for immunity on that basis.[14]

These rulings set the stage for what Washington lawyer Beth Wilkinson, the prosecutor in the Oklahoma City bombing case, called, "*the* trial," saying that if Judge Ellis were to rule for the defense and suppress Lindh's confessions, "it will make the case much more difficult for the government" because Lindh's confessions were the heart of the case against him.[15] Conversely, Wilkinson predicted, if Judge Ellis were to decide that a jury could hear the incriminating statements, Lindh's counsel would find it a "challenge" to put up any kind of viable defense for him.

The facts, as usual, were disputed. Lindh's lawyers took the position that Lindh had not been warned of his rights before the commencement of focused questioning and also (by consequence) had been denied access to the lawyer his father had already hired. Thus, his confessions were coerced. The government countered that Lindh did not request a lawyer until December 12, 2001, and that when approached by the military, FBI, or even media interviewers, "Lindh chose to communicate his story to anyone and everyone who would listen."

Prosecutor Randy Bellows also argued that it was Lindh's "own astoundingly bad decisions that led to the conditions and circumstances about which he now so loudly complains. . . . Lindh was not entitled to a *Miranda* warning. No court has ever held that *Miranda* applies to American soldiers in a war zone engaged in debriefing captured enemy combatants."[16]

The trial—the arguments on both sides to determine just how *Miranda* should apply in this extraordinary situation—would have been interesting, to say the least. On July 15, 2002, however, Lindh himself rendered moot his pending motion to suppress his confessions and in so doing rendered his *Miranda* challenge unnecessary as well: He pled guilty to reduced charges in exchange for a stipulated prison term, and Judge Ellis accepted the plea and signed an appropriate order to that effect.[17]

One can only surmise that the fervor Lindh had displayed in the CNN interview, and his candor in talking to the FBI, had since then mellowed. At least by September 2002, he wanted "his countrymen to know that he is not a terrorist and never joined Osama bin Laden's network, even though he met bin Laden in a military training camp in Afghanistan." Perhaps he has learned something since his return to America, although, unfortunately, it is not how to avoid incriminating himself. Acknowledging that "[he] made a terrible mistake," Lindh recently said, "No one wants to be judged by the worst mistake they made when they were 20 years old."[18]

The Other American Taliban—Jose Padilla and Esam Hamdi

As it turned out, Lindh was not the only American Taliban. Several other young Americans have also adopted militancy and violence in the name of Islam, and at least two have emerged from the shadowy world of al Qaeda to be confronted with their own legal battles. Yaser Esam Hamdi and Jose Padilla were "out of school, unemployed, loose molecules in an unstable social fluid that threatened to ignite," according to Robert D. Kaplan.[19] Another analyst, Dr. Don Beck, expanded on the growing instability of this disenfranchised segment of the population Kaplan was referring to:

> Here is a simplistic, seventh-century, puritanical and closed value structure that is locked in a pre-modern mind-set. Unhappily, it's the next step for millions of youth who have been shut out, frustrated, and left behind as they see their counterparts, both next door, and in other societies, thriving and prospering. And it transcends racial or ethnic categories, which is why it is such a threat.[20]

Yaser Esam Hamdi was born in Louisiana, raised in Saudi Arabia, and detained in the United States while his suspected ties to al Qaeda were investigated. It seems that Hamdi, armed with a Kalashnikov rifle, had been captured in Afghanistan in December 2001 when his Taliban fighter group surrendered. At that time, he told military investigators that he had come to Afghanistan several months before to train and fight with the Taliban.[21] Initially airlifted to the U.S. Marine base at Guantanamo Bay, Hamdi was transferred to a military jail in the United States after his claim of birth in Louisiana was confirmed. Secretary of Defense Donald Rumsfeld quickly determined that Hamdi had been both armed and fighting with enemy forces on foreign soil, and President Bush classified Hamdi as an "enemy combatant" and confined him indefinitely to the American military prison camp.

Hamdi's lawyers, who had not actually talked to him, argued that his Fifth Amendment rights were violated. The Fourth Circuit Court of Appeals disagreed, twice.[22] The law is clear that trial judges are obliged to accord "great deference" to the executive branch's classification of men like Hamdi as enemy combatants. Is Hamdi entitled to remain silent and to the presence of an attorney? It is well beyond the scope of this book to enlarge upon Hamdi's role as the second American Taliban beyond the core issue of *Miranda*.

Jose Padilla, born in Puerto Rico but raised in Chicago, was also detained in the United States while his alleged attempt to detonate a "dirty bomb" was investigated. Padilla had changed his name twice—first to Ibrahim and then to Abdullah al Muhajir, which means "the emigrant"— to reflect his affiliation with Islam. By the time he became infamous in American society, he was a Chicago street-gang member, an ex-convict, and a convert to Islam. Georgie Anne Geyer of the *Tulsa World* described him as "an immigrant between ideologies, between ways of life and surely between loyalties."[23]

Padilla had served time in jail in both Chicago and south Florida before moving to Egypt, then to Pakistan, and finally to Afghanistan as part of the al Qaeda network.[24] On May 8, 2002, he was arrested as he stepped off a plane in Chicago after flying in from Zurich and was held for an indeterminate period in military custody as a suspected terrorist. In alleging that Padilla belonged to an al Qaeda cell that had plotted to detonate a radioactive explosive device in the United States, government officials reported that Padilla had discussed the bomb plot with al Qaeda leaders in Pakistan and Afghanistan.

Defense Secretary Donald Rumsfeld said the government wanted to question, rather than prosecute, Padilla.[25] It is, of course, the government's duty to protect its citizens and prevent al Qaeda terrorists from delivering the nuclear devastation that they have threatened. Consequently, following Padilla's initial detention at O'Hare, federal agents subpoenaed him to testify before a grand jury. When he refused, President Bush declared him an "enemy combatant" under the War Powers Act. This subjected Padilla to arrest, not as a suspect but as a material witness.[26] Under the War Powers Act, a material witness can be held indefinitely. As of the time this book went to print, Padilla was still in custody in a South Carolina military brig.

Chapter 8

A BROADER PERSPECTIVE

Looking Back on *Miranda*

I began this book with a preface that I hoped would set the stage for the story of how America won the right to remain silent. That story, I felt, involved not only Ernesto Miranda but also Danny Escobedo, Charles Dickerson, and a host of other people. I also wanted to offer an account of what has happened to the *Miranda* doctrine since the 1966 Supreme Court ruling and a brief look at *Miranda*'s future. An easy prediction, based entirely on the past, is that *Miranda* will continue to generate debate. As America's global influence increases, new questions will surely arise. In this chapter, I hope to provide a broad sense of *Miranda*'s social, political, and historical legacy. For me personally—when I first began to gather the background material I needed to tell this story—understanding that legacy involved gaining a certain perspective, one derived not merely from a single, subjective viewpoint but from all the various viewpoints that turn a short story into a book. Consequently, I sought to interview many uniquely situated individuals, people who represent the different groups directly concerned in the *Miranda* decision and its aftermath—the lawyers, the judges, and the police officers, as well as suspects, scholars, teachers, and ordinary citizens. Fortunately, only one or two who promised to get back to me never did. Most of those I contacted graciously answered my questions, and a few spoke at length. Because I believe I did acquire from talking with these people a broader understanding of how *Miranda* has altered our recent history—and what it has meant to our society and form of government—in the following sections, prefaced by brief biographical notes, I offer boiled-down versions of their observations and opinions, as well as a summary of selected answers to several fundamental questions I put to most of them.

John P. Frank, Esq.

John P. Frank was the single most important person involved in establishing America's right to remain silent. It is likely that without his insight, scholarship, and reputation, we would never have seen the historic evolution of the *Miranda* warnings from 1966 to 2000. My several in-depth interviews with him provided a perspective that likely pervades many parts of this book. My most insistent questions had to do with his views on *Dickerson*'s affirmation of *Miranda* and what he thought that meant to America today. He reminded me that he had written his views on this specific topic in May of 2000, just a few days after the *Dickerson* case was argued in the Supreme Court but a full month before the decision was handed down. He also explained to me why he took the time to record his views of *Miranda*'s importance in light of the *Dickerson* attack on its constitutional status.

Notwithstanding the thirty-four-year span in time and the three-thousand-mile geographical separation, he saw *Miranda* and *Dickerson* as legal twins. Just as Ernesto Miranda had been taken by police from his home, so had Charles Dickerson. Both were minimally educated and neither was gainfully employed in any long-term sense of the word. During custodial interrogation, Miranda had confessed to rape and robbery without being told he had the right to an attorney or that he could remain silent. Thirty years later, Charles Dickerson was subjected to custodial interrogation by the police and confessed to his crime without being informed of his constitutional rights. And the inexorable tie that bound Ernesto Miranda to Charles Dickerson, according to Frank, was the fact that both became unknowing witnesses against themselves—neither knew they had the right to say "no."

"Miranda, and by extension everyone else, including Dickerson, was entitled to *know* he had a constitutional right not to be a witness against himself," Frank concluded. Expanding the thought, Frank said, "The Constitution should not be kept secret from anyone, but *especially* from those who cannot read well enough to inform themselves."

I also asked Frank whether he agreed that the Fifth Amendment was the "heart" of the Bill of Rights. In answer, Frank recalled that one of its authors, James Madison, considered it essential to civilized society. "So did Chief Justice Earl Warren," he added, "and Justices Hugo Black, William Douglas, William Brennan, and Abe Fortas when they decided *Miranda* in 1966, and I still think so today."

When I asked him about Earl Warren, Frank said, "Chief Justice Warren traced the self-incrimination privilege to the Bible and from there to England when the forces of King James sought to compel John Lilburne to testify against himself." This long lineage of religious and judicial precedents, Frank believed, "in itself argued the veracity of the idea." This idea was the subject of an editorial published in the *Arizona Daily Star* on May 7, 2000, where Frank wrote, "The fact remains that George Washington, James Madison, and Thomas Jefferson thought that no person should be forced into testifying against himself. *Miranda* represents the American tradition of justice at its best."[1]

Peter D. Baird, Esq.

Peter Baird, the quintessential big-city, big-firm, and big-idea lawyer, is both an insider with respect to the *Miranda* case and a vociferous advocate of *Miranda*'s most basic message: All of us have a right to know our rights. As a protégé of John Frank and John Flynn, Baird was directly involved in defending Miranda after the Supreme Court's historic opinion in 1966. Accordingly, he has seen *Miranda*'s many faces and believes that the case's legacy lies in the "street side tutorials" it created. "Because of *Miranda*, thousands of times every day, tense police officers confront dangerous suspects and give them a thirty-second lesson on constitutional law," Baird said. He also observed that while cops did this reluctantly in 1966, most of them now see issuing the warning as a valuable routine—a more objective, uniform standard for the admissibility of the confession they hope to obtain.

He then went on to note that the basic rights protected by *Miranda* are no longer rationed to restricted classes of Americans; *Miranda* insures that everyone is told what his rights are at the moment he most needs the information—upon his arrest. *Miranda,* said Baird, "thus has meant the equalization of information about the most publicly important document in our country—the United States Constitution."

Dean Paul Bender

Paul Bender, a constitutional scholar and the former dean of the Arizona State University College of Law, first became immersed in constitutional law as the *Supreme Court Law Review* editor at Harvard Law School in 1957. He clerked for one of America's most famous jurists, Judge Learned Hand, in 1958, and then for Justice Felix Frankfurter on the Supreme Court, in 1960. He was the principal deputy solicitor general of the United States in the mid-nineties and has argued more than twenty cases before the United States Supreme Court. Bender had a great deal to say about *Miranda*'s legacy. He believes *Miranda* is important because it shows that the U.S. Supreme Court can take the realities of law enforcement into account in applying the Constitution. Prophylactic rules, he contended, can prevent constitutional violations and need not limit the law by looking only at relief where rights have already been violated and cannot be restored.

Judge J. Thomas Brooks

Tom Brooks was a prosecutor in a rural Arizona county at the time of the *Miranda* decision, and then, in sequence, became a defense lawyer and a trial judge, and was eventually elevated to the Arizona Court of Appeals. Not surprisingly, his forty-year perspective on *Miranda* provides a sophisticated understanding of the law blended with a compassionate understanding of the foibles and faults in all us, and particularly in rural law enforcement. Although he saw *Miranda* as important, he continued to worry about its negative impact on society. He said that his years on a criminal court bench had given him a firsthand look at the chaos that comes from an abrupt change in standard operating procedures. He remembered that, when first handed down, *Miranda* caused a great deal of confusion and frustration. Trial courts were often inconsistent. What one judge accepted as sound procedure by a police officer would cause another judge to suppress the evidence. Without doubt, especially early on, and notwithstanding good faith on the part of police officers, many guilty persons went either free or successfully negotiated plea agreements to substantially lesser crimes.

Captain Carroll Cooley

Carroll Cooley, the Phoenix police officer who arrested Ernesto Miranda and secured his confession, had been a policeman for about five years when he became the lead detective on what looked like a serial rape case in March 1963. His trial testimony helped send Miranda to prison, but he is most remembered for his failure to inform Miranda of his constitutional rights. Cooley met Miranda several times over the years and has given numerous interviews about their interactions. His written account of the arrest and his interrogation procedures are still used by the Arizona Peace Officer Standards and Training Board.

Thus, arguably, Cooley can remember Miranda's case more clearly than anyone else in the legal community. Indeed, his memories of Miranda as a man are oddly like those of a casual friend, not those of the arresting officer. "The case is important," Cooley said, "because after the decision lots of guilty defendants went free." On this point then, he agreed with Judge Brooks.

Justice Robert J. Corcoran

Arizona Supreme Court Justice Robert Corcoran, the man who gave birth to the *Miranda* case, sees "waiver" as *Miranda's* most important legacy. "How can you actually waive something unless you know what it is," he asked rhetorically. And the knowledge, to be just, must come from a police officer at the right time (custodial interrogation) for the right reason (because it is the law). Only then can there be a true "waiver" and only then can one understand *Miranda's* full importance.

John Dowd, Esq.

John Dowd is a senior partner in one of America's most prestigious law firms. While based in Washington, D.C., he has tried important criminal cases all over America, including Phoenix. His perspective of *Miranda's* importance stems from his long career both prosecuting and defending countless high-profile criminal cases. His clientele includes those who are famous and those who are about to become so. Both hire him because of his consummate courtroom skills, his deep knowledge of law and procedure, and most of all, his professional tenacity.

For Dowd, the *Miranda* case captured "the struggle between the need for truth to operate the criminal justice system and the right to remain silent." And "there is a subsidiary struggle between the police officer's desire to discover what happened and the suspect's fear of implication through interrogation," he observed, explaining that his experience suggested that police will use any tactic available to obtain a confession. With the advent of DNA testing, he said, "We can get a clearer picture of the ongoing corruption of the system in which innocent persons are convicted. *Miranda* is a great shield against abuse and hysteria."

Judge Joseph Howe

Joseph Howe was Chief Judge Richard Chambers' clerk on the Ninth Circuit Court of Appeals and taught law at Iowa, Case Western, and Harvard before settling down to practice in Arizona at the time Miranda was working his way through the system. Appointed to the Maricopa County Superior Court in 1982, he retired in 2000 but remains active, teaching trial advocacy to lawyers all over America.

He argued an important criminal case before the Arizona Supreme Court the day after it received word from the United States Supreme Court of the reversal in the *Miranda* case. Recalling an unhappy bench that day, he saw a "fundamental problem" in the *Miranda* decision. In proving that the "holding" of a case may be seen differently on the bench than from the pit of the courtroom, he said, "[*Miranda*] held that lack of informed consent is equivalent to coercion. The illogic of this leads to the present problem: A truly coerced confession is excluded, not just because of the constitutional 'rights' but because it is unreliable. Similarly unreliable is the confession obtained by promise of benefit. The confession obtained without a recitation of *Miranda* rights is not unreliable simply because of the omission of the recitation."

There is much to worry about in the criminal justice system, irrespective of where one sits in the courtroom. The "fruit of the poisoned tree" doctrine is one such worry, and Judge Howe was concerned that confessions rejected or suppressed because of *Miranda* should not be considered "poisoned fruit" but rather simply technically inadmissible. Otherwise, its fruit "is just as wholesome as all get out."

Robert Jensen, Esq.

Bob Jensen became a lawyer in Minnesota and moved to Arizona in the fall of 1965 to join Lewis and Roca. While waiting for the results of the Arizona bar examination, he and Paul Ulrich performed the bulk of the exhaustive legal research necessary to prepare and file the petitioner's brief in the United States Supreme Court. Now a senior but still very active member of the Arizona bar, Jensen remembers Miranda through John Flynn's eyes. He did only a little criminal defense work in Arizona and consequently views *Miranda* primarily from a historical perspective.

Jensen worked with John Flynn on a number of cases after the *Miranda* decision came down. Not unexpectedly, Jensen thought *Miranda*'s importance stems from the fact that "John Flynn handled the oral arguments." He quickly recalled "Flynn's instinctive and extremely personal approach to trial work," and believed Flynn translated that instinct for understanding juries to his instinct for what the High Court wanted to hear in 1966. *Miranda* is also important for another reason: "It sharply focused the issue of *choice* under the Constitution." As Jensen put it, "When push comes to shove, do we tip the balance to the individual or society?"

Chris Johns, Esq.

Chris Johns, a Phoenix public defender, knows well the inherent probability of constitutional violation because most criminal suspects are "trusting souls." He brings a lifetime of both trial and appellate advocacy to his vigorous defense of indigent defendants. Well known for his devotion to poor, uneducated clients like Miranda, Johns believes that "we might not even have public defenders had not a courageous Supreme Court handed down the rights trilogy of *Gideon, Escobedo,* and *Miranda.*

"As long as police need confessions to make their cases and as long as suspects accept the promises made by the police," Johns argued, "unwarned confessions will be made." He sees the *Miranda* doctrine as a "critical weapon in the fight for defendants' rights."

Barry Kroll, Esq.

Barry Kroll might be said to be a prime mover in the *Miranda* saga because, as Danny Escobedo's appellate lawyer, he stood before the bar of the Supreme Court and made history in 1965. At the time of my interview with him, in 2002, he had not seen Danny Escobedo since his release from prison. During that entire time, Kroll never handled another criminal case or appeared again before the United States Supreme Court.

Predictably, Kroll said the most significant aspect of *Miranda* is that the Supreme Court reconfirmed and clarified the basic holding of *Escobedo.* He also saw *Dickerson* in the same light. The importance of constitutional litigation often vibrates from its predecessors and its successors.

Senator Jon Kyl, R-Arizona

Jon Kyl, like Dowd, is based in Washington, D.C., but visits his old friends and law partners in Phoenix quite regularly. He was an outstanding lawyer long before he became a highly respected member of the United States Senate. A former classmate of mine at the University of Arizona College of Law and my law partner for many years at Jennings, Strouss and Salmon, Jon has both a legal and political perspective on the *Miranda* case. Kyl's dedication to national legal and social issues earned him a seat on the United States Senate's Judiciary Committee. Along with nine other senators,[2] he filed an amici curia brief with the Supreme Court urging it to affirm the Fourth Circuit's decision in *Dickerson* and to repeal *Miranda*. He has, in his political life, earned a reputation as a severe critic of liberal Supreme Court decisions, so I wasn't surprised to hear that he believed many of the Warren Court decisions favored the criminal over the victim. Nor was I surprised to find that he believed the *Miranda* decision should not govern the admissibility of confessions in federal court—because "the *Miranda* rules are not mandated by the Constitution." At least in federal courts, Kyl contended in his legal brief, *Miranda* is unimportant because the prophylactic safeguards devised in the case are not materially altered in the federal legislation [Section 3501] that was intended to "repeal" the decision.

Rex E. Lee, Esq.

Rex Lee was already a constitutional law scholar when he became the chairman of Jennings, Strouss and Salmon's recruiting committee in 1965. He was instrumental in bringing Jon Kyl to the firm in 1966 and me in 1967. As noted earlier in this book, Rex Lee[3] reluctantly turned Bob Corcoran down as lead appellate counsel in the *Miranda* case. He knew the *Escobedo* case intimately because he had been Justice Byron White's law clerk in 1964, the year *Escobedo* came down. He predicted that the Supreme Court would likely accept certiorari in the case and reverse Miranda's conviction, and in 1966, told Bob Corcoran that he was "unenthusiastic" about the rules of law approach (in *Escobedo*) because he did not believe it would be good constitutional law (in *Miranda*).

As it turned out, Lee's views in 1966 became the reality of the *Miranda* doctrine's search for constitutional acceptance. He was right about *Miranda*, in that the "rules of law" approach would be controversial. He would likely have welcomed *Dickerson*'s final anointment of *Miranda* as a "constitutional" decision, for he was a strong believer in the concept of settled law and the value of stare decisis. Those beliefs, along with his stellar academic record and his practice skills, led him to become the first dean of the Brigham Young University Law School, the solicitor general of the United

States, and, ultimately, the President of Brigham Young University.[4] Neither John Frank nor Rex Lee lived to see my project come to fruition as a book. They were two of America's finest lawyers and inexorably linked by their vast knowledge of constitutional litigation and their respective roles in the *Miranda* doctrine.

Professor Tom Mauet

Tom Mauet holds the Milton O. Riepe Professorship of Law at the University of Arizona College of Law. He is a frequent national lecturer and has written a great deal on criminal procedure and trial advocacy. Before joining the faculty, he was a criminal defense lawyer in Chicago. This rare mixture of solid courtroom experience and high academic scholarship produced a seemingly inconsistent response to my question about *Miranda*'s importance. "Yes," he said, "of course it's important; it's just not significant."

Then Mauet cautioned me to remember that "Today, *Miranda*'s warnings are an accepted part of arrest procedure. However, they have not accomplished what the decision seemingly intended. There has not been a reduction in either the number of interrogations or the number of confessions." He is one of a large number of nationally ranked faculty who believe the Supreme Court "must have hoped that confessions would go down once suspects learned that they had a right to remain silent."

"Isn't it entirely possible," I responded, "that the Supreme Court wanted to bring about reform in the police department and did not really focus on the quantity of confessions?" "No," Mauet insisted. "Their judicial hope was that 'coerced' confessions would decrease. Wasn't that the real point of the case?"

Craig Mehrens, Esq.

Craig Mehrens was a public defender in Maricopa County, Arizona, when Ernesto Miranda's criminal case was winding its way through the criminal justice system. He watched much of the early process with young eyes and a suspicion of police interrogation techniques, one that comes naturally to criminal defense lawyers. He cautioned me that the Miranda story is important "only if told compellingly."

Easy enough for him to say, I countered; he was not writing the book. On a more serious note, Mehrens agreed with *Miranda*'s leading critic, Professor Grano, and its leading proponent, Professor Kamisar, on the inescapable conclusion that *Miranda* was the most important criminal procedure case in American history. *Miranda* has generated scores of books, thousands of articles, and millions of references in mainstream print and broadcast media. It is cited more than any other constitutional law case and known more widely in the lay world than any other case, with the possible exception of *Roe v. Wade*.

Mehrens argues for *Miranda's* importance by reminding us that although an American suspect always had the right to remain silent, suspects did not often assert that right because they did not know they had it. *Miranda's* importance thus lay in the earth-shattering requirement that a cop in an interrogation room actually tell the suspect that he *can* remain silent.

Attorney General Gary K. Nelson

As the head of the appeals section of the Arizona Attorney General's office in 1966, Gary Nelson wrote the brief and argued the prosecution's case in the United States Supreme Court. Nelson was later elected Arizona's attorney general and was subsequently appointed to the Arizona Court of Appeals. After lamenting the fact that he is now known as the "losing" lawyer in the *Miranda* case, he contended that the *Miranda* case "showed just how far the Warren Court was willing to go to implement its 'assumed' right of silence." The case was important because "unless you cross all the t's and dot all the i's you are out of luck."

Nelson remained true to the opinion of some prosecutors and police officers in the 1960s that criminal defense lawyers always represented guilty clients; however, he refined that opinion somewhat by candidly admitting the "something" they were guilty of was sometimes a different crime than the one they were charged with at the time of arrest. He also recalls the common practice of "overcharging" by zealous prosecutors. His long-held view of *Miranda's* big mistake was that bringing defense counsel into the interrogation room always "ends interrogation."

Detective Ron Quaife

Ron Quaife was the man who "Mirandized" the man who murdered Ernesto Miranda. There is great irony in the simple fact that Mirandizing this suspect allowed him to exercise his *Miranda* rights, notwithstanding the solid proof that he had killed Miranda. Lacking a confession or other evidence on the day of the murder, Quaife had to release the suspect, who promptly fled to Mexico. Perhaps he never returned, but neither Quaife nor anyone else on the Phoenix Police Department really knows because no one ever checked. The Miranda murder case was "cleared" by closing the file a few months after it was opened. Consequently, Miranda's murder went unsolved and his murderer unprosecuted. Moreno, at least, was warned that he had constitutional rights. Perhaps this is the only significant thing that really distinguished him from the man he allegedly killed.

With only two years on the force under his belt at the time Miranda was murdered, Quaife thought the *Miranda* case made his job "harder and more time consuming." He recalled those early years as "exasperating, because small mistakes in the stationhouse became big problems in the courthouse." Quaife's post-*Miranda* experience, however, both inside the stationhouse as well as out on the street, has led him to believe that lawyers played "at best, only a minor role in the investigation of crime in Phoenix."

Charles Roush, Esq.

Charles Roush[5] was a young lawyer at Lewis and Roca when its two famous senior partners, John Frank and John Flynn, took Miranda's case to the Supreme Court. While he did not play a direct role in the case, he learned the craft of advocacy from two of the best. Later, Roush moved from Lewis and Roca to the Maricopa County Superior Court. His first assignment as a trial judge was "a very long year taking pleas in confession cases." As a member of a prominent family of lawyers, he saw "Phoenix in the fifties as a society entirely dependent on the police department to control crime." The Eisenhower/J. Edgar Hoover "tough-on-crime" mentality overlooked police abuse, which, he thought, "ultimately forced the courts to step in. The judiciary had to force procedural changes necessary to protect the guilty as well as the innocent." *Miranda* is important, Roush believes, "because it was sorely needed, wisely used, and has stood the test of time."

Chief Judge Mary Schroeder

Mary Schroeder is the chief judge of the United States Court of Appeals for the Ninth Circuit. Like Peter Baird and Governor Janet Napolitano, she was a protégé of John Frank and spent her formative years at Lewis and Roca. She never worked on the *Miranda* cases while at the firm but has seen *Miranda*'s progeny at several different levels. As the first woman to become the Ninth Circuit's chief judge, she oversees the largest and busiest federal appellate court in the country.

"*Miranda* is important," Judge Schroeder said, "because it sharply delineates two very different periods of legal history. In the first, police relied on confessions obtained through coercive interrogation. In the later period, lawyers told their clients to be quiet. The perception of *Miranda* "is that it made it harder to get suspects to talk after they were given their rights; the reality of *Miranda* is that the entire criminal justice system now has significantly fewer problems with coerced confessions."

Mara Siegel, Esq.

Mara Siegel, another of Arizona's best trial lawyers, spent her entire professional life defending indigent clients in felony criminal cases. A colleague of Chris Johns, she has strong feelings about the *Miranda* doctrine. When asked about its importance to America, she said, "*Miranda* is the biggest shovel in the trench warfare of our criminal justice system. I use it every day to dig my clients out of the messes they put themselves in by swallowing the line that the police really want to help."

Siegel also said she believed that the Fifth Amendment would be violated daily "but for *Miranda*." She is not alone in that belief. As a general proposition, public defenders are not routinely assigned to suspects at the custodial stage, but privately retained lawyers are often involved. Whether public or private, the several score of defense lawyers I interviewed about *Miranda* share a common belief: Because the *Miranda* decision is still alive and well in America, "police officers have to investigate rather than merely interrogate." When challenged on the plausibility of that statement, most defense lawyers back off. They nevertheless believe that, but for *Miranda*, most defendants would unknowingly incarcerate themselves and give the police little to do except type up the confessions.

Judge Barry Silverman

Barry Silverman sits on the United States Court of Appeals for the Ninth Circuit. A native of Phoenix, Judge Silverman is perhaps the only federal judge in America who actually knew Ernesto Miranda. Silverman interviewed family members, lawyers, witnesses, and police officers in the early 1980s and wrote a nonfiction narrative of the case. Later, as he moved up from lawyer to state court judge to federal magistrate, and finally, to federal appellate judge, Silverman watched the *Miranda* doctrines evolve. Judge Silverman believes the pivotal question *Miranda* answered is not *whether* rights should be given but *when*. He asked me, "What happens in the event of an unintentional violation of the rule?" It is a frequently asked question in current criminal procedure cases. Judge Silverman worried that federal magistrates and state trial judges had no discretion in the matter. He would argue for exceptions to the necessity for *Miranda* warnings, in cases were the confession is "unquestionably voluntary."

Robert Storrs, Esq.

Bob Storrs graduated with me in 1967 from the University Of Arizona College of Law. He became the prosecutor in the retrial of Miranda's robbery case in 1971. He spent the first two decades of his career prosecuting criminals in Phoenix and the last decade defending them. His perspective on Ernesto Miranda gives him a larger view of the legacy created by the *Miranda* doctrine.

Miranda is important, he noted, "in principle but no longer of any practical significance." In explaining this, he pointed out that without *Miranda*, no one would have known about the right to remain silent. "Now everyone knows about it," he said. We all think we have a personal right of silence because of *Miranda*. What could be more important than that?

Paul Ulrich, Esq.

Paul Ulrich was a clerk at Lewis and Roca, awaiting admission to the bar, in the fall of 1965. Together with Bob Jensen, he was responsible for the exhaustive legal research necessary to prepare and file the petitioner's brief in the United States Supreme Court. Paul now views *Miranda* from an exclusively historical perspective because he no longer takes criminal cases. Ulrich believed that *Miranda* took some of the fear of lawyers out of police stations. Prior to the historic decision, Ulrich recalled, "Lawyers were unwelcome in police stations because they tended to slow down the clearing of cases through confessions, voluntary or not. Many defendants confessed to crimes not even under investigation, as was the case with Ernesto Miranda."

Ulrich sensed that "many police officers subscribed to the theories propounded by Inbau and Reid[6] in their book on police interrogation technique. That book is a catalogue of deceptive practices justified under the rubric that a suspect is likely guilty of something—even if he is not guilty of the current charge." He observed that even a casual reading of Inbau and Reid reveals that "extracting confessions from guilty suspects is entirely warranted because it expedites their punishment."

Judge Warren Wolfson

Warren Wolfson, Escobedo's "other" lawyer, represented Danny Escobedo at the time of his arrest in Chicago in 1962. He was the young lawyer pounding on the door at the Chicago police station trying to see his client while he was being interrogated inside the building. Because he was listed as the primary witness at Escobedo's suppression hearing, he insisted that Escobedo have new counsel. The new lawyer, Barry Kroll, was appointed by the trial judge to represent Escobedo. Wolfson continued to practice criminal law for many years, was appointed to the trial bench in Cook County, Illinois, and eventually became a highly respected appellate judge in Illinois.

Judge Wolfson believes *Miranda*'s importance lies in its durability. He went on to explain that, although it is not often an issue in state court criminal matters because of its wide acceptance, the *Miranda* doctrine relies on the good faith of the people who are in the system. Like other experienced judges, Wolfson sees the legacy of *Miranda* more as a waiver issue than anything else.

He also said that he believes *Escobedo*'s reliance on the Sixth Amendment to extend the right of counsel to pretrial custodial interrogation procedures is best examined in light of *Miranda*. There the Fifth Amendment was extended to custodial interrogation, thereby both affirming and expanding the *Escobedo* doctrine.

Did *Miranda* Retard Law Enforcement?

Many of the people I interviewed, especially those who observed *Miranda* in real time as prosecutors, continue to believe what was widely thought in the sixties, namely that *Miranda* would put an increasing number of criminals on the street. Some acknowledge that, although statistically this may appear to be the case, the cause cannot be traced to *Miranda*. However, they contend that law enforcement is still retarded simply because lawbreakers who would have been justly tried and convicted on the basis of confession go free solely because of *Miranda.* On the other hand, as Craig Mehrens points out, "An American suspect had always had the right to remain silent. How could one say that law enforcement was retarded by *Miranda?* In fact, if more people knew their rights, one could argue that law enforcement was being *advanced.*" It seems an undeniably valid point, in effect arguing that breaking the law in order to uphold the law results in no positive outcome.

Did we know that informing innocent suspects of their rights would diminish confessions? "Of course we knew," former Attorney General Gary Nelson said. "The career criminal might speak to the police but the more knowledgeable types, i.e., the new breed of criminal, after *Miranda,* would listen only to his lawyer." Inevitably, then, lawyers trumped police officers. That in turn minimized the impact of the typical police officer's advice to "talk now—it will be better for you."

Detective Quaife represents the dissenting minority on this question. "No," he said, "we didn't really believe that confessions would drop. In fact, a large percentage of suspects continued to confess *after* we gave them their warnings. *Miranda* did not impede confessions as long as you treated the suspect with respect. He still wanted to talk." This assertion, that respect for the suspect makes a difference, seems important, for it suggests that police should adhere to the basic edict of American law—you are innocent until proven guilty. Such a philosophy may seem axiomatic, but it is not. Police, like most Americans, more often unconsciously equate suspicion with guilt. Some would argue that guilt is even more assured today than in the past, given the current methods police use to gather information and the extensive databases they maintain. Also, it could be argued that *Miranda* has caused police to gather more information before arrest, knowing that they will need to justify the arrest to an attorney. In short, the vast majority of suspects arrested turn out to be guilty as charged. That reality, however, does not alter Quaife's contention that treating a suspect as innocent encourages the suspect to cooperate.

On the related question of whether *Miranda* has become a "waiver" case and is no longer a "rights" case, Professor Mauet opines that later Supreme Court opinions have watered down *Miranda* and thus diluted the original meaning of a "knowing and intelligent waiver" of right to counsel or to remain silent. Consequently, Mauet, like most experienced criminal defense lawyers, uses motions to suppress based on "voluntariness" rather than a failure to comply with *Miranda.*

This seems a natural byproduct of the many modifications and adjustments to *Miranda* that took place during the Berger and Rehnquist years. Nevertheless, the *Miranda* warnings, effective or not, continue to be routinely given. That is tremendously important. It is, as Peter Baird dubbs it, a thirty-second constitutional tutorial given by police thousands of times every day all over America. It may be that not enough listen, or even that too many listen. Of course in the final analysis, that does not matter. What does matter is that the warnings are *routinely* given and that professional police officers know that more than coerced confessions are needed to clear their case logs.

Judge Howe, in responding to the question of whether *Miranda* has retarded law enforcement, observed, "Eventually we will need to hire a law professor to review all possible scenarios for the defendant before any evidence may be used against him except that obtained without any statements by the defendant at all."

Setting aside the temptation to blend suspicion with guilt, there remains another dichotomy. What people believed would happen as a result of informing suspects of their constitutional rights seemed to depend on the differences between the "gatehouse" (the often-drab interrogation room in the local police station) and the "courthouse." The gatehouse is where, in the pre-*Miranda* era, suspects talked, one way or the other. Of course, the conversation was private, no lawyers allowed. What the suspect said was typed up by the police and handed to the prosecutor. The prosecutor in turn carried the conversation, now labeled a "confession," up to the courthouse, which was often a majestic building where former suspects—now full-fledged defendants—became public persons. Now all those freshly typed words were read into the record. At least that was the case for the minority of suspects who insisted on a trial. The majority of unwarned suspects, when confronted privately with their confessions, adopted a much more efficient resolution: They pled guilty.

Before *Gideon,* before *Escobedo,* and certainly before *Miranda,* the vast majority of suspects checked their information bags at the gatehouse. These were not reopened until they appeared, as if by magic, in the courthouse when the magistrate asked if the confession were freely and voluntarily given. After *Gideon, Escobedo,* and especially *Miranda,* America engaged in the great debate over how to reconcile what apparently went on in the gatehouse with what obviously happened in the courthouse. The most glaring difference was that one was private and the other public. What came to light in the courthouse was often very different from the dark tales told in the gatehouse.

Another difference can be found in the lack of respect for one and the power of the other. Courts were places of dignity where rights were respected, victims had lawyers (called prosecutors), and defendants were repeatedly told of their rights, in public, by impartial judges. The gatehouse was more often a place where rights were ignored, suspects did not have lawyers, and no one was impartial.

America also struggled with the reality that many suspects, guilty or not, spent more time in the gatehouse than the courthouse. For example, Miranda's arrest and interrogation took longer than his trial. Many suspects, guilty or not, contributed to their own incarceration through what they said, notwithstanding the fact that they might not have actually committed the specific crime to which they confessed.

Why the Constitution was so important in the courthouse but largely ignored in the gatehouse became the dilemma faced by the Supreme Court in the *Miranda* case. Some of the justices found the answer in the evil ways of those cops who extracted confessions with rubber hoses and fraudulent promises. Others obviously believed that policing was a difficult, dangerous business and required stern, disciplined officers just to keep pace with a growing crime rate and a less-than-tolerant political climate. Clearing cases by encouraging suspects to confess was acceptable to most "law-abiding" citizens—a logic explained by the simple fact that most law-abiding citizens and criminal suspects had one thing in common: Neither really knew that you *could* remain silent in the gatehouse and that you *could* have a lawyer sitting at the interrogation table with you if you wanted one.

Detective Carroll Cooley steadfastly maintains that Ernesto Miranda "knew his rights, just as he knew his way around the criminal justice system." In fact, "Miranda knew as much as I did," he insisted. When I asked Cooley if he knew when he interrogated a suspect that the suspect did not have to talk and that a lawyer could be present in that little room any time he wanted, he said, "No, that came down on us from the Supreme Court years later."

False Confessions, the Temple Murder Case, and the Tucson Four

Psychologists and sociologists recognize three distinct types of false confession. A voluntary false confession occurs when a suspect falsely confesses to a crime without influence from others. The most common situation that explains voluntary false confessions is mental abnormality. Mentally defective individuals tend to offer confessions in countless high-profile crimes.[7] By "high-profile" I mean personal crime, not corporate crime. It is almost unheard of in "white-collar" criminal cases for a suspect to even be interrogated, much less for one to confess.

Another type of false confession, called "coerced-compliant," usually occurs when the suspect feels he must avoid duress or seeks to benefit from the confession. Long interrogations conducted late at night or on the promise of a favorable plea bargain account for many coerced-compliant false confessions.

The third type of voluntary false confession, the "coerced-internalized false confession," invariably involves police coercion. Instead of confessing to get out of an undesirable situation or to tie down a lenient plea bargain, the suspect unconsciously incorporates into his own memory the information given to him during police interrogation. Consequently, the suspect comes to believe he is truly responsible for the crime, notwithstanding the fact that no initial memory of the crime ever existed. The psychology literature suggests that these coerced-internalized memories can last for days or weeks, depending on the length of police interrogation.[8]

False confessions derive from several psychological conditions. A suspect may feel guilty about something he has done or failed to do, something completely unrelated to the crime in question. A suspect's ability to reason may be impaired by drug addiction, or he may be unduly frightened of the police or possess a disordered or inadequate personality. Some suspects simply can't resist the notoriety they know will result from confessing to a high-profile crime.

The frequency of false confessions is a vigorously debated question in the legal world. An even more complicated question arises in trying to determine how many wrongful convictions are based on false confessions. Estimates range from a low of 35 to a high of 840 annually.[9] There do not appear to be any definitive studies. Since social scientists have thus far not compiled conclusive data, I will offer anecdotal evidence to illustrate the perfidious nature of so-called voluntary false confessions. The case concerns a multiple murder that, once again, put Arizona in the national headlines.

In August of 1991 nine bodies were discovered inside the Wat Promkunaram Buddhist Temple in the desert near Phoenix. The victims, including six Buddhist monks, lay face down in a circle, each shot in the head. The killers had ransacked the temple and stolen a small amount of money, cameras, and stereo equipment. Based on forensic science, the

Maricopa County sheriff's department quickly identified the murder weapon as a Marlin Model 60, .22-caliber rifle. The rifle was not found but the make, model, and caliber were clear from crime-scene evidence.

A few weeks later, in September 1991, an anonymous tip implicated four young Tucson men. The Maricopa County sheriff's office immediately arrested them and subjected each one to lengthy questioning. All four confessed, in writing, to the Temple murders. Then they talked to their parents and their lawyers. The next day they recanted their confessions and professed their innocence.

In October 1991, while the men, now dubbed the "Tucson Four" were still in jail, Maricopa County sheriff's deputies located the murder weapon in Phoenix. Its owner identified it as such, but denied involvement in the crime, and told the deputies that two young Phoenix men, Jonathan Doody and Alex Garcia, had borrowed his rifle shortly before the murders. The deputies located Doody at a high school football game on October 25 and took him in for questioning.

Doody, a seventeen-year-old juvenile, was advised of his *Miranda* rights but told the deputies he wanted to talk to them without an attorney and without his parents present.[10] His interrogation began at 9:25 in the evening. Two and one-half hours later, he made "inculpatory statements, and after approximately four more hours of questioning, admitted to being at the temple on the night of the murders."[11] His interrogation lasted for almost thirteen consecutive hours without significant breaks. During this time, Doody implicated four other young men, including Alex Garcia, but *not* the Tucson Four already in custody.

Garcia was also questioned on the night of October 25, 1991. He initially invoked his right to remain silent but, after talking to his father, agreed to give a statement about his involvement in the murders. In essence, Garcia claimed that Doody had planned the robbery, insisted that they leave "no witnesses," and shot each of the victims in the head with the Marlin rifle.[12] Garcia insisted that he and Doody were the only two involved and denied that the other two Phoenix juveniles or any of the Tucson Four had been involved.

It was ultimately revealed that the sheriff's focus on the Tucson Four had begun when one of them, a mental patient, called the police and falsely confessed. The other three young men, actually innocent, had broken down under interrogation and confessed to the killings. The prosecutor described the investigation of the Tucson Four as "bungled" by the sheriff's office.[13]

The Tucson Four, having recanted their confessions and professed their innocence, were released after three months of incarceration. They promptly filed wrongful-arrest civil suits against the sheriff's office. In September 1994, the Tucson Four accepted a $2.8 million dollar out-of-court settlement offered by Maricopa County.

Garcia accepted a plea bargain that saved him from the death penalty, conditioned on his agreement to testify against Doody at trial. Doody unsuccessfully attempted to suppress his confession. Since the prosecutors already had a plea from Garcia and his promise to testify, they did not offer a plea bargain to Doody.

Following a media-intensive trial, Doody was convicted of felony murder, but the jury rejected the charge of premediated murder. He appealed his conviction on multiple grounds, including that his confession was coerced and that Garcia's confession, like those given by the Tucson Four, was false. He also argued that his confession was false because it had been extracted by the same interrogators, who had used on him the same technique that they had used to extract false confessions from the Tucson Four.

Nevertheless, Doody's conviction and sentence of 281 years in the Arizona State Penitentiary were affirmed by the Arizona Court of Appeals. Arizona's Supreme Court denied review and the United States Supreme Court rejected his petition for a writ of certiorari on June 16, 1997.[14] Doody received ten more years than the judge gave Garcia on his plea bargain.

The Arizona Supreme Court has expressed grave concern with respect to juvenile confessions. The leading Arizona Supreme Court case on the subject says, "[The] greatest care must be taken to assure that [a juvenile's] admission was voluntary, in the sense not only that it was not coerced or suggested, but also that it was not the product of ignorance of rights or of adolescent fantasy, fright or despair."[15]

In the Temple Murder case, the interrogators secured six confessions from juveniles after securing waivers of their *Miranda* rights. All six recanted their confessions. Four of those confessions were indisputably *false*.

Of course, not all false confessions are the product of police misconduct. However, when police misconduct cases are evaluated on a national scale, it appears that 42 percent of the cases involve allegations of undue suggestiveness in pretrial identification procedures and coerced confessions arising out of custodial interrogation.[16]

The motive or the psychological explanation for the confessions by the Tucson Four may never be known, but in acknowledgement that such false confessions do occur, and not infrequently, the criminal justice system must be skeptical of all confessions. The false confession will never disappear, even when the right to remain silent is offered.

If *Miranda* Was a Liberal Decision, Why Was *Dickerson* a Conservative Decision?

This question, of course, concerns the meaning of the words *liberal* and *conservative*. For purposes of this book, I use both in the political sense. Politically, if not linguistically, liberalism took root in the early nineteenth century as an attempt to reach the maturity level of the more "advanced" Whigs. The ideology flowered in England with the Reform Act of 1832 and blossomed in America when FDR took on the Great Depression. As a political philosophy, liberalism is concerned with the development of personal freedom and social progress. Liberalism and democracy are generally thought to have common aims, although, in the past, many liberals considered democracy unhealthy because it encouraged mass participation in politics. Nevertheless, liberalism eventually became identified with movements seeking to change social order through the extension of democracy.

The growth of the liberal wing of the Republican Party in New York in the late 1950s distressed conservative-minded Republicans in the state and led to the formation of the Conservative Party as a more distinct alternative to liberalism. As a voting block, the Conservative Party was initially planted in New York State three years before the *Miranda* decision came down. Although today numerous candidates throughout the nation seek office as conservatives, the Conservative Party of New York State is the only party legally constituted as such in the United States. The party stresses a firm belief in the American tradition of individual initiative and liberty.

In our justice system, the courts, particularly the United States Supreme Court, tend to take on the character of the chief justice, especially when the chief's legal ideology is consistent with at least four other justices. Thus, we often describe a court as "the Warren Court" or "the Rehnquist Court."

The acceptance, at least by the public, of a ruling by the Supreme Court depends, in part, on how far the Court departs from public opinion. When the Court is perceived to be pursuing an "activist" agenda rather than simply interpreting the Constitution, the voicing of public opinion—or the media's representation of it—increases. More consternation ensues when it appears that justices are writing their own values into the Constitution. More often than not, those who object to an activist Court are politically conservative, and those who favor judicial activism support liberal politics.

However, judicial activism and conservatism do not always reflect a liberal-conservative political split. Judicial politics, like judicial opinions, are decidedly more complex than that. Conservatives frequently oppose the Court's expansion of procedural rights for criminal defendants. That largely explains the uproar in the 1960s when conservatives attacked the Warren Court's decisions as both activist *and* politically liberal. Critics of the Taft Court's suppression of the government's power to regulate commerce in the 1920s, on the other hand, complained that those decisions were activist and politically conservative.

Perhaps the most illuminating treatment of the larger subject—the appropriate balance between individual liberties and community concerns at the Supreme Court level—is found in Jim Simon's *The Center Holds*. The preface to Simon's book introduces "the story of a conservative judicial revolution that failed."

> It was led by the chief justice of the United States, William H. Rehnquist, and actively encouraged by two conservative Republican presidents, Ronald Reagan and George Bush. They hoped to reverse the liberal legacy of the Warren Court and its successor, the Burger Court, which had given the broadest scope in the nation's history to the civil rights and civil liberties protections of the Bill of Rights and the Fourteenth Amendment.[17]

Simon uses the term *liberal* to describe a justice who gives the political branches of our government wide latitude to effect social and economic reform while insisting that those political branches do not interfere with individual rights.[18] Likewise, Chief Justice Rehnquist, in describing the justices of the Court in the *Miranda* era, distinguishes "liberal" from "conservative" by noting that the liberal wing "conceded to the government great authority under the Constitution to regulate economic matters, but . . . sharply circumscribed that power when it was pitted against claims of individual rights." The "conservative" wing, on the other hand, he held was "inclined to sustain government action pretty much across the board." [19]

Definitions in hand: Why was establishing a suspect's right to remain silent considered "liberal" in 1966 but confirming that right was considered "conservative" in 2000?

Dean Paul Bender answered by observing that in the sixties *anything* that aided criminal suspects was a "liberal" thing to do. Conversely, or perhaps conservatively, the Rehnquist Court adhered to precedent, which is a supposedly "conservative" action. Bender, having not noticed whether conservatives believe in precedent any more than liberals do, then urged me to forget "liberal" and "conservative" and concentrate on "correct."

Criminal defense lawyers John Dowd and Craig Mehrens answered the question more bluntly. Dowd said "labeling something as liberal is part of the hysteria created by politicians who use crime as a scare tactic to win votes." Mehrens observed that "giving a suspect any rights—because he is viewed as guilty—is always labeled liberal—until, of course, it is your spouse or child who is under suspicion."

Senator John Kyl referred me to the sizable volume of published work by Professor Cassell, now a U.S. district court judge. I was not surprised that Cassell declined to label courts or decisions as either liberal or conservative. However, the media coverage regarding his confirmation in the U.S. Senate to a federal district court seat in Utah suggests that he was himself at least perceived as a "conservative."[20]

Ever the pragmatist, former Attorney General Gary Nelson shunned political labels altogether. As he saw it, the Rehnquist Court merely recognized and approved of—erroneously, in his opinion—the reality that several generations of lawyers and cops have lived with *Miranda,* and therefore saw no reason for a change.

Judge Schroeder, as usual, got right to the point. "Anything contrary to established practice was liberal," she stated flatly, implying that anything "in accordance" is, by default, "conservative."

Perhaps the answer lies in the simple logic that affirming a decision is, by definition, the more conservative measure. We should not forget, however, that perception matters at least as much as objective truth. Chief Justice Rehnquist, who earned master's degrees in political science from Stanford and Harvard, spent several years working in a Republican administration's justice department before then-President Nixon nominated him as a "conservative" candidate to the Supreme Court. In the estimation of many, his personal history alone justifies labeling his affirmation of *Miranda* in the *Dickerson* opinion as a conservative action.

Why Did the Court Switch from the Sixth Amendment in *Escobedo* to the Fifth Amendment in *Miranda*?

Craig Mehrens believes the Sixth Amendment promotes a very different legal principle than does the Fifth. "The Sixth guarantees the right to counsel, the Fifth the right to silence," he said. "The latter is useless unless you know about it and you will not know about it without the former."

Another defense lawyer, Chris Johns, gave a more pragmatic answer. "It is not practical to have lawyers involved in every custodial interrogation, so the right to remain silent will have to do until a lawyer shows up."

The man who represented Arizona in the *Miranda* case, Gary Nelson, was even more practical. "The Warren Court had not had much success changing police conduct with the Sixth Amendment. They hoped that the Fifth Amendment would get the attention of the cops."

Dean Paul Bender's scholarly yet brief answer essentially contradicted the question's premise. "It wasn't a change," he said. "The earlier cases involved rights *after* indictment, when the Sixth Amendment right had attached. The Sixth Amendment right doesn't attach at mere arrest and custody." Apparently, he meant to suggest that the Fifth Amendment *does* attach when the suspect is taken into custody.

To add to these authoritative answers, Thomas Jefferson believed that the Bill of Rights in total puts into the hands of the judiciary a check against any tyranny committed by the legislative or executive branches of the government. As such, the Sixth provides the rights and the Fifth provides the means for implementing those rights. Thus, both *Gideon* and *Escobedo* looked to the Sixth Amendment's provisions for justification: *Gideon* holding that the right to counsel requires state governments to provide attorneys for indigent criminal defendants, and *Escobedo* that the Sixth Amendment gives a suspect the right to counsel when being interrogated in police custody as well as during a trial. *Miranda* departed from the provisions of the Sixth because it was the Fifth Amendment that would require police officers to inform a suspect of his right to counsel *and* his right to invoke the privilege against self-incrimination.

It bears repetition here that the *Miranda* warnings do not include a warning that a suspect has "a privilege against self-incrimination." To require a suspect to invoke that privilege in order to halt a custodial interrogation makes no sense whatsoever. But requiring a police officer to tell a suspect that he has a "right to remain silent" makes the privilege against self-incrimination available in the most meaningful possible way.

Was It Police Methodology or Political Ideology?

Some see *Miranda*'s historic birth as a product of flawed police methodology. Others claim the Court was motivated by political ideology. Certainly, when one examines Chief Justice Warren's majority opinion, a distrust of police becomes evident:[21]

- In the early 1930s, extensive factual studies confirmed that police violence and the "third degree" flourished.
- Long after these studies, this Court confirmed that the police resort to physical brutality, beatings, hanging, and whippings—and to sustained and protracted questioning incommunicado in order to extort confessions.
- The 1961 Commission on Civil Rights found much evidence that some policemen still resort to physical violence to obtain confessions.
- The use of physical brutality and violence is not, unfortunately, relegated to the past or to any part of the country.
- The modern practice of in-custody interrogation is psychologically rather than physically oriented.
- Interrogation still takes place in privacy. Privacy results in secrecy. Secrecy results in a general lack of knowledge about what goes on in interrogation rooms.
- Police officers are told in their training manuals that the principal psychological factor contributing to a successful interrogation [a confession] is privacy.
- Police officers are taught to display an air of confidence in the suspect's guilt. . . . The guilt of the suspect is to be posited as a fact.
- The officers are instructed to minimize the moral seriousness of the offense, to cast blame on the victim or on society.
- These tactics are designed to put the suspect in a psychological state where his story is but an elaboration of what the police purport to know already—that he is guilty.
- The interrogators sometimes are instructed to induce a confession out of trickery.
- When the techniques described above prove unavailing, the texts recommend they be alternated with a show of some hostility.
- Unless a proper limitation upon custodial interrogation is achieved . . . there can be no assurance that practices of this nature will be eradicated in the foreseeable future.

Last but not least, the *Miranda* opinion notes: "Even without employing brutality, the third degree or the specific stratagems described above, the very fact of custodial interrogation exacts a heavy toll on individual liberty and trades on the weakness of individuals."[22]

As clear as the Warren Court's distrust appears, it is not clear that this mistrust is a product of the Court's political ideology, that "ideology" being extremely difficult to peg. Courts are cohorts of individual concepts, but Courts also change with new elections or appointments. The Warren Court was characterized by most as "liberal" because its most controversial opinions seemed more acceptable to liberals than conservatives—yet the justices serving under Chief Justice Warren's administrative leadership could never be pinned down as either liberal or conservative. Each was an outspoken, independent thinker who did not seem to cling to any defined political ideology. Each made the effort to decide each case on its specifics and merits.

Furthermore, the ancestries of Chief Justice Warren and Justices Brennan, Black, Clark, Douglas, Fortas, Harlan, Stewart, and White made their court emblematic of America as a melting pot of political and social mores. They were Catholic, Protestant, and Jewish and from every region in America. Their early lives were spent in the cities of the Northeast, the rural South, the emerging Southwest, the homespun Midwest, and the West Coast paradise. They were Republicans and Democrats who owed their high-bench seats to the presidential politics and merit selection tendencies of both parties. The youngest was forty-nine, the oldest eighty. Justice Black's tenure on the Court had spanned five presidents whereas Justice White was of a new generation and had joined the bench during the presidency of John F. Kennedy.

It is worth noting that *Miranda* was decided by a five-to-four majority of the Court. That split demands a look at the five who voted to reverse the convictions. Did Chief Justice Warren and Justices Brennan, Black, Douglas, and Fortas share a common set of concepts about human life or culture? Alternatively, did they have integrated assertions, theories, or aims that might constitute a sociopolitical program?

Liva Baker, author of one of the most comprehensive books written on the *Miranda* case, believes that the essential commonality among the majority of five was their socioeconomic status while growing up. "Once again," she writes of the *Miranda* vote, "the Court had divided along class lines, the justices born to families in humbler circumstances looking at the interrogation room through the eyes of the defendant, those born to families accustomed to privilege and influence looking at it through the eyes of the policeman."[23]

"Class lines," alone, however, do not seem to provide a full explanation. Families of modest means constitute over 80 percent of the American population. Liva Baker's alternative thesis was that the five were connected by way of their "humble origin." Were they in fact all of an origin that can be defined as humble?

Chief Justice Earl Warren was born in Los Angeles in 1891. Educated at the University of California, he was admitted to the bar in 1914 and served one term as attorney general of California and three terms as governor of California before becoming the Republican candidate for vice president in Thomas E. Dewey's 1948 campaign. President Eisenhower appointed Warren as the fourteenth chief justice in 1953, and he served on the Court until his retirement in 1969. No one ever described him as humble or as a man of modest means.

Justice Hugo Lafayette Black was born in Harlan, Alabama, in 1886. He was educated at the University of Alabama and served in the United States Senate. President Roosevelt appointed him to the Supreme Court in 1937. He certainly favored individual freedom and was best known for his literal interpretation of the First Amendment. He authored the *Gideon* opinion, dissented in *Griswold v. Connecticut,* and served on the Court until 1971. He can fairly be described as a man of the people and perhaps even as self-effacing.

Justice William Brennan served on the Court for thirty-four years under eight presidents. Born in Newark, New Jersey, and educated at the University of Pennsylvania and Harvard Law School, he rose to the rank of colonel in the U.S. Army. President Eisenhower appointed him to the Court in 1956. He was an intellectual and a fierce advocate against capital punishment.

Justice William O. Douglas hailed from Maine, Minnesota, and was educated at Whitman College and Columbia University. He taught law at Columbia and Yale before being appointed to the Court by President Roosevelt. He served on the Court for thirty-six years, longer than any other justice did. He was said to be liberal on social issues, balanced on economic issues, and conservative on international issues. His clerks thought him proud, not humble.

Justice Abe Fortas was born in Tennessee and educated at Yale. First in his class, he was appointed to the faculty at Yale upon his graduation. He served the government in various capacities from 1937 to 1946 and was a regular adviser to many national leaders, including President Johnson, who appointed him to the Supreme Court in 1965. Fortas may have had the shortest tenure on the Court with his resignation in 1969. His role in academics, government, and high-end law practice hardly qualified him as a man of the people.

Two of the five majority justices were Republicans, three were from large cities, and three attended prestigious private law schools. All did well financially and all were experienced in the ways of politics and business at the time they formed the majority in the *Miranda* decision. They were not consistently on the same side of controversial issues and often dissented in cases where one or the other wrote the majority decision.

At least from this limited look at their lives, one can not easily conclude that a common ideology drove their decisions. That moves the debate to the other question: Was the Court's stated mistrust of the police establishment well founded?

Dean Bender believes it was. He worked with several of the justices in the *Miranda* majority and believes that none had a pro-criminal or anti-law-enforcement agenda. Most had been prosecutors—none had been defense lawyers—and all were well read and conscientious about the factual predicates for every case they heard. John Dowd also believes that the Warren Court had "good reason" to distrust police.

Craig Mehrens, on the other hand, wondered if I was serious in even asking the question. He sees the empirical data on police abuse as "overwhelming" and wonders why 99 percent of all suspect statements to police are not recorded. *Miranda* makes police interrogators "knock and announce," he said, but it "overlooks the rummaging and pillaging that goes on after the first knock." Since *Miranda* requires warnings but approves of "waiving and chatting," the police warn, the suspects waive and then confess. Subsequent recanting pits the guilty man in the gray jumpsuit against the man in the blue uniform.

Chris Johns raised a different concern with regard to police mistrust: "intentional" violations of *Miranda*. Such violations occur when the police intentionally fail to warn a suspect of his rights and then secure a confession knowing that it is not admissible in the prosecutor's case. They never even try to get it admitted. *Miranda's* progeny allow such an unwarned statement to be admitted for impeachment in the defendant's case *if* he elects to take the stand. His clients may be trusting souls, but Chris Johns is not. "Hell," he says, "they don't want his confession; they just want to keep him off the witness stand. The defendant is afraid to take the stand because then his unwarned confession is admitted under the guise of impeachment."

Gary Nelson thinks that the majority in the *Miranda* case did distrust the police but rejects the notion that their decision was ideologically based. He wonders whether it was the product of "worst case scenarios." The Supreme Court naturally takes only those cases that seem to cry out for the intervention of the court of last resort. "That experience might make them see things a bit worse than they really are," he said.

I gave Detectives Cooley and Quaife the last word on this question because their combined experience on the streets and in the interrogation rooms clearly gives them a firsthand perspective. Both were career policemen who routinely used subtle and admittedly deceptive techniques when they honestly felt they had the right man in the interrogation room. Cooley had extracted the confession from Miranda and Quaife had tried to extract a confession from the man who allegedly murdered Miranda. Neither thought the Court's mistrust was misplaced and neither thought it was politically motivated.

When Did *Miranda* Become a "Constitutional" Decision?

The literal answer to this question is Monday, June 26, 2000, at about nine o'clock in the morning. That is the date and time that the *Dickerson* opinion was released by the clerk of the Court to the public. Writing for the majority of the Court, Chief Justice Rehnquist said in the first paragraph: "We hold that *Miranda*, being a *constitutional decision* of this Court, may not be in effect overruled by an Act of Congress, and we decline to overrule *Miranda* ourselves."[24] This is the first time that any court or commentator flatly said that *Miranda* was a "constitutional" decision. As noted earlier in this book, the decades-long debate about *Miranda* focused on whether the case was mandated by the Constitution or was merely a rule of law or a prophylactic solution to a criminal procedure problem. By such a forceful declaration, Chief Justice Rehnquist put the debate to bed.

Perhaps this unequivocal rhetoric was necessary to deal with the extremely unusual path Charles Thomas Dickerson took to get to the United States Supreme Court. The Fourth Circuit took it upon itself to support the extraction of a confession from Dickerson by applying a long-forgotten statute that no one in the lower court even mentioned. But, once the Fourth Circuit released its potentially explosive opinion, some of America's most prolific publishers of legal arcana wrote hopeful articles predicting the overturning of *Miranda*.

As it turned out, the doctrine of stare decisis,[25] combined with the declaration that *Miranda* was a "constitutional" decision, made some law review writers reconsider their prognosis. This time it was by a vote of seven to two, and this time, no one said that political ideology carried the day.

My question, *when* does an opinion become "constitutional," seemed profound in the asking but largely innocuous in the reply. Neither of my expert detectives knew the answer. My friends on the bench either did not know or wouldn't say. Most of the lawyer experts had not read the *Dickerson* opinion, much less the law review articles it generated.

Dean Bender provided the only real insight. "The law review writers who predicted *Miranda*'s demise were mostly whistling in the dark. Most of them apparently knew very little about the current Court or its sense of the value of precedent in constitutional litigation."

With *Dickerson,* the Fourth Circuit Court of Appeals did something quite unheard of in constitutional litigation. It raised, on its own motion, the thin promise of using Section 3501 of the federal code to overrule a thirty-four-year-old Supreme Court decision. It not only raised the issue when the government did not, but it also gave the government a ruling it never wanted. Bender called that "outrageous." He is joined by many others who share a similar opinion but were too kind to say so.

Anyone who predicted that the Supreme Court would affirm the Fourth Circuit and overrule *Miranda* must have thought that Justices Scalia and Thomas were the *only* members of the Supreme Court. Since *Dickerson* did not change anything in police administration or constitutional warnings, or advance any new application of either the Fifth or Sixth Amendments, it did not retard or advance the individual liberties of suspects, nor did it retard or advance the power of the police to investigate.

Chapter 9

THE FUTURE

Gideon's Legacy

While many Americans feared the consequences of the *Gideon* decision and shuddered at *Miranda*, both cases have stood the test of time as compelling contributions to legal and cultural history. And for good reason. Until *Gideon*, a suspect did not have a clearly defined constitutional right to counsel in state courts. Until *Miranda*, a suspect did not have a clearly announced constitutional right to counsel *prior* to questioning by state police. As Attorney General Robert F. Kennedy said of *Gideon*, "The whole course of American legal history has changed."[1] Criminal defense lawyers, like Craig Mehrens, were also profoundly impacted by *Gideon*. "I cannot imagine an accused facing the judicial system without an attorney," said Mehrens. "Even with counsel, the fight is always uphill: a Sisyphusian affair. In addition, although notoriety is usually spotlighted on retained counsel, I know that it is the public defenders of this country that do the heavy lifting—who protect every day the constitutional rights of so many people, for so little pay, for little thanks, and in such adverse conditions. Gideon's trumpet still plays for them. And what a clarion call it is."[2]

For those interested in learning the full story, I suggest Anthony Lewis's awarding-winning study, *Gideon's Trumpet*. Justice Arthur Goldberg called Lewis's account "as absorbing as the best fiction" and predicted the book would "take its place in the annals of distinguished literature about the law."[3] Harvard law professor Paul Freund called it a "warm, intimate, and moving account of a lowly man's case that became a Constitutional landmark."[4] The most distinguished trial lawyer of the time, Edward Bennett Williams, proclaimed it a "book which should be read by every American interested in the administration of justice."[5]

Dickerson's Legacy

Dickerson reaffirmed one of the most famous decisions in American jurisprudence. It also struck down a congressional act that was a thinly disguised political attempt to overrule *Miranda*. Section 3501 did not guarantee the same rights that *Miranda* did. Although its passage in 1968 was, at best, merely nettlesome—which explains why it was largely ignored—its application by a federal circuit court in 1999 made it a challenge to both the separation of powers doctrine and stare decisis within the judicial branch. The Fourth Circuit's sua sponte transfusion of life into a dead statute gave the United States Supreme Court little choice but to strike it down. In doing so, the Court effectively told the Fourth Circuit that *Miranda* was, for the last time, a "constitutional" decision, and the message radiated out from Richmond to the congressional salons across the Potomac.

However, *Dickerson* was not a loss for Congress any more than it was a win for the Supreme Court. In its ruling, the Supreme Court had revealed that the "constitutional" *Miranda* was quite different from the old prophylactic-rule *Miranda,* but their opinion was *obiter,* or "by the way," and *dictum,* that is, tangential to the Court's holding.

A final irony produced by *Dickerson* also merits noting: The cases that justified *Miranda*—thirty-four years' worth—had relied almost entirely on the thesis that it was merely a prophylactic rule and not a constitutional requirement. In striking down Section 3501, the Court made the *Miranda* warnings constitutional. That, of necessity, upgrades *Miranda*'s progeny to constitutional status as well.

However, *Dickerson* also reaffirmed the notion that a Fifth Amendment *Miranda* violation will not apply to the fruit-of-the-poisonous-tree doctrine in the same way that a Fourth Amendment violation will. Only the confession itself can be suppressed by a technical violation of *Miranda*. Absent coercion, any other evidence derived from the confession can still be admitted. Thus, for example, the money found on the bed in Charles Dickerson's apartment was admitted because the prosecution could show sufficient "purging" of the tainted confession.

In the final analysis, *Dickerson* is a first-class decision for two reasons: One, it eliminates the ambiguity that clouded *Miranda* for thirty-four years. Two, it had no adverse practical impact on law enforcement because prosecutors can still purge the taint of an unwarned confession.

The Evolution of *Miranda*

Suspects will continue to come to the attention of the police and show up, willingly or not, in America's interrogation rooms. Once there, knowing no better regardless of any warnings, many will incriminate themselves directly into jail, and the privilege against self-incrimination will be trumped by the certainty of self-incarceration. Although most police interrogators are more interested in doing the job than clearing the docket, some will want the confession badly enough to ignore the Supreme Court's rules about warning suspects. In time, those who make the rules and fund police protection will prevail, and the entire American police force will be comprised of professionals; everyone in the interrogation rooms will be college educated, highly trained, and respectful of America's right to remain silent.

To what extent that right should be respected when applied to non-Americans, however, is an entirely different question. The devastation wreaked upon New York City and, psychologically, on the rest of the nation on September 11, 2001, understandably created a need for changes in the ways we prosecute foreign criminals such as the al Qaeda terrorists. What we see as a constitutional right for ourselves may have to be withheld from those who would take all rights away by terror and violence rather than by the due process of the democratic system. We would do well to remember, however, that, if in the effort to solve the problems *Miranda* has posed to law enforcement, we return to the days when law enforcement was silent on the rights of suspects, be they homegrown simple thieves or foreign-trained terrorists, then the hate-America campaign will have obtained one of its objectives. These people seek to destroy democracy itself and replace it with a radically fundamental theocracy run by their God, not their government.

The good news: Technology will provide some solutions. In time, the same kinds of monitoring devices that have modernized courtrooms may become standard equipment in interrogation rooms. Video cameras have already revolutionized many aspects of police surveillance and arrest procedures, providing evidence that can often be more convincing than eyewitness accounts (isolated occurrences such as the Rodney King affair notwithstanding). Some day, video cameras in the interrogation room will provide evidence of similar verisimilitude and serve to monitor the conduct of suspect and interrogator.

On the other hand, open meeting laws, public records legislation, and "sunshine" budgets may motivate the executive branch to the point that confessions are not the mainstay of police work. Also, DNA testing, vastly improved fingerprinting, and crime scene forensics are already producing physical evidence that can supersede eyewitness testimony and even the suspect's own admissions of guilt. It likely will come to pass that the mapping of the human genome and further advancements in DNA testing will change both the methodology and the law of confessions. Such changes are probably already justified, as Barry Scheck, Peter Neufeld, and Jim Dwyer suggest in their startling book, *Actual Innocence*. Reporting on a large data-gathering endeavor called the "Innocence Project," Scheck et al. cite sixty-two criminal convictions that were later overturned based on posttrial examination and DNA testing. In each of these cases, the actual innocence of the convicted man is now accepted fact. In 24 percent of those cases, innocent men confessed to crimes they did not commit.[6] In every one of these cases, *Miranda* warnings were duly given and promptly waived. In every single case, "actually innocent" men confessed.

Regardless of whether or not improved methods for gathering evidence will serve to condemn or exonerate, people will, through some natural compulsion perhaps, continue to unburden their souls in the misguided belief that confessing to their crimes will set them free of the law just as surely as confessing their sins can clear their consciences. Such confessions, if they comply with the Fifth and Sixth Amendments, will be admissible and will remain a valuable tool for finding the truth, but they will not be the only evidence offered at trial. And unwarned confessions will more easily remain in the prosecutor's briefcase—unless and until the defendant tries, once again, to talk himself into jail by taking the witness stand.

Just as surely as more crimes are committed in the dark than in the light of day, suspects will continue to confess more often than they assert their right to remain silent. Crime will, of course, continue as well, just as surely as poverty and ignorance. The indigent miscreant, unable to defend himself or hire a lawyer experienced and talented enough to argue his case successfully, will have to rely on the public defender's office, which is too often understaffed and laboring under a crushing caseload. Prosecutors will push for the admission of statements and judges will follow the law, like it or not. And the courts will continue to process the poor and ignorant, like fast food to be consumed by the penal system.

For this reason alone, *Miranda* should stand. We would do well to remember that the Constitution, the Bill of Rights, all of the Amendments, and the thousands of cases defining and interpreting statutes and codes still do *not* recognize a *general* right of silence. Freedom of speech, religion, and assembly are generally recognized rights but silence is not. That is a good thing: The right to choose not to incriminate yourself while in police custody *should* be a much narrower right than, say, free speech or freedom of religion. It should apply only to a thankfully smaller group: those suspected of committing a crime.

The right to remain silent should never be rescinded in the interests of national security, either, or on the strength of any other reason. It is a fundamental value in American society, one that distinguishes us, for no other government recognizes the right of its citizens to tell government officials "no" and make them abide by it. Whether we choose silence or choose to confess is not really the point. *Knowing* that we can choose one or the other is the point. In upholding this right, we license our government to protect all of us, innocent and guilty alike. In knowing that we have the right to say "no," we will, as a nation, stand the test of time.

Thank you, *Miranda*.

ACKNOWLEDGMENTS

If Cicero was right and gratitude is the mother of all virtues, then my confession of appreciation will surely pave my path with rose petals. This book is about the instinct to confess tempered by the knowledge that you have the right to remain silent. I am deeply grateful for the unwarned admissions of hundreds of people not named in the book but whose thoughts and anecdotes are secreted in every chapter. There is no way to prioritize the generosity of my friends and colleagues or to apologize to those whose names are lost in my research files. That said I will start at the beginning.

The late John P. Frank was the first to encourage the writing of this book. His passing three years later was felt by thousands. My most fervent wish was to see him with this book in his generous hands. He was central to the decision itself, the debate surrounding it, and many of the books it spawned. This one would not have been written without his personal approval; his generous contributions of time, energy, and perspective; and his never-fading encouragement along the way. In many ways, this was John's book to write but he insisted that I could do it in a way he could not. I can only hope he was right.

A great many judges, lawyers, cops, citizens, and suspects gave great color to the big picture and shaded the gray-on-gray world of procedural rights and constitutional litigation. If the book seems authentic and grounded it is because they were insistent that it be so. They curbed my impatience, demanded forbearance, shared their insight, and warned of quicksand and bottomless quagmires of inconsistency. Thanks to Chuck Ares, Peter Baird, Paul Bender, Craig Blakey, Tom Brooks, Carroll Cooley, Bob Corcoran, John Dowd, Paul Fish, Craig Futterman, Joe Howe, Bob Jensen, Chris Johns, Mike Kimerer, Barry Kroll, Jon Kyl, Fred Martone, Tom Mauet, Craig Mehrens, Jim Moeller, Gary Nelson, Ron Quaife, Chuck Roush, Mary Schroeder, Mara Siegel, Barry Silverman, Bob Storrs, Tom Thinnes, Dick Treon, Larry Turoff, Paul Ulrich, and Warren Wolfson. I am especially grateful to Craig Mehrens for his patience as he labored to give me a soupçon of the subtlety inherent in the life of a criminal defense specialist.

Writers, editors, scriveners, and criticasters worked feverishly with me and, often, on me, to make this a good read, to instill plausibility, and to explain the disingenuous. They include Marianne Alcorn, Craig Blakey, Tom Davison, Paul Fish, Dave Knopp, Katie Kallsted, Mary Rodarte, Al Schroder, Dean Smith, Kathleen Stuart, and Susan Turngate. They helped me find my voice, overlooked my grammar, searched for active verbs, and deep-sixed many an inapt metaphor.

Three very talented people read every line and every page many times. They are the quid pro quo of the writing itself. Without Kathleen Gilbert's polished eye over every line and word, this manuscript would likely not have passed academic muster. Without Dan Thrapp's experienced and penetrating look at structure, form, content, style, and pace, this manuscript would read like your run-of-the-court appellate opinion. Special gratitude must go to Christine Szuter. Without her encouragement, even before the first word of text came into being, this book would have remained a fantasy.

While I have made every effort to accurately state both fact and law, this book is nevertheless laced with opinions about *Miranda*'s legal and social underpinnings and its cultural and political legacy. Except as specifically noted, the opinions and attitudes are entirely mine. Some readers might be puzzled as to what qualifications a civil trial lawyer has to write a book dealing with constitutional litigation and America's love-hate relationship with the Fifth Amendment and its expansive interpretation by the Warren Court. The answer is to remember the comic who wanted to play Hamlet. A great many lawyers are frustrated writers; as far as I know, I am the only writer extant who is a frustrated constitutional litigator.

To close on my opening note, without John Frank's good humor and eternal optimism about the project, I might still be researching and exercising my right to remain silent.

NOTES

Chapter 1. Crimes, Confessions, and Convictions

1. See *The Inside Story of Miranda—Arizona Peace Officer Standards and Training Board,* by Carroll Cooley and Joseph Farmer, 1980.

2. Ibid., 73.

3. City of Phoenix Police Department Form Number 2000-66-D, labeled, "Witness/Suspect Statement." Revised, November 1959.

4. The original Miranda confession was marked as "State's Exhibit 1" in his trial before Judge Yale McFate on June 20, 1963. See *State v. Miranda,* 98 Ariz. 18, 401 P.2nd 721 (1965) and Transcript of Record in the Supreme Court of the United States, October Term, 1965, No. 759, styled Ernesto A. Miranda, *Petitioner v. Arizona,* on *writ of certiorari* to the Supreme Court of the State of Arizona (certiorari granted November 22, 1965).

5. See Cooley and Farmer, *The Inside Story of Miranda,* 77.

6. Ibid., 78.

7. See opinion, *State v. Miranda,* 98 Ariz. 11, 401 P.2nd 716 (1965).

8. See letter of May 20, 1963, from Judge Henry S. Stevens to Drs. Rubinow and Kilgore. Both letters are filed as exhibits in the trial record. Maricopa County Superior Court Cause Nos. 41947 and 41948.

9. See psychiatric report of James M. Kilgore, M.D., May 28, 1963, Transcript of Record, p. 7, Supreme Court of the United States, October Term, 1965, Docket No. 759, Ernesto A. Miranda, *Petitioner v. Arizona,* on writ of certiorari to the Supreme Court of the State of Arizona.

10. See report of Dr. Rubinow, filed as exhibit in Maricopa County Superior Court Cause Nos. 41947 and 41948, May 1963.

11. Cooley's trial testimony is excerpted from the typed transcript prepared by the official court reporter, Velma Shanks, and filed with the Arizona Supreme Court as part of the appellate record in the case.

12. Miranda confessed to both crimes on March 13, 1963; however, he was asked to write down only the rape confession. Accordingly, the photo became Exhibit 1 in the robbery case and the handwritten confession became Exhibit 1 in the rape case.

13. See record on appeal, *State v. Miranda,* 98 Ariz. 11, 401 P.2nd 716 (1965).

14. See trial transcript, Maricopa County Superior Court, *State v. Miranda,* Cause No. 41947, June 18, 1963, 62.

15. Id., 64.

16. Id., 105.

17. Id., 109.

18. The sixty-page official transcript of Miranda's trial can be found in most public libraries in Phoenix, both of Arizona's law school libraries, the Maricopa County law library, and the archives of the Arizona Supreme Court. The copy used to extract the testimony in this book is contained in the official Transcript of Record in the United States Supreme Court, October Term, 1965, Docket No. 759, styled Ernesto A. Miranda, *Petitioner v. Arizona,* on writ of certiorari to the Supreme Court of the State of Arizona. All references to this transcript hereinafter made will be to the page number assigned in the Transcript of Record (hereinafter TR-Docket 759).

19. TR-Docket 759, 33.

20. TR-Docket 759, 36.

21. TR-Docket 759, 38.

22. TR-Docket 759, 41.

23. TR-Docket 759, 42.

24. TR-Docket 759, 45.

25. TR-Docket 759, 50.

26. TR-Docket 759, 51.

27. TR-Docket 759, 58.

28. TR-Docket 759, 59.

29. TR-Docket 759, 63.

30. The New Jersey lower court opinion and judgment are not reported. See *State of New Jersey v. Johnson and Cassidy,* 43 N.J. 572, 206 A.2nd 737 (1965).

31. See *State v. Johnson,* 31 N.J. 489, 158 A.2nd 11 (1960).

32. See *People v. Vignera,* 21 App. Div.2nd 752, 252 NYS2nd 19 (1964), aff'd, 15 NYS2nd 970, 207 N.E.2nd 527, as amended, 16 NY2nd 614, 209 NE2nd 110 (1965).

33. See *Vignera v. Wilkens,* Civ. 9901 (D.C.W.D.N.Y. December 31, 1961).

34. U.S. 478 (1964).

35. *People v. Dorado,* 62 Cal.2nd 338, 398 P.2nd 361, cert denied, 381 U.S. 937 (1965).

36. See *People v. Stewart,* 62 Cal.2nd 571, 400 P.2nd 97 (1964).

37. See *Westover v. U.S.,* 342 F.2nd 684 (1965).

38. Id., 686.

Chapter 2. The Law

1. For a more detailed discussion of the political climate in the early sixties and the impact of the Warren Court's criminal procedure decisions, see Liva Baker's excellent treatment of the subject in chapters 3, 4, and 5 of her book—*Miranda: Crime, Law and Politics,* Atheneum, NY, 1983.

2. See Baker, *Miranda,* 40.

3. Ibid.

4. Ibid., 200.

5. See Richard J. Medalie, *From Escobedo to Miranda.*

6. See Baker, *Miranda,* 221.

7. The Constitution was drafted in 1787. The Bill of Rights was added in 1789 and ratified in 1791.

8. *Barron v. The Mayor and City Council of Baltimore,* 7 Pet. 243, 8 L.Ed. 672 (1873).

9. See, generally, *Constitutional Law,* by Noel Dowling and Gerald Gunther, 7th ed., NY: The Foundation Press, Inc., 1965.

10. *Powell v. Alabama,* 287 U.S. 45 (1932). The case actually involved four prisoners: Ozie Powell, Willie Roberson, Andy Wright, and Olen Montgomery. They were consolidated under case Nos. 98, 99, and 100. All three cases were argued on October 10, 1932, and decided on November 7, 1932.

11. The Alabama trial judge appointed all the members of the local bar for the purpose of arraigning the defendants and claimed that all of them would continue to help the defendants if no counsel appeared at the trial.

12. See *Powell v. Alabama,* 287 U.S. 45 (1932).

13. U.S. 455 (1942).

14. Gideon's remand to the trial court in Florida, with the assistance of appointed counsel, resulted in his acquittal. See Dowling and Gunther, *Constitutional Law,* 768.

15. Abe Fortas graduated first in his class from Yale Law School in 1933. He earned a Phi Beta Kappa key, was editor-in-chief of the *Yale Law Journal,* and became a protégé of then-Professor William O. Douglas. He eventually became a close friend of and advisor to Lyndon Johnson.

16. See Lewis, *Gideon's Trumpet,* 64.

17. U.S. 278 (1935).

18. Chief Justice Hughes, appointed by President Hoover, served from February 1930 to June 1941.

19. *Lisbena v. California,* 314 U.S. 219 (1941).

20. *Ashcraft v. Tennessee,* 322 U.S. 143 (1944).

21. *Watts v. Indiana,* 338 U.S. 49 (1949).

22. *Haley v. Ohio,* 332 U.S. 596 (1984).

23. See *Payne v. Arkansas,* 356 U.S. 560 (1958).

24. See *Thomas v. Arizona,* 356 U.S. 390 (1958).

25. Justice Whittaker, speaking for the Court, said: "The use in a state criminal trial of a defendant's confession obtained by coercion—whether physical or mental—is forbidden by the Fourteenth Amendment."

26. Justice Clark, speaking for the court, said: "Deplorable as these ropings are to the spirit of a civilized administration of justice, the undisputed facts before us do not show that petitioner's oral statement was a product of fear engendered by them. . . . His statement appears to be the spontaneous exclamation of a guilty conscience."

27. U.S. 368 (1964).

28. There were three dissenting opinions: one by Justice Black, joined in part by Justice Clark; one by Justice Clark; and one by Justice Harlan, joined by Justices Clark and Stewart. Justice Black's dissent stated that the ruling affected at least fifteen states.

29. *Twining v. New Jersey,* 211 U.S. 78 (1908).

30. *U.S. v. Murdock,* 284 U.S. 141 (1931).

31. *Feldman v. U.S.,* 322 U.S. 487 (1944).

32. *Adamson v. U.S.,* 332 U.S. 46 (1947).

33. *Knapp v. Schweitzer,* 357 U.S. 371 (1958).

34. *Malloy* may be best remembered for its tangential discussion of the view of many, but not all, of the justices that the Fourteenth Amendment incorporates the rights enumerated in the first eight amendments. Justice Brennan's majority opinion notes that those views had "not thus far prevailed."

35. Writing for the majority, Justice Goldberg said: ". . . the constitutional privilege against self-incrimination protects a state witness against incrimination under federal as well as state law and a federal witness against incrimination under state as well as federal law."

36. U.S. 591 (1896). *Walker* involved an investigation of Interstate Commerce Act violations.

37. U.S. 422 (1956).

38. Justice Black joined the dissent.

39. U.S. 478 (1964).

40. See *Time, the Weekly News Magazine,* April 29, 1966, p. 54.

41. DiGerlando ultimately served a long prison sentence for the murder of Manuel Valtierra.

42. See 378 U.S. 478.

43. Id.

44. The reversal resulted in Escobedo's release from the Statesville Penitentiary, where he had spent four and one-half years of his twenty-year sentence. He was not recharged or retried for the crime although his friend and accuser, Benny DiGerlando, did serve a long term for shooting Escobedo's brother-in-law.

45. Ironically, Escobedo was also the only one of the three who completely avoided the consequences of the crime, which was the subject of his true but inadmissible confession. After the Supreme Court remanded his case to the Illinois state courts, he was never prosecuted for the murder of his brother-in-law. Escobedo's case was largely based on conspiracy law, as he aided and abetted the actual "shooter" in the case. The shooter was subsequently convicted of the murder and was sentenced to life in prison.

46. Cal. Rptr. 169, 398 P.2nd 361 (California Supreme Court, 1965).

47. One of the photos contained a caption that read, "To balance public safety against private rights." See page 52.

48. The photo had a caption that read, "With equal and exact justice for all." See page 53.

49. See page 54.

50. The photo had a caption that read, "Almost at once forced to clarify." See page 57.

51. The photo had a caption that read, "Posing the retroactivity riddle." See page 58.

52. Barry Kroll was twenty-nine years old at the time of his famous appearance in the United States Supreme Court. He had successfully argued many appeals before Escobedo, but all were in the Military Court of Appeals as a JAG lawyer. Somewhat ironically, Kroll was the successful lawyer in *U.S. v. Kanter* two years earlier. He argued in *Kanter* that a confession was admissible in evidence because the military suspect had not asked for a lawyer and thus there was no reason to provide one for him at the custodial stage.

53. See *Time*, April 29, 1966, p. 60.

54. Ibid., 57.

55. Ibid., 58.

56. Mr. Fortas was appointed to the U.S. Supreme Court on July 28, 1964, by President Lyndon Johnson. He was confirmed by the U.S. Senate and took his seat on the Court in October 1964.

57. The Dyer Act, which made auto theft a federal crime, was enacted by Congress on October 29, 1919. See Chapter 89, 41 Stat. 324.

58. Id., 721.

59. See *State of Arizona v. Miranda*, 98 Ariz. 11, 401 P.2nd 716 (the robbery case) and 98 Ariz. 18, 401 P.2nd 721 (the rape case), both decided on April 22, 1965.

60. See 98 Ariz. 79.

61. See *Massiah*, 377 U.S. 201 and *Escobedo*, 378 U.S. 478, both decided in 1964.

62. "Lewis and Roca" is used throughout this book for ease of reference. In the interests of historical accuracy, the full name of the firm at the time of the filing of the petition for a writ of certiorari in the *Miranda* case was "Lewis, Roca, Scoville, Beauchamp, and Linton." The firm name was modified several times over the years until the "permanent" name of Lewis and Roca was adopted.

63. Corcoran's nonpaid position as counsel to the Arizona Civil Liberties Union began in 1964, when he left his job as a prosecutor with the Maricopa County Attorney's office to form Dushoff, Sacks, and Corcoran. In his July 12, 1979, letter to Ms. Liva Baker (author of *Miranda: Crime, Law and Politics*, NY: Atheneum, 1983) he explained that he took the ACLU position because many people were not represented in criminal cases in Arizona at the time. "Some of them had substantial constitutional and legal claims for redress. My main interest was to secure attorneys for as many people as I could. This is how I got involved in the Miranda case."

64. See *California v. Dorado*, 40 Cal. Rptr. 264, 394 P.2nd 952 (1965).

65. All of Corcoran's correspondence to Miranda, his lawyers, and others has been provided to the author as a courtesy and an aid in historical accuracy. His two-page letter of June 15, 1965, contains his handwritten research notes on the constitutional issues involved in the case, seven months before the petition for certiorari was accepted by the United States Supreme Court.

66. An LL.D is an earned doctorate in law degree and is academically equivalent to a Ph.D.

67. See Corcoran's letter of July 12, 1979, to Liva Baker.

68. See *Johnson v. Zerbst*, 304 U.S. 458 (1938).

69. See *Mallory v. U.S.*, 354 U.S. 449 (1957).

70. See Nelson's Brief for Respondent, February 1966, 2–3.

71. See Mr. Hirshowitz's Amici Curiae brief, February 21, 1966, 4.

72. Id., 4.

73. Case No. 584 (*California v. Stewart*) and Case No. 759 (*Miranda v. U.S.*) raised questions pertaining to the assistance of counsel, and the absence, or adequacy, of the warnings given. Case No. 760 (*Vignera v. New York*) involved a twenty-four-hour period of detention prior to arraignment. Case No. 761 (*Westover v. United States*) was a federal court case raising statutory and supervisory issues as well as constitutional

factors. Case No. 762 (*Johnson and Cassidy v. New Jersey*) raised questions pertaining to self-incrimination through comment to the jury, severance, and improper prosecution argument and summation.

74. *Davis v. North Carolina*, 339 F.2nd 770 (4th Cir. 1965), transferred as U.S. Supreme Court Docket No. 815, was slotted for oral argument later in the October 1996 term.

75. Mr. Hirshowitz, First Assistant Attorney General of the State of New York, is believed to be the lead author of the brief filed by Louis J. Lefkowitz, New York Attorney General. This brief was filed in all five of the combined cases on behalf of "The State of New York, joined by the states of Arizona, Colorado, Delaware, Florida, Georgia, Idaho, Illinois, Kansas, Kentucky, Louisiana, Maine, Maryland, Missouri, Montana, Nebraska, North Carolina, North Dakota, Oregon, Pennsylvania, Rhode Island, South Carolina, Texas, Virginia, Washington, West Virginia and Wyoming, The Commonwealth of Puerto Rico, and the Territory of the Virgin Islands." Mr. Telford Taylor was Special Counsel to the New York Attorney General and likely had a lead role in the crafting of the brief. It was filed with the United States Supreme Court on February 21, 1966.

76. Ibid., 2, where the "interest of the Amici" is said to be: "The petitions for certiorari in the above cases raise such questions as whether criminal suspects must be advised, prior to arraignment, of a right to be silent, or a right to have counsel; whether counsel must be furnished to suspects upon request, or even in the absence of request; whether pre-arraignment standards of an accused taken in the absence of counsel must be excluded at trial; and whether newly-established constitutional rules limiting the admissibility of statements made by a defendant prior to his arraignment must be applied retroactively."

77. *Watts v. Indiana*, 338 U.S. 49, 59 (1949).

78. See Mr. Hirshowitz's Amici Curiae brief, February 21, 1966, 30.

79. See *Escobedo*, 378 U.S. 492 (1965).

80. See *People v. Dorado*, 398 P.2nd 361 (California 1965); *People v. Neely*, 398 P.2nd 482 (Oregon, 1965); *State v. Dufour*, 206 A.2nd 82 (Rhode Island, 1965). The Pennsylvania Supreme Court said in *Commonwealth v. Negi*, 213 A.2nd 670 (1965), that it would follow the ruling in the Third Circuit Court of Appeals in United States ex rel Russo New Jersey, 351 F.2nd 429 (1965). In addition, Texas provided by statute (Tex. Code Cr. Proc. Art. 727) that a defendant's confession is excludable where he had not been previously warned of his right to remain silent.

81. See Bator and Vorenberg, "Arrest, Detention, Interrogation and the Right to Counsel; Basic Problems and Possible Legislative Solutions," 66 *Col. L. Rev.* 62, 71–76 (1966).

82. Rights ought to be stated in the affirmative as opposed to obligations, which are usually stated in the negative.

83. See William J. Schafer, *Confessions and Statements*.

84. William J. Schafer III, A.B., LL.B., served as an assistant U.S. district attorney in Alaska and as a trial attorney with the U.S. Dept. of Justice in Washington, D.C., before his election as county attorney in Pima County, Arizona.

85. See William J. Schafer, *Confessions and Statements*, 35–36.

86. See Otis H. Stephens Jr., *The Supreme Court and Confessions of Guilt*, 64.

Chapter 3. The Oral Arguments

1. Thomas Jefferson, in his letter to James Madison of July 31, 1788.

2. Alexander Hamilton, in his speech to the United States Senate in August of 1788.

3. See *American Federation of Labor v. American Sash & Door Co.*, 355 U.S. 538, 557 (1949).

4. The Supreme Court consists of the chief justice of the United States and such number of associate justices as may be fixed by Congress. The number of associate justices is currently fixed at eight (28 U.S.C., §1). Power to nominate the justices is vested in the president of the United States, and appointments are made with the advice and consent of the Senate. Article 3, §1 of the Constitution further provides that "[t]he Judges, both of the supreme and inferior Courts, shall hold their Offices during good Behaviour, and shall, at stated Times, receive for their Services, a Compensation, which shall not be diminished during their Continuance in Office." "The president, vice president, and all civil officers of the United States, shall be removed from office on impeachment for, and conviction of, treason, bribery, or other high crimes and misdemeanors (U.S. Constitution, art. 2, §4.)." Technically, impeachment is the Senate's quasicriminal proceeding instituted to remove a public officer, not the actual act of removal. Most references to impeachment, however, encompass the entire process, beginning with the House's impeachment inquiry. The term will be used in that broader sense here. By design, impeachment is a complex series of steps and procedures undertaken by the legislature. The process roughly resembles a grand jury inquest, conducted by the House, followed by a full-blown trial, conducted by the Senate, with the chief justice presiding. Impeachment is not directed exclusively at presidents. The constitutional language, "all civil officers," includes such positions as federal judgeships. The legislature, however, provides a slightly more streamlined process for lower offices by delegating much of it to committees. See *Nixon v. U.S.*, 506 U.S. 224 (1993), involving the removal of a federal judge. Presidential impeachments involve the full, public participation of both branches of Congress.

5. See handout: "The Supreme Court of the United States—The Court Building," Supreme Court Historical Society.

6. The lead advocates and their cases are: *Miranda*—John P. Frank, John J. Flynn, and Gary K. Nelson; *Vignera*—Victor M. Earle III and William I. Siegel; *Westover*—F. Conger Fawcett and Solicitor General Thurgood Marshall; *Johnson*—Stanford Shmukler, M. Gene Haeberle, and Norman Heine; *Stewart*—Gordon Ringer and William A. Norris; *Amicus Curiae*—General Telford Taylor, Duane R. Nedrud, Professors Anthony G. Amsterdam and Paul J. Mishkin.

7. The majority opinion in *Miranda* was authored by Chief Justice Warren and joined by Justices Black, Brennan, Douglas, and Fortas. Dissenting opinions in *Miranda* were filed by Justices Clark, Harlan, Stewart, and White. The majority opinion in *Johnson* was authored by Chief Justice Warren. Mr. Justice Clark filed a concurring opinion in which Justices Harlan, Stewart, and White joined. Justice Black wrote a dissenting opinion.

8. Mr. Nedrud's argument was an apparent effort to focus the Court on the rights of the people as opposed to the rights of a single individual. The majority opinion of the

Court focused on the rights of all people who might be accused of a crime. The court of public opinion was first molded by the *Saturday Evening Post*. The editors posed the issue in the title of the lead story two weeks after the Court's opinion was handed down as "The Court v the Cops." See the *Saturday Evening Post,* June 30, 1966, 66.

9. *McNabb v. U.S.,* 318 U.S. 332 (1943).

10. *Mallory v. U.S.,* 354 U.S. 449 (1957).

Chapter 4. The Aftermath

1. The *Miranda* opinion handed down on June 13, 1966, includes two sentences on page 442 that contain an astounding 180 words: "The maxim 'Nemo tenetur seipsum accusare' had its origin in a protest against the inquisitorial and manifestly unjust methods of interrogating accused persons, which [have] long obtained in the continental system, and, until the expulsion of the Stuarts from the British throne in 1688, and the erection of additional barriers for the protection of the people against the exercise of arbitrary power, [were] not uncommon even in England. While the admissions or confessions of the prisoner, when voluntarily and freely made, have always ranked high in the scale of incriminating evidence, if an accused person be asked to explain his apparent connection with a crime under investigation, the ease with which the questions put him may assume an inquisitorial character, the temptation to press the witness unduly, to browbeat him if he be timid or reluctant, to push him into a corner, and to entrap him with fatal contradictions, which is so painfully evident in many of the earlier state trials, notably in those of Sir Nicholas Throckmorton, and Udal, the Puritan minister, made the system so odious as to give rise to a demand for total abolition" (*Brown v. Walker,* 161 U.S. 591 [1896]).

2. "The cases before us raise questions which go to the roots of our concept of American criminal jurisprudence" (384 U.S. 439).

3. See 384 U.S., footnote 27 at page 459.

4. See 384 U.S., footnote 4 at page 444.

5. "The quality of a nation's civilization can be largely measured by the methods it uses in the enforcement of its criminal law." See Opinion at page 480, citing one of America's most distinguished jurists (Schaefer, "Federalism and State Criminal Procedure" 70 *Harv. L. Rev.* 1, 26 [1956]).

6. See *Miranda* Opinion at page 492.

7. See Baker, *Miranda,* 166.

8. See *Miranda* Opinion at page 467.

9. Four cases were joined in a single written opinion. They were Docket 759 (*Miranda v. Arizona*); Docket 760 (*Vignera v. New York*); Docket 761 (*Westover v. United States*); and Docket 584 (*California v. Stewart*). The opinion of the Court, authored by Chief Justice Warren, is reported at 384 U.S. 436, 86 S.Ct. 1062, 16 L. Ed. 694, 1966 U.S. Lexis 2817, 10 A.L.R.3rd 974. The opinion was released on June 13, 1966.

10. See Medalie, *From Escobedo to Miranda,* 36.

11. See Opinion at page 495 (Schaefer, "Federalism and State Criminal Procedure" 70 *Harv. L. Rev.* 1, 26 [1956]).

12. Ibid.

13. See Medalie, *From Escobedo to Miranda*, 41.

14. Stewart also claimed that he confessed only because the police were holding his ailing wife in a cell and had threatened to hold her there until he confessed. The Supreme Court did not reach that allegation. See *Miranda* Opinion at page 798.

15. *Linkletter v. Walker*, 381 U.S. 618 (1965) and *Tehan v. Shott*, 382 U.S. 406 (1966).

16. See *Johnson and Cassidy v. New Jersey*, 384 U.S. 719, 726.

17. See Medalie, *From Escobedo to Miranda*, 39.

18. See Medalie, *From Escobedo to Miranda*, xix.

19. See *Ownbey v. Morgan*, 256 U.S. 94 (1921).

20. See *Coler v. Corn Exchange Bank*, 250 N.Y. 136, 164 N.E. 882 (1928).

21. See *Palko v. Connecticut*, 302 U.S. 319 (1937).

22. See *Griswold v. Connecticut*, 381 U.S. 484 (1965).

23. Id.

24. See *Roe v. Wade*, 410 U.S. 113 (1973). Roe is barely noteworthy in the *Miranda* context because (a) it came down after *Miranda* and (b) it does not cite *Miranda* in the history of cases that can be said to create "new" rights because they are part of the penumbra, letter, spirit, or emanations of one or more of the specific rights explicit in the first fourteen amendments to the Constitution.

25. See *NAACP v. Alabama*, 357 U.S. 357 (1958), in which the Court protected the freedom to associate and privacy in one's associations. The Court observed that the freedom of association was a "peripheral" First Amendment right. In other words, the First Amendment has a penumbra where privacy is protected from governmental intrusion.

26. Id., 462.

27. See the Hon. Nathan R. Sobel, *The New Confession Standards*. Judge Sobel's 153-page book is an excellent primer on the legal underpinnings of *Miranda*, running from *McNabb* to *Massiah* to *Escobedo* to *Denno*. His factual dissection is exquisitely precise.

28. Ibid.

29. See 384 U.S. 467–69.

30. Id.

31. Id.

32. Id.

33. Id.

34. 384 U.S. 469.

35. Id.

36. See 384 U.S. 469–70.

37. Id.

38. Id.

39. See 384 U.S. 470.

40. Id., 471.

41. Id., 472.

42. Id.

43. See *Johnson v. Zerbst*, 304 U.S. 458 (1938).

44. See 384 U.S. 475.

45. Id.

46. Id., 476.

47. See *People v. Gunner*, 15 N.Y.2nd 266 (1965).

48. See *People v. Price*, 63 Cal.2nd 370.

49. See *People v. Cotter*, 63 Cal.2nd 386.

50. See *Stowers v. U.S.*, 351 F.2nd 301.

51. See *Evalt v. U.S.*, 359 F.2nd 534.

52. See 308 U.S. 341.

53. See *State of Arizona v. Miranda*, 104 Ariz. 174, 450 P.2nd 364 (1969).

54. See *State of Arizona v. Miranda*, 109 Ariz. 337, 509 P.2nd 607 (1973).

55. Bob Storrs, a 1967 graduate of the University of Arizona College of Law, was a highly regarded young prosecutor at the time of Miranda's retrial in 1971. His recollections of the trial and Miranda were relayed to the author in an interview in the spring of 2002 in Phoenix, Arizona.

56. Tom Thinnes, a 1965 graduate of the University of Arizona College of Law, was an associate in John Flynn's firm at the time of the retrial of Miranda's robbery case. Although Flynn was present at the beginning of the trial and made the opening statement to the jury, Thinnes did the bulk of the defense work, including the witness examinations and the final argument to the jury. His recollections of the trial were relayed to the author in an interview in the spring of 2002 in Phoenix, Arizona.

57. See *Arizona v. Miranda*, 109 Ariz. 337, 509 P.2nd 607 (1973).

58. See Baker, *Miranda*, 192.

59. See Appellant's Opening Brief, *State of Arizona v. Miranda*, Supreme Court of Arizona Case No. 1802, by John P. Frank, 4.

60. See 104 Ariz. 183.

61. Id.

62. See Phoenix Police Departmental Report DR#76-011123, supplement dated 2-1-76, by Detective Quaife, pp. 6–8.

63. Officer Miller called the station at 1:30 A.M. on 2-1-76. Officer Miller, accompanied by Officer Jere Miller and Officer G. Maxwell, took Esquelle Moreno into custody and transported him to the Phoenix Police Station Interrogation Room Number Two to be interviewed by Detective Quaife.

64. DR#76-011123, supplement dated 2-1-76, by Detective Quaife, p. 7.

65. DR#76-011123, supplement dated 2-1-76, by Detective Quaife, p. 7. Signed by Detective Quaife and Detective Marcus Aurelius (Badge # 1653).

66. DR#76-011123, supplement dated 2-1-76, by Detective Quaife, p. 8.

67. See Deputy County Attorney Rizer's signed report, dated 2-2-76. Mr. Rizer asked Detective Quaife to clear up the discrepancies in the witness statements before a formal complaint would be filed by his office.

68. DR#76-011123, supplement dated 2-3-76, by Detective Quaife, p. 1.

69. DR#76-011123, supplement dated 2-3-76, by Detective Quaife, p. 3.

70. DR#76-011123, supplement dated 2-1-76, by Detective Lash, p. 1.

71. DR#76-011123, supplement dated 2-1-76, by Detective Lash, p. 2.

72. Detective Quaife's memory of Fernando Zamura Rodriguez is quite distinct. In his interview with the author on February 6, 2002, he accurately relayed the details

notwithstanding the thirty-five-year gap since he had last seen his detailed departmental report. Quaife candidly noted that he knew that his suspect was involved in the killing of the famous Ernesto Miranda but that the irony of giving Rodriguez his *Miranda* warnings did not occur to him at the time. Quaife also noted the linguistic irony of a good cop named "Bueno" reading *Miranda* warnings to the suspect in Miranda's murder (author's interview with Ron Quaife on 2/6/02 and Carroll Cooley on 1/25/02).

73. DR#76-011123, supplement dated 2-3-76, by Detective Quaife, p. 4.

74. As confirmed in the interviews with Detective Quaife and Captain Cooley by the author in January and February of 2002.

Chapter 5. The Ongoing Debate

1. See *Crooker v. California*, 357 U.S. 433, 441. The full quote from this notable decision is: "Refusal by state authorities of the request to contact counsel necessarily would then be an absolute bar to conviction. On the other hand, where an event has occurred while the accused was without his counsel which fairly promises to adversely affect his chances, the doctrine suggested by petitioner would have a lesser but still devastating effect on enforcement of criminal law, for it would effectively preclude police questioning—fair as well as unfair—until the accused was afforded opportunity to call his attorney. Due process, a concept 'less' rigid and more fluid than those envisaged in other specific and particular provisions of the Bill of Rights." *Betts v. Brady*, 316 U.S. 455, 462 (1942) demands no such rule.

2. Mr. Meese was a graduate of the University of California at Berkeley's Boalt Hall College of Law. After service as a prosecutor, he became Governor Ronald Reagan's chief of staff. When Governor Reagan became President Reagan, he made Meese his attorney general.

3. See *U.S. News and World Report*'s interview with Edwin Meese, October 14, 1985.

4. Baird is a prominent member of the Arizona bar and a senior partner in the law firm (Lewis and Roca) that once included John Flynn, Michael Kimerer, and Jim Moeller. All of them worked under the tutelage of the legendary John P. Frank, the architect of the *Miranda* case in the U.S. Supreme Court. Baird's published works on *Miranda* include: "Miranda Memories," *ABA Litigation Magazine*, Vol. 16, No. 2 (winter 1990); "Miranda Was the Right Decision," *The Wall Street Journal*, June 13, 1991, A15; "The Confessions of Ernesto Arturo Miranda," *Arizona Attorney*, October 1991, 20; "You Have the Right to Remain Silent," *Phoenix Magazine*, June 1996, 38.

5. See *The Wall Street Journal*, June 13, 1991, A15, paragraph 5.

6. See *Harris v. New York*, 401 U.S. 222 (1971).

7. See *Newsweek*, July 1988.

8. See, for example, the Amici Curiae briefs filed in *Dickerson v. United States*, where the law enforcement community largely supported the retention of *Miranda*.

9. See FINDLAW.COM, Monday, May 13, 2002, By Thomas Ferraro (Washington, Reuters).

10. 90 *Northwestern Univ. Law Rev.* 387 (1996).

11. See 90 *Northwestern Univ. Law Rev.* 387, p. 498.

12. Welsh S. White, *Miranda's Waning Protections*.

13. Ibid., 8.

14. See *Miranda v. Arizona*, 384 U.S. 436, dissent by J. Harlan at page 517.

15. See *The Miranda Debate: Law, Justice, and Policing*, edited by Richard A. Leo and George C. Thomas III, essay No. 19: "Remembering the Old World of Criminal Procedure: A Reply to Professor Grano," 268.

16. Edited by Richard A. Leo, assistant professor of criminology at the University of California at Irvine and George C. Thomas III, professor of law at Rutgers University, this comprehensive book was published by Northeastern University Press, Boston, MA, in 1998.

17. Ibid., 315.

18. Mr. Frank's extended views on this subject were relayed to the author in a series of personal interviews in the spring of 2001 in his office suite at Lewis and Roca, in Phoenix.

Chapter 6. The *Dickerson* Case

1. Dickerson testified at his suppression hearing that he did not feel he had a choice about whether to accompany the agents to the field office. See *Dickerson v. USA*, 166 F.3rd 667, 676 (4th Cir. 1999).

2. See petitioner's brief, U.S. Supreme Court Case No. 99-5525, styled Charles Thomas Dickerson, Petitioner, v. United States of America, Respondent, on writ of certiorari to the United States Court of Appeals for the Fourth Circuit, footnote 3.

3. See *United States v. Dickerson*, 166 F.3rd 667, 677 (4th Cir. 1999).

4. See *Dickerson v. USA*, 166 F.3rd 667, 680 (4th Cir. 1999).

5. See *Dickerson v. USA*, 166 F.3rd 667, 679 (4th Cir. 1999).

6. Id., footnotes 5 and 6.

7. See *Dickerson v. USA*, 166 F.3rd 667, 670 (4th Cir. 1999).

8. See petitioner's brief, U.S. Supreme Court Case No. 99-5525, supra at page 11, styled Charles Thomas Dickerson, Petitioner, v. United States of America, Respondent, on writ of certiorari to the United States Court of Appeals for the Fourth Circuit.

9. See, generally, *Davis v. United States*, 512 U.S. 452, 457 (1994).

10. Id., 463–64 (J. Scalia, concurring, noting that the "provision has been studiously avoided by every Administration . . . since its inception 25 years ago.")

11. See *Dickerson v. USA*, 166 F.3rd 667, 672 (4th Cir. 1999).

12. See, generally, *Davis v. United States*, 512 U.S. 452, 457 (1994).

13. See *Dickerson v. USA*, 166 F.3rd 667, 673 (4th Cir. 1999)

14. See *Dickerson v. USA*, 166 F.3rd 667, 671, footnote 1 (4th Cir. 1999).

15. See Wechsler, "Toward Neutral Principles of Constitutional Law," 73 *Harv. L. Rev.* 1, 7, 9, and "Selected Essays 1938–62," 463, 468 (1963).

16. See Bickel's foreword, "The Passive Virtues," 75 *Harv. L. Rev.* 40 (1963).

17. John P. Frank's hopes for *Miranda* were expressed in his January 4, 2000, letter to Richard Orton. In one of his several interviews with the author, Mr. Frank offered the letter as reflective of his lifetime interest in constitutional litigation as well his concerns for the future of *Miranda*, the right to counsel, and the political realities of changing standards.

18. Professor Dripps holds the James A. Levee Professorship in Criminal Procedure

at the University of Minnesota Law School. His comments are more fully set forth in his lengthy law review article entitled "Is Miranda Caselaw Really Inconsistent? A Proposed Fifth Amendment Synthesis," 17 *Const. Commentary* 19, spring 2000.

19. Professor Blaine's article is entitled "Miranda under Fire." See 10 *Seton Hall Constitutional L. Journ.* 1007 (summer 2000).

20. See *United States v Dickerson*, 166 F.3rd 667, 686–87 (4th Cir. 1999) (concluding, "Congress enacted 3501 with the express purpose of returning to the pre-Miranda case-by-case determination of whether a confession was voluntary).

21. See United States Official Transcript, *Dickerson v. United States*, No. 95-5525, Washington, D.C., at page 1. Hereinafter denoted "*Dickerson* OA-TR at___." A written version of this transcript is available at www.soc.umn.edu/.

22. *Dickerson* OA-TR at 1.

23. Justice Scalia was presumably referring to a civil action under 18 USCA 1983.

24. *Dickerson* OA-TR at 7.

25. Title VII of the Civil Rights Act of 1964 (42 U.S.C. §2000e et seq.) prohibits covered employers from discriminating based on race, color, sex, religion, or national origin.

26. *Marbury v. Madison,* 5 U.S. 137, 1 Cranch 137 (1803).

27. See *Garner v. United States*, 424 U.S. 648 (1976). The Court held that the defendant's Fifth Amendment privilege against self-incrimination was not violated by the admission in evidence of his tax returns. The defendant was prosecuted for gambling-related crimes, not for filing false tax returns.

28. *Dickerson* OA-TR at 15.

29. Professor Cassell received his law degree from Stanford, clerked for then-Judge Antonin Scalia on the U.S. Court of Appeals for the D.C. Circuit and for Chief Justice Warren Burger of the U.S. Supreme Court. He taught at the University of Utah College of Law and supervised the prosecutor criminal process course. He wrote frequently in opposition to the *Miranda* case. His web site (www.law.utah.edu/Faculty/bios/cassell.html) contains a page labeled "Overhaul Miranda?" and links to several other sites on the legal and social issues embedded in *Miranda*. Professor Cassell became Judge Cassell in 2002, when President Bush nominated him to the United States District Court in Utah.

30. See Cassell, "The Statute That Time Forgot: 18 U.S.C. §3501 and the Overhauling of Miranda," 85 *Iowa L. Rev.* 175 (1999).

31. *Dickerson* OA-TR at 19.

32. See 417 U.S. 433 (1974).

33. *Dickerson* OA-TR at 26.

34. *Dickerson* OA-TR at 40.

35. *Dickerson v. United States,* 530 U.S. 428, 147 L. Ed.2nd 405, 120 S.Ct. 2326, 2000 Lexis 4305, 68 U.S.L.W. 4566, 13 Fla. L. Weekly Fed. S 488, 2000 Cal. Daily Op. Service 5091, 2000 Colo. J. C.A.R. 3855, 2000 D.A.R. 6789 (2000).

36. 530 U.S. 428, p. 432.

37. Citing *King v. Rudd*, 1 Leach 115 (1783), stating that the English courts excluded confessions obtained by threats and promises.

38. *Hopt v. Territory of Utah,* 110 U.S. 574 (1884).

39. *Brown v. Mississippi,* 297 U.S. 278 (1936).

40. 530 U.S. 428, p. 435.

41. 530 U.S. 428, p. 439.

42. 530 U.S. 428, p. 442.

43. See *United States v. Dickerson,* 27 Fed. Appx. 236, 2001 U.S. App. LEXIS 27236, December 27, 2001, at page 6.

44. See *United States v. Elie,* 111 F.2nd 1135 (1997).

45. See *John J. Fellers v. United States,* U.S. Supreme Court Docket No. 02-6320, 2003 LEXIS 1977, March 10, 2003.

46. See *Fellers v. United States,* 285 F.3rd 721, 722 (2002).

47. Id., 723.

48. Id., 724.

49. Id., 725.

50. The facts and chronology of the case are detailed in the opinion of the United States Court of Appeals for the Tenth Circuit Court of Appeals. See *U.S. v. Patane,* 304 F.3rd 1013 (10th Cir. 2002).

51. Id., 1014.

52. See petitioner's brief in *U.S. v. Patane,* Supreme Court Docket No. 02-1183, filed July 14, 2003.

53. See *State v. Seibert,* 92 S.W.3rd 700, at 701 (Supreme Court of Missouri, 2002).

54. Id., 702.

55. Id., 706.

Chapter 7. The Global Reach

1. See *U.S. v. Usama Bin Laden,* aka Usamah Bin-Muhammad Bin-Ladin, 132 F. Supp.2nd 168 (2001).

2. See "Miranda's Final Frontier—the International Arena: A Critical Analysis of U.S. v. bin Laden, and a Proposal for a New Miranda Exception Abroad," by Professor Mark Godsey. 51 *Duke L. J.* 1703 (April 2002).

3. Ibid., 1755.

4. See *International Herald Tribune/Washington Post* Service—The IHT Online, by Dan Eggen and Brooke A. Masters, January 17, 2002.

5. See Attorney General Transcript, John Walker Lindh Press Conference, Department of Justice, January 15, 2002.

6. Special Agent Asbury's sworn affidavit dated January 15, 2002, confirms that Walker remained in the "custody of U.S. military forces" from his capture on November 25, 2001, until the date of her affidavit, which includes the dates of his interviews with FBI agents on December 9 and 19, 2001. In addition, paragraph 10 of the United States District Court for the Eastern District of Virginia, Alexandria Division, Criminal Number 02-37A, styled, United States of America v. John Philip Walker Lindh, a/k/a "Suleyman al-Faris," a/k/a "Abdul Hamid," Defendant avers that John Philip Walker Lindh was first brought into the United States on or about January 23, 2002.

7. See Attorney General Transcript, John Walker Lindh Press Conference, Department of Justice, January 15, 2002.

8. See *The Washington Post,* June 15, 2002, p. A11.

9. See Special Agent Asbury's sworn affidavit dated January 15, 2002.

10. Ibid.

11. See *The New York Times,* June 15, 2002, section A, p. 14, col. 1.

12. See *USA Today,* July 15, 2002, News, p. 7A, dateline Alexandria, Va., by Toni Locy.

13. See *U.S. v. Lindh,* 2002 U.S. Dist. LEXIS 12683.

14. Id.

15. Id.

16. See *The Washington Post,* July 2, 2002, p. A03, by Tom Jackson.

17. Judge T. S. Ellis III signed the court order accepting the plea bargain struck by counsel for the parties on July 15, 2002. See *U.S. v. Lindh,* Cr. No. 02-37A.

18. See comments of Lindh lawyer Tony West as reported in *Newsday,* September 1, 2002, p. A07.

19. See *The Tulsa World,* June 14, 2002, "Opinion," by Georgie Anne Geyer, Universal Press Syndicate, Ankara, Turkey.

20. Ibid.

21. See *National Review,* Vol. 54, No. 17, September 16, 2002, by Kate O'Beirne.

22. Ibid.

23. See *The Tulsa World,* June 14, 2002, "Opinion," by Georgie Anne Geyer, Universal Press Syndicate, Ankara, Turkey.

24. See *The Orlando Sentinel,* June 16, 2002, "Editorial," p. G3.

25. See *The Record,* Bergen County, NJ, June 14, 2002, "Opinion," p. 10.

26. See *The Los Angeles Times,* June 14, 2002, California Metro, part 2, p. 14.

Chapter 8. A Broader Perspective

1. See *Arizona Daily Star,* May 7, 2000, "Op-Ed," "The Miranda Rule," by John P. Frank.

2. See Amicus Curiae brief of Senators Orrin G. Hatch, Trent Lott, Don Nickes, Strom Thurmond, Bob Smith, Larry E. Craig, Paul Coverdell, Fred Thompson, Jon Kyl, and Jeff Sessions urging affirmance in U.S. Supreme Court Docket No. 99-5525, *Dickerson v. U.S.,* on writ of certiorari to the United States Court of Appeals for the Fourth Circuit, filed March 9, 2000. The interest of the ten senators signing the brief is stated: "As members of the United States Senate, Amici contend that 18 USC §3501 represents a valid and constitutional exercise of Congress' legislative authority to establish the rules of procedure and evidence for the federal courts. [We] also believe [we] will bring to the Court's attention relevant information the parties have not addressed."

3. Rex Lee's views of the *Miranda* case and his reasons for turning it down are detailed in Justice Corcoran's correspondence files. Particularly important is the letter Justice Corcoran wrote to Liva Baker on July 12, 1979. That letter and all of Justice Corcoran's files were graciously given to the author by Justice Corcoran in the spring of 2001.

4. Lee died in March of 1996. He argued fifty-nine cases before the Supreme Court in roles as a private attorney, the assistant attorney general in charge of the Justice Department's Civil Division, and as solicitor general of the United States. He agreed to

accept the presidency of Brigham Young University on the condition that he could continue to argue cases in the Supreme Court. His views, as cited in this book, are found in his published work and his correspondence in the *Miranda* case and reflect long conversations with the author in the late 1960s.

5. Mr. Roush is one of Arizona's most respected trial lawyers. His experience on the bench, in the classroom, and his early training at Lewis and Roca make him widely sought after as a specialist in civil trial law.

6. See Inbau and Reid, *Criminal Interrogation and Confession* (1962). John Frank characterized Professor Inbau as the principal publicist for secret inquiries and said that his book makes a poor case for itself. See petitioner's brief in the *Miranda* case file, at page 45, note 40.

7. See *The Journal of Credibility Assessment and Witness Psychology*, by Krista D. Forrest, Theresa A. Wadkins, and Richard L. Miller, Vol. 3, No. 1, 23–45 (2002).

8. Ibid., 25.

9. See Barry Scheck et al., *Actual Innocence*, 92.

10. The details of Doody's arrest, confession, efforts to recant, trial, conviction, sentencing, and appeal are set forth in detail in *State of Arizona v. Doody*, 187 Ariz. 363, 930 P.2nd 440 (1996).

11. Id., 367.

12. Id., 368.

13. See *The Arizona Republic*, July 19, 1994, p. A1, by Brent Whiting.

14. See *State of Arizona v. Doody*, 187 Ariz. 363, 930 P.2nd 440, cert denied, 520 U.S. 1275, June 16, 1997.

15. See *State v. Jimenez*, 165 Ariz. 444, 449, 799 P.2nd 785, 790 (1990).

16. Id., appendix 2, 265.

17. Simon, *The Center Holds*, 11.

18. Ibid., 14.

19. Ibid., 15.

20. Professor Cassell was confirmed by a vote of sixty-seven to twenty. All twenty negative votes were from Democrats who noted that he tried to topple a pillar of American justice—"the requirement police inform suspects of their right to remain silent and have an attorney." Professor Cassell wrote the lead brief and delivered the principal argument in the *Dickerson* case urging the Rehnquist Court to strike down *Miranda*. At his confirmation hearing, Cassell said that as a federal judge he would uphold *Miranda*, vowing it "is the law of the land and that's the law I will follow." See FindLaw, *Legal News and Commentary*, Monday, May 13, 2002.

21. These and other factual confirmations are found in the body of the *Miranda* opinion—384 U.S. 1613–17.

22. Id., 455. In footnote 24, the Court described a 1964 New York case confirming that a suspect falsely confessed to two brutal murders that he had not committed. When this was discovered, the prosecutor said: "Call it what you want—brainwashing, hypnosis, fright. They made him give an untrue confession. The only thing I don't believe is that Whitmore was beaten." The Court also directed interested readers to Borchard, *Convicting the Innocent* (1932) and Frank and Frank, *Not Guilty* (1957).

23. See Baker, *Miranda*, 166.

24. See *Dickerson v. U.S.*, 530 U.S. 427, 431 (2000).

25. See *A Dictionary of Modern Legal Usage*, by Bryan A. Garner, Oxford University Press, 1987. *Stare decisis* is Latin for "to stand by things decided," the doctrine of precedent, under which it is necessary to abide by former judicial decisions when the same points arise again in litigation.

Chapter 9. The Future

1. From his address to the New England Law Institute, November 1, 1963.

2. See book review by Craig Mehrens of Lewis's *Gideon's Trumpet*.

3. Ibid.

4. Ibid.

5. Edward Bennett Williams was also quoted on the dust cover and said that *Gideon's Trumpet* was an absorbing account of one of the most important cases to come out of the Supreme Court in years.

6. See Scheck et al., *Actual Innocence*, 246.

BIBLIOGRAPHY

Primary Sources

Affidavits, Reports, Witness Statements, Photographs, and Transcripts

Asbury, Anne. Affidavit filed in *United States v. John Philip Walker Lindh,* U.S. Dist. Ct., Eastern Dist. of Virginia, Criminal No. 02-347A. Styled, "In Support of Criminal Complaint and Arrest Warrant." Verification of facts regarding suspect's admissions and waiver of *Miranda* rights.

Ashcroft, John. Transcript of press conference given by United States Attorney General John Ashcroft on January 15, 2002, regarding criminal charges against John Walker Lindh based on voluntary statements made to FBI.

Congressional Record. 90th Cong., 1st sess., 1967. Vol. 1120. Controlling Crime through More Effective Law Enforcement: Hearings before the Subcommittee on Criminal Laws and Procedure of the Senate Committee on the Judiciary.

Cooley, Carroll F., with Joseph R. Farmer. *The Inside Story of Miranda—Arizona Peace Officer Standards and Training Board.* 1980.

Frank, John P. Review of *The New Legality—1932–1968 (U.S. Supreme Court Decisions).* 58 *American Bar Association Journal* 394 (1972).

———. "Miranda Today, Appleton, Wisconsin." Lawrence University convocation address, November 5, 1985.

Phoenix Police Departmental Reports 62-40126, November 1962; 63-07180, February 1963; 63-08380, March 1963; 74-07204, July 1974; and 76-011123, January 1976.

Smith, Darrell F. "Seminar On Miranda." Seminar materials prepared by Smith, attorney general of Arizona, Phoenix, AZ, August 12, 1996.

Subcommittee on Criminal Justice Oversight of the Committee on the Judiciary of the United States Senate. *Statement of Professor Paul G. Cassell.* 86-page statement concerning the enforcement of 18 U.S.C. §3501 as of May 13, 1999.

U.S. Senate Judiciary Committee. *The Clinton Justice Department's Refusal to Enforce the Law on Voluntary Confessions under 18 U.S.C. §3501.* 106th Cong., 1st sess., Senate Hearing 106237, May 13, 1999.

Personal Records, Correspondence, and Notes

Miranda, Ernest A. Materials referenced: signed "Miranda Rights Card" dated 6-13-66; Phoenix booking photos, 1960 and 1963; prison records; FBI Record No.

879313C regarding arrests and convictions between October 29, 1957, and July 16, 1974; handwritten confession signed by Ernest Miranda on March 13, 1963.

Personal Correspondence and Notes provided by: Justice Robert Corcoran, John P. Frank, Carroll F. Cooley, Peter D. Baird, Judge Barry Silverman, and Gary Nelson.

Court Filings and Records

Brennan, William, Justice. Signed memorandum to the chief justice regarding the *Miranda* opinion, May 11, 1966.

Judgment of Guilt and Sentence, Nos. 41497 and 41498, signed by the Hon. Yale McFate.

Maricopa County Superior Criminal Information, Nos. 41947 and 41948, filed April 16, 1963.

Northeast Phoenix Justice Court, No. 7345, criminal complaint, filed March 14, 1963.

Notice of Intent to Prove Insanity or Mental Defectiveness, filed by Alvin Moore, May 11, 1963.

Pleadings and transcripts filed in Maricopa County Superior Court, Docket No. 41498, February 15–17, 20–23, 1967, before the Hon. Laurence T. Wren.

Pleadings and transcripts filed in Maricopa County Superior Court, Docket No. 41497, 1969, before the Hon. William H. Gooding and the Hon. Philip W. Marquardt.

Pleadings and transcripts filed in the United States District Court for the District of Arizona, No. Civ 69-10, before the Hon. C. A. Muecke.

Pleadings, briefs, and opinions filed in the Arizona Supreme Court, Docket Nos. 1394, 1397, 1397-1, 1397-2, 1802.

Pleadings, briefs, and opinions filed in the United States Supreme Court, Docket No. 759, October Term, 1965, Ernesto A. Miranda, Petitioner; and Docket No. 2176, October Term, 1968, Ernesto A. Miranda, Petitioner.

Pleadings, briefs, and opinions filed in the United States Supreme Court, Docket No. 99, October Term, 2000, *Dickerson v. United States of America*.

Pleadings, briefs, and opinions filed in the United States Court of Appeals for the Fourth Circuit, No. 99-5525.

Psychiatric Report of James M. Kilgore Jr., M.D., May 28, 1963.

Psychiatric Report of Leo Rubinow, M.D., June 4, 1963.

Reporter's transcript of trial in Maricopa County Superior Court Docket Nos. 41497 and 41498, June 19 and 20, 1963, before the Hon. Yale McFate.

State's Exhibit 1 in Docket No. 41498 (typed, signed confession by Ernest Miranda, witnessed by Carroll Cooley and Wilfred M. Young).

Warren, Earl, Chief Justice. Handwritten notes prepared in advance of releasing the *Miranda* opinion in May 1966.

Author Interview Notes and Correspondence Files

Alcorn, Marianne, Esq., Librarian, Arizona State University College of Law.

Ares, Charles, Dean, University of Arizona College of Law.

Baird, Peter, Esq., Phoenix, Arizona.

Bender, Paul, Dean, Arizona State University College of Law.

Blakey, Craig, Judge, Maricopa County Superior Court.

Brooks, Thomas, Judge. Coconino County Superior Court.

Cooley, Carroll, Captain, Phoenix Police Department.

Corcoran, Robert, Justice, Arizona Supreme Court.

Dowd, John, Esq. Washington, D.C.

Fish, Paul, Esq. Albuquerque, New Mexico.

Frank, John P., Esq. Phoenix, Arizona.

Futterman, Craig, Esq. Chicago, Illinois.

Howe, Joseph, Judge, Maricopa County Superior Court.

Jensen, Robert, Esq. Phoenix, Arizona.

Johns, Christopher, Esq. Phoenix, Arizona.

Kimerer, Michael, Esq. Phoenix, Arizona.

Kroll, Barry, Esq. Chicago, Illinois.

Kyl, Jon. U.S. Senator, R-Arizona.

Lee, Rex, Esq. Former solicitor general of the United States, president of Brigham Young University, deceased.

Martone, Fred. Judge, U.S. District Court for the District of Arizona and former justice of the Arizona Supreme Court.

Mauet, Tom. Professor, University of Arizona College of Law.

Mehrens, Craig, Esq. Phoenix, Arizona.

Moeller, John. Justice, Arizona Supreme Court.

Napolitano, Janet, Esq. Governor, State of Arizona, former Arizona attorney general.

Nelson, Gary. Arizona attorney general and judge of the Arizona Court of Appeals.

Quaife, Ron. Detective, Phoenix Police Department.

Roush, Charles, Esq. Former judge of the Maricopa County Superior Court.

Schroeder, Mary. Chief Judge, U.S. Court of Appeals, Ninth Circuit.

Siegel, Mara, Esq. Phoenix, Arizona.

Silverman, Barry. Judge, U.S. Court of Appeals, Ninth Circuit.

Storrs, Robert, Esq. Phoenix, Arizona.

Thinnes, Thomas, Esq. Phoenix, Arizona.

Turngate, Susan, Esq. Santa Fe, New Mexico.

Turoff, Larry, Esq. Phoenix, Arizona.

Ulrich, Paul, Esq. Phoenix, Arizona.

Wolfson, Warren. Judge, Illinois Court of Appeals.

Audio, Video, and Multimedia Materials

Cassell, Paul. *Overhaul Miranda?* http://www.law.utah.edu/Cassell.

Focus on the Fifth: Miranda v. Arizona. FindLaw Constitutional Law Center, http://supreme.lp.findlaw.com.

Gideon v. Wainwright and Miranda vs. Arizona. Narrated by Ramsey Clark, Guidance Associates, Mt. Kisco, NY, 1986.

Grant, Michael, Moderator. *Miranda v. Arizona.* Panelists: Dean Paul Bender, Attorney General Gary Nelson, Assistant Attorney General Steve Twist, and Judge Rudolph Gerber, KAET, Channel 8, Arizona State University, 1987.

Gribben, Mark. *All about Miranda v. Arizona—The Crime That Changed American Justice.* http://www/crimelibrary.com.

Guidelines for Interrogations: Waiver of Rights under Miranda, Obtaining and Proving Waiver of Rights as an Element of Durable Convictions. Narrated by Daliel J. Penofsky, Aqueduct Books, Rochester, NY, 1967.

Irons, Peter, and Stephanie Guitton, Eds. *May It Please the Court—Historic Recordings of 23 Leading Supreme Court Cases.* Published in conjunction with the Earl Warren Bill of Rights Project of the University of California, San Diego and the Northwest Public Affairs Network, 1993.

Warren, Earl, Chief Justice, and Justice William Brennan. *Miranda Rights.*http://lcweb.locl.gov/exhibits.

Secondary Sources

Books

Baker, Liva. *Miranda: Crime, Law and Politics.* NY: Antheneum Press, 1983.

Brandt, Charles. *The Right to Remain Silent.* NY: St. Martin's Press, 1988.

Cohen, Stanley. *Law Enforcement Guide to United States Supreme Court Decisions.* Springfield, IL: Charles C. Thomas Publishing, 1971.

Cray, Ed. *The Big Blue Line: Police Power vs. Human Rights.* NY: Coward-McCann Inc., 1967.

Dash, Samuel. Foreword to *From Escobedo to Miranda: The Anatomy of a Supreme Court Decision,* by Richard J. Medalie. Washington, D.C.: Lerner Law Book Company, 1996.

Dowling, Noel T., and Gerald Gunther. *Constitutional Law.* 7th Ed. NY: The Foundation Press, Inc., 1965.

Frank, John P. *Mr. Justice Black: The Man and His Opinions.* NY: Alfred A. Knopf, 1949.

———. *Cases on Constitutional Law.* Chicago: Callaghan & Co., 1950.

———. *Cases on Constitutional Law.* 2nd ed. Chicago: Callaghan & Co., 1950.

———. *Cases on the Constitution.* NY: McGraw-Hill Book Co., Inc, 1951.

———. *The Marble Palace: The Supreme Court in American Life.* NY: Alfred A. Knopf, 1958.

———. *American Law: The Case of Radical Reform—Lectures upon the Dedication of the Earl Warren Legal Center.* NY: MacMillan Co., 1964.

———. *Justice Daniel, Dissenting.* Cambridge: Harvard University Press, 1964.

———. *The Warren Court: A Personality and Photographic Portrait of the Justices on Today's United States Supreme Court.* NY: MacMillan Co., 1964.

———. *Clement Haynsworth: The Senate and the Supreme Court.* Charlottesville: University of Virginia Press, 1991.

George, James B., Jr., Stephen Glasser, and Yale Kamisar. *A New Look at Confessions: Escobedo—The Second Round.* Ann Arbor: Institute of Continuing Legal Education, Hutchins Hall, 1967.

Grano, Joseph D. *Confessions, Truth, and the Law.* Ann Arbor: The University of Michigan Press, 1993.

Huff, Ronald C., Rattner Arye, and Edward Sagarin. *Convicted but Innocent: Wrongful Conviction and Public Policy.* Beverly Hills: Sage Publications, 1996.

Kamisar, Yale. *Police Interrogation and Confessions*. Ann Arbor: University of Michigan Press, 1980.

Leo, Richard A., and George C. Thomas III., Eds. *The Miranda Debate: Law, Justice, and Policing*. Boston: Northeastern University Press, 1998.

Levy, Leonard. *Origins of the Fifth Amendment: The Right against Self-Incrimination*. NY: MacMillan Co., 1986.

Lewis, Anthony. *Gideon's Trumpet*. NY: Random House, 1964.

Medalie, Richard J. *From Escobedo to Miranda: The Anatomy of a Supreme Court Decision*. Washington, D.C.: Lerner Law Book Company, 1966.

Mersky, Roy, and Jenni Parrish. *The Supreme Court in Current Literature Overview 1964–74*. Supreme Court Historical Society, Yearbook 1977.

Milner, Neal A. *The Court and Local Law Enforcement: The Impact of Miranda*. Beverly Hills: Sage Publications, 1971.

————. *Some Common Themes in Police Responses to Legal Change in Police in Urban Society*. Harlan Hahn, ed. Beverly Hills: Sage Publications, 1971.

Schafer, William J., III. *Confessions and Statements*. Springfield, IL. Charles C. Thomas Publishing, 1968.

Scheck, Barry, Peter Neufeld, and Jim Dwyer. *Actual Innocence: Five Days to Execution, and Other Dispatches from the Wrongly Convicted*. NY: Doubleday, 2000.

Simon, James F. *The Center Holds: The Power Struggle inside the Rehnquist Court*. NY: Simon & Schuster, 1995.

Sobel, Nathan R. *The New Confession Standards, Miranda v. Arizona: A Legal Perspective, a Practical Perspective*. NY: Criminal Law Bulletin, Inc., Gould Publications, 1996.

Sokol, Ronald. *Law Abiding Policeman: A Guide to Recent Supreme Court Decisions*. Charlottesville, NC: Michie, 1966.

Stephens, Otis H., Jr. *The Supreme Court and Confessions of Guilt*. Knoxville: The University of Tennessee Press, 1973.

Swindler, William F. *The New Legality, 1932–1968*. NY: Bobbs & Merrill, 1970.

White, Welsh S. *Miranda's Waning Protections: Police Interrogation Practices after Dickerson*. Ann Arbor: University of Michigan Press, 2001.

Wigmore, John H. *Evidence in Trials at Common Law*. Boston: John T. Mcnaughton Inc., 1961.

Principal Supreme Court Cases and Federal Statutes

Admissibility of Confessions   18 USC §3501 (1968)

Betts v. Brady   316 U.S. 455 (1942)

Brown v. Mississippi   297 U.S. 278 (1936)

Crooker v. California   357 U.S. 433 (1958)

Dickerson v. United States   530 U.S. 428 (2000)

Edwards v. Arizona   451 U.S. 477 (1981)

Escobedo v. Illinois   378 U.S. 478 (1964)

Fulminante v. Arizona   499 U.S. 279 (1991)

Gideon v. Wainwright   372 U.S. 355 (1962)

Harris v. New York   401 U.S. 222 (1978)

Jackson v. Denno   378 U.S. 368 (1964)

Mallory v. United States   354 U.S. 449 (1957)

Malloy v. Hogan   378 U.S. 1 (1964)

Mapp v. Ohio   367 U.S. 643 (1961)

Massiah v. United States   377 U.S. 201 (1964)

McNabb v. United States   318 U.S. 332 (1943)

Miranda v. Arizona   384 U.S. 436 (1966)

People v. Dorado   398 P.2nd 361 (1964)

Powell v. Alabama   287 U.S. 45 (1932)

Spano v. New York   360 U.S. 315 (1959)

United States v. Dickerson   166 F.2nd 667 (2000)

USA PATRIOT Act of 2001   Act. P.L. 107–56 (2001)

Law Review Articles

Alschuler, Albert W. "A Peculiar Privilege in Historical Perspective: The Right to Remain Silent." 94 *Michigan Law Review* 2625, 1996.

Altman, David B. "Fifth Amendment—Coercion and Clarity: The Supreme Court Approves Altered Miranda Warnings." 80 *Criminal Law and Criminology* 1086, 1990.

Bateman, Connor G. "Dickerson v. United States: Miranda Is Deemed a Constitutional Rule, but Does It Really Matter?" 55 *Arkansas Law Review* 1277, 2002.

Benner, Laurence A. "Requiem for Miranda—The Rehnquist Court's Voluntariness Doctrine in Historical Perspective." 67 *Washington University Law Quarterly* 59, 1998.

Blaine, Jonathan L. H. "Miranda under Fire." 10 *Seton Hall Constitutional Law Journal* 1007, summer 2000.

Brennan, Timothy. "Silencing Miranda: Exploring Potential Reform to the Law of Confessions in the Wake of *Dickerson v. United States.*" 27 *New England Journal on Criminal and Civil Confinement* 253, 2001.

Caplan, Gerald M. Review of *Miranda: Crime, Law and Politics,* by Liva Baker. 93 *Yale Law Journal* 1375, 1984.

Cassell, Paul G. "Miranda's Social Costs: An Empirical Reassessment" 90 *Northwestern University Law Review* 387, 1996.

———. "The Statute That Time Forgot: 18 U.S.C. §3501 and the Overhauling of Miranda" 85 *Iowa Law Review* 175, 1999.

Cassell, Paul G., and Bret S. Hayman. "Police Interrogation in the 1990's: An Empirical Study of the Effects of Miranda" 43 *UCLA Law Review* 839, 1996.

Cassell, Paul G., and Richard Fowles. "Handcuffing the Cops? A Thirty-Year Perspective on Miranda's Harmful Effects on Law Enforcement" 50 [4] *Stanford Law Review* 1055, 1998.

Crawford, K. A. "Intentional Violations of Miranda: A Strategy for Liability" 66[8] *FBI Law Enforcement Bulletin* 27, 1997.

Donohue, John J., III. "Did Miranda Diminish Police Effectiveness?" 50[4] *Stanford Law Review* 1147, 1998.

Dripps, Donald A. "Is Miranda Caselaw Really Inconsistent? A Proposed Fifth Amendment Synthesis" 17 *Constitutional Commentary* 19, spring 2000.

———. "Constitutional Theory for Criminal Procedure—Dickerson, Miranda and the Continuing Quest for Broad-But-Shallow" 43 *William & Mary Law Review* 1, 2001.

Garrison, Arthur H. "Rehnquist v. Scalia—The Dickerson and Miranda Cases: A Debate on What Makes a Decision Constitutional" 91 *American Journal of Trial Advocacy* 2001.

Gerhardt, Michael. "The Rhetoric of Judicial Critique: From Judicial Restraint to the Virtual Bill of Rights" 10 *William & Mary Bill of Rights Journal* 585, 2002.

Grano, Joseph, William H. Erickson, and Philip Johnson. "Miranda Symposium: Four Essays Critical of Miranda v Arizona" 24[2] *American Criminal Law Review* 193, 1987.

Hancock, Catherine. "Due Process before Miranda" 70 *Tulane Law Review* 2195, 1996.

Harris, Allen. "Miranda v. Arizona: Is It Being Applied?" 3[3] *Criminal Law Bulletin* 135, 1967.

Huh, Richard H. "Interrogation of Criminal Defendants: Some Views on Miranda v. Arizona" 35 *Fordham Law Review* 233, 1968.

Huitema, David. "Miranda: Legitimate Response to Contingent Requirements of the Fifth Amendment" 8 *Yale Law & Policy Review* 261, 2000.

Inbau, Fred E. "Police Interrogation—A Practical Necessity" 52 *Journal of Criminal Law—Criminology and Police Science* 16, 1961.

Ingram, Roderick R. "A Clash of Fundamental Rights: Conflicts between the Fifth and Sixth Amendments in Criminal Trials" 5 *William & Mary Bill of Rights Journal* 299, 1996.

Kamisar, Yale. 1984 Survey of Books Relating to the Law: *Crime and Punishment: Miranda the Case, the Man and the Players,* by Liva Baker, 82 *Michigan Law Review* 1974.

———. "Can (Did) Congress Overrule Miranda?" 4 *Cornell Law Review* 883, 2000.

———. "Miranda Thirty-Five Years Later: A Close Look at the Majority and Dissenting Opinions in Dickerson" 33 *Arizona State Law Journal* 387, 2001.

———. Foreword to "From Miranda to §3501 to Dickerson." 99 *Michigan Law Review* 879, 2001.

Kauper, Paul G. "Judicial Examination of the Accused—A Remedy for the Third Degree" 30 *Michigan Law Review* 1224, 1932.

Langbein, John H. "The Historical Origins of the Privilege against Self-Incrimination at Common Law" 92 *Michigan Law Review* 1047, 1994.

Leiken, Lawrence S. "Police Interrogation in Colorado: The Implementation of Miranda" 47[1] *Denver Law Journal* 1, 1970.

Luban, David. "The Warren Court and the Concept of a Right" 34 *Harvard Civil Rights—Civil Liberties Law Review* 7, 1999.

Macnair, Michael R. T. "The Early Development of the Privilege against Self-Incrimination" 10 *Oxford Journal of Legal Studies* 66, 1990.

Markman, Stephen J. "The Fifth Amendment and Custodial Questioning: A Response to 'Reconsidering Miranda'" 54 *University of Chicago Law Review* 938, 1987.

———. "Truth in Criminal Justice: The Law of Pre-trial Interrogation" 21[1] *Prosecutor* 23, 1987.

Mason, Christopher. "Dickerson v. United States—The Supreme Court's Holding in

Miranda v Arizona Was a Constitutional Decision That Cannot Be Overruled by an Act of Congress" 31 *University of Baltimore Law Forum* 57, 2000.

Medalie, Richard J., et al. "Custodial Police Interrogation in Our Nation's Capital: The Attempt to Implement Miranda" 66 *Michigan Law Review* 1347, 1968.

Morgan, Edmund M. "The Privilege against Self-Incrimination" 34 *Minnesota Law Review* 1, 1949.

Muller, Andrew W. "Congress' Right to Remain Silent in *Dickerson v. United States*— Or, How I Learned to Stop Worrying and Love *Miranda v. Arizona*" 34 *Creighton Law Review* 801, 2001.

Payne, Brian K., and Victoria M. Time. "Support for Miranda among Police Chiefs: A Qualitative Examination" 1 *American Journal of Criminal Justice* 65, 2000.

Pearce, Gene A. "Constitutional Law—Criminal Law: The United States Supreme Court Affirms the Use of "Miranda" Rights by Police to Determine the Admissibility of Statements Made during Custodial Interrogation in *Dickerson v Untied States*" 77 *North Dakota Law Review* 153, 2001.

Pepinsky, Harold E. "A Theory of Police Reaction to *Miranda v Arizona*: Crime and Delinquency" 16[4] *Crime and Delinquency* 379, 1970.

Prebble, Amanda L. "Manipulated by Miranda: A Critical Analysis of Bright Lines and Voluntary Confessions under *United States v. Dickerson*" 68 *University of Cincinnati Law Review* 555, 2000.

Robinson, Cyril D. "Police and Prosecutor Practices and Attitudes Relating to Interrogation as Revealed by Pre- and Post-Miranda Questionnaires: A Construct of Police Capacity to Comply" 3 *Duke Law Journal* 425, 1968.

Schulhofer, Stephen J. "Reconsidering Miranda" 54 *University of Chicago Law Review* 435, 1987.

————. "Miranda, Dickerson and the Puzzling Persistence of Fifth Amendment Exceptionalism" 99 *Michigan Law Review* 941, 2001.

Seeburger, Richard H., and R. Stanton Wettick. "Miranda in Pittsburgh: A Statistical Study" 29 *University of Pittsburgh Law Review* 1, 1967.

Seidman, Louis Michael. "Brown and Miranda" 80 *California Law Review* 673, 992.

Stephens, Otis H. "Police Interrogation and the Supreme Court: An Inquiry into the Limits of Judicial Policy-making" 17[2] *Journal of Public Law* 241, 1968.

Stephens, Otis H., Robert L. Flanders, and J. Lewis Cannon. "Law Enforcement and the Supreme Court: Police Perceptions of the Miranda Requirements" 39[3] *Tennessee Law Review* 407, 1972.

Ulrich, Jackie. "Criminal Procedure: The Court Distinguishes between the Sixth Amendment Right to Counsel and the Fifth Amendment Miranda Right against Self-Incrimination" 31 *Washburn Law Journal* 629, 2000.

White, Welsh S. "Defending Miranda: A Reply to Professor Caplan" 39 *Vanderbilt Law Review* 1, 1986.

Witt, James W. "Non-Coercive Interrogation and the Administration of Criminal Justice—The Impact of Miranda on Police Effectuality" 64 *Journal of Criminal Law & Criminology* 320, 1973.

Zeitlin, Jonathan B. "Voluntariness with a Vengeance: Miranda and a Modern Alternative" 14 *St. Thomas Law Review* 109, 2001.

Zeitz, Leonard, Richard J. Medalie, and Paul Alexander. "Anomie, Powerless and Police Interrogation" 60[3] *Journal of Criminal Law—Criminology and Police Science* 314, 1967.

Selected Print Media

1965: "High Court Will Review Rapist's Case." *The Arizona Republic,* November 23.

1966: "Danny Escobedo—Moving the Constitution into the Police Station." *Time Magazine,* Vol. 87, No. 17, April 29, cover story.

1966: *Miranda v. Arizona,* ACLU news release, No. 207, June.

1966: "Some Moderation (Miranda Not Retroactive)." *The Arizona Republic,* June 23.

1967: "Homicides Increase in Chicago but Confessions Drop by 50%." *The New York Times,* by Donald Janson, July 24, p. 24.

1968: "Right of Confession." *The Phoenix Gazette,* January 29.

1968: "Criminal Justice: Doubts about Miranda." *Time Magazine,* November 1.

1976: "Police Search for Suspect in Miranda Death." *The Arizona Republic,* January 25, 1976.

1976: "Ernesto Miranda Is Killed; Subject of Landmark Case." *The Arizona Republic,* February 1.

1976: "Miranda Dies of Stabbing." *Mesa Tribune,* February 2.

1976: "Parole Officer Says Miranda Was Adjusting." *The Arizona Republic,* February 3.

1982: "Miranda—To the High Court and Back." *The Harvard Law Record,* Vol. 75, No. 6, by John Morris, October 29.

1982: "Court's Decision Leaves Miranda in Jail." (Part Two) *The Harvard Law Record,* by John Morris, November 5.

1990: "Miranda Memories." *ABA Litigation Magazine,* Vol. 16, No. 2 (winter), by Peter D. Baird, p. 43.

1991: "The John J. Flynn Award." *The Defender—Arizona Attorneys Criminal Justice,* by Michael Kimerer, April.

1991: "Critics Must Confess, Miranda Was the Right Decision." *The Wall Street Journal,* Counterpoint, by Peter D. Baird, June 13.

1991: "The Confessions of Arturo Ernesto Miranda." *The Arizona Attorney,* by Peter D. Baird, October, p. 20.

1994: "Ten People Who Changed the Way You Live—John Flynn." *American Heritage Magazine,* December.

1996: "A Member of the Legal Team Recalls the Landmark Miranda Case." *Phoenix Magazine,* by Peter D. Baird, June, p. 38.

1996: "Police vs. Miranda: Has the Supreme Court Really Hampered Law Enforcement?" *The Wall Street Journal,* by Wayne E. Green, December 15, p. 16.

1999: "High Court Should Leave Miranda Rule." *The Arizona Republic,* Editorial, January 15.

1999: "Miranda Law Benefits Most Vulnerable, Needs to Stay." *The Arizona Republic,* by Steve Wilson, February 2.

1999: "Miranda Rights Up for Review—Should Police Have Some Leeway?" *The Arizona Republic,* by Jon Kamman, December 7.

2000: "The Miranda Rule: It Works Well So Let's Keep It." *The Arizona Daily Star,* by John P. Frank, May 7.

2001: "Judges and the GOP: The Rehnquist Court, Miranda v. Arizona and Dickerson v. United States." *The Wall Street Journal,* by Kenneth W. Starr, May 3.

2002: "Will [John Lindh] Walker's Statements Be Admitted against Him?" *Jurist, The Legal Education Newspaper,* by Prof. Marjorie Cohn, January 18.

INDEX

questioning and, 11, 14, 19–20, 55; pivotal nature of, 70, 75–76, 182n76; police advising suspects of, 25, 38–39, 48, 54–56, 58, 64, 72–73, 75, 80, 84, 187n1; police investigation and, 25, 37–38, 40, 46–47, 77, 83, 88; purpose of defense attorney and, 61–62; Supreme Court test cases and, 23–24, 31, 73, 169; waiving, 90. *See also* Sixth Amendment

right of privacy, 85

right to remain silent: advisement of, 48, 56, 68, 81, 84, 85–86; attorney-client privilege and, 103; constitutional basis for, 35, 72–73; fair trial and, 25; questioning by authorities and, 26, 37, 172–73; right of counsel and, 76, 161–62; Supreme Court test cases and, 30–31, 55. *See also* Fifth Amendment; self-incrimination, privilege against

Ringer, Gordon, 74–75, 183n6

Rizer, James, 97

Rochester, James, 107, 108, 124–25

Rodriguez, Fernando Zamura, 96–99, 186–87n72

Roe v. Wade, 85, 148, 185n24

Roush, Charles, 149, 192n5

Rubinow, Leo, 9

Rumsfeld v. Padilla, xx

Sand, Leonard B., 131

Saudi Arabia, 131, 136

Scalia, Antonin, 110–11, 114–19, 121, 123, 168, 189n29

Schafer, William J., III, 49, 182n84

Scheck, Barry, 172

Schroeder, Mary, 149–50, 161

Section 3501, 109–11; federal separation of powers and, 191n2; *Miranda* doctrine and, 112–13, 120, 122, 146, 189n20; Supreme Court and, 114–15, 124, 169–70

Seibert, Darian, 129

Seibert, Jonathan, 129

Seibert, Patrice, xviii–xix, 129–30

self-incrimination, privilege against: absence of counsel and, 82; advisement of, 80; *Brown v. Mississippi* and, 33; constitutional basis for, 46, 75; *Escobedo* decision and, 69; marital privilege and, 94; *Miranda* warnings and, 162; precedents for, 141; questioning by police and, 40, 56, 123, 124, 180n35; tax returns and, 189n27

September 11, 2001, 132, 171

Shmukler, Stanford, 76–77, 183n6

Siegel, Mara, 150

Siegel, William I., 67–69, 183n6

Silverman, Barry, 150–51

Simon, Jim, 160

Sixth Amendment: interpretation of, 31, 104, 162; *Miranda* and, 41, 47; right of counsel and, 22, 25, 43, 55–56, 72, 74–75, 152, 161–62; Supreme Court decisions and, 32, 43, 46, 47. *See also* right of counsel

Sobel, Nathan R., 185n27

Souter, David, xx, 114, 115, 122

stare decisis, 124, 146, 167, 192n25

states' rights, 29, 30. *See also* federalism

State v. Seibert, xviii–xix

Stephens, Otis, 49

Stevens, John Paul, 114, 115

Stewart, Potter, 55, 56, 57, 64, 66, 75, 81, 164, 179n28, 183n7

Stewart, Roy Allen, 25, 74, 84, 125, 183n6, 185n14

Storrs, Robert, 92, 151, 186n55

Struckmeyer, Fred, 41

Taft Court, 160

Taliban, 132, 133, 137

Taylor, Telford, 182n75, 183n6

Tenth Circuit, 128

Thinnes, Tom, 92, 186n56

Thomas, Clarence, 114, 115, 123, 168

Westover, Carl Calvin, 25–26, 69, 70–
71, 81, 84, 125
Westover v. United States, 69–74, 81,
181–82n73, 183n6
White, Byron, 44, 57, 67, 71, 81, 146,
164, 183n7
White, Welsh, 102

Wilkinson, Beth, 135
Williams, Edward Bennett, 169
Wolfson, Warren, 35–36, 152
Wren, Lawrence, 93, 125

Yarborough v. Alvarado, xix
Young, Wilfred, 5–6, 7–8, 14, 20, 41, 43

ABOUT THE AUTHOR

Mr. Stuart's publishing career began as an editor of the *Arizona Law Review* while attending the University of Arizona College of Law (J.D., 1967). He wrote scores of legal appellate briefs, law review articles, and monographs on legal advocacy and ethics during his thirty years as a partner in one of Arizona's largest law firms, Jennings, Strouss and Salmon. His first legal textbook, *The Ethical Trial Lawyer* (Arizona State Bar, 1994), was followed by a national treatise, *Ethical Litigation,* in 1998 (Lexis-Nexis Publishing Company). Mr. Stuart served for ten years as chair of the Arizona State Bar's Committee on Rules of Professional Conduct and retains an active role in all aspects of lawyer and judicial discipline and regulation.

He is a founding fellow of the Arizona Bar Foundation and an elected member of the American Board of Trial Advocates, and he is listed in numerous reference works, including *Who's Who in American Law, Martindale-Hubbell's Premier American Lawyers,* and *The Best Lawyers in America.* Mr. Stuart tried more than one hundred jury cases to a conclusion in several states and federal jurisdictions. He is a frequent lecturer and a faculty member at the National Institute for Trial Advocacy and the Arizona College of Trial Advocacy. He teaches ethics, trial practice, and creative writing as an adjunct law professor at the University Of Arizona's James E. Rogers College of Law and at the Arizona State University College of Law.

His first novel, *The Gallup 14,* was published by the University of New Mexico Press in 2000. Mr. Stuart divides his time among his higher education interests as a member of the Arizona Board of Regents, his part-time law practice in Phoenix, Arizona, and his emerging career as a novelist at his writing studio in Placitas, New Mexico.